The Gamer's Brain

HOW NEUROSCIENCE AND UX CAN IMPACT VIDEO GAME DESIGN

The Gamer's Brain

HOW NEUROSCIENCE AND UX CAN IMPACT VIDEO GAME DESIGN

Celia Hodent

CRC Press
Taylor & Francis Group
Boca Raton London New York

CRC Press is an imprint of the
Taylor & Francis Group, an **informa** business

A FOCAL PRESS BOOK

CRC Press
Taylor & Francis Group
6000 Broken Sound Parkway NW, Suite 300
Boca Raton, FL 33487-2742

© 2018 by Celia Hodent
CRC Press is an imprint of Taylor & Francis Group, an Informa business

No claim to original U.S. Government works
Printed on acid-free paper

International Standard Book Number-13: 978-1-4987-7550-2 (Paperback)
978-1-1380-8996-9 (Hardback)

Visit the Taylor & Francis Web site at
http://www.taylorandfrancis.com

and the CRC Press Web site at
http://www.crcpress.com

To the scientists, artists, designers, and game developer magicians out there. You never cease to inspire me.

Contents

Foreword   xiii

Author   xv

1 Why You Should Care about the Gamer's Brain   1

   1.1   Disclaimer: The "Neuro-Hype" Trap 2
   1.2   What This Book Is about and Who It Is for..4

Part I Understanding the Brain

2 Overview about the Brain   9

   2.1   Brain and Mind Myths 9
        2.1.1   "We Only Use 10% of Our Brains" 10
        2.1.2   "Right-Brained People Are More Creative than
                  Left-Brained People" 10
        2.1.3   "Men and Women Have Different Brains"............................11
        2.1.4   Learning Styles and Teaching Styles 11
        2.1.5   "Video Games Are Rewiring Your Brain and Digital
                  Natives Are Wired Differently"... 12
   2.2   Cognitive Biases... 12
   2.3   Mental Models and the Player-Centered Approach 15
   2.4   How the Brain Works, in a Nutshell 16

3 Perception   19

3.1   How Perception Works..19
3.2   Limitations of Human Perception 20
3.3   Application to Games.. 24
    3.3.1   Know Your Audience.. 24
    3.3.2   Playtest Your Game Regularly and Test
            Your Iconography.. 26
    3.3.3   Use Gestalt Principles of Perception 26
    3.3.4   Use Affordances 31
    3.3.5   Understand Visual Imagery and Mental Rotation............32
    3.3.6   Be Aware of the Weber–Fechner Bias 32

4 Memory   35

4.1   How Memory Works..35
    4.1.1   Sensory Memory 36
    4.1.2   Short-Term Memory 37
    4.1.3   Working Memory... 38
    4.1.4   Long-Term Memory... 40
4.2   Limitations of Human Memory 42
4.3   Application to Games.. 45
    4.3.1   Spacing Effect and Level Design 46
    4.3.2   Reminders 48

5 Attention   51

5.1   How Attention Works...51
5.2   Limitations of Human Attention 52
5.3   Application to Games..55

6 Motivation   59

6.1   Implicit Motivation and Biological Drives 60
6.2   Environmental-Shaped Motivation and Learned Drives..................61
    6.2.1   Extrinsic Motivation: Of Carrots and Sticks 61
    6.2.2   Continuous and Intermittent Rewards............................ 63
6.3   Intrinsic Motivation and Cognitive Needs............................. 65
    6.3.1   Undermining Effect of Extrinsic Incentives 65
    6.3.2   Self-Determination Theory.................................... 66
    6.3.3   The Theory of Flow.. 67
6.4   Personality and Individual Needs... 68
6.5   Application to Games...70
6.6   Quick Note on the Importance of Meaning 71

7 Emotion   73

7.1   When Emotion Guides Our Cognition....................................75
    7.1.1   The Influence of the Limbic System 75
    7.1.2   The Somatic Markers Theory 76

7.2   When Emotion "Tricks" Us 77
7.3   Application to Games.. 80

8 Learning Principles   83

8.1   Behavioral Psychology Principles 83
    8.1.1   Classical Conditioning 84
    8.1.2   Operant Conditioning... 84
8.2   Cognitive Psychology Principles 86
8.3   Constructivist Principles... 86
8.4   Application to Games: Learning by Doing with Meaning............... 87

9 Understanding the Brain: Takeaway   91

9.1   Perception 92
9.2   Memory... 93
9.3   Attention 93
9.4   Motivation... 93
9.5   Emotion... 94
9.6   Learning principles... 94

Part II   A UX Framework for Video Games

10 Game User Experience: Overview   97

10.1   A Short History of UX 98
10.2   Debunking UX Misconceptions.. 100
    10.2.1   Misconception 1: UX Will Distort the Design
            Intents and Make the Game Easier 100
    10.2.2   Misconception 2: UX Will Restrict the Creativity
            of the Team...101
    10.2.3   Misconception 3: UX Is Yet Another Opinion 103
    10.2.4   Misconception 4: UX Is Just Common Sense 104
    10.2.5   Misconception 5: There Is Not Enough Time
            or Money to Consider UX.................................... 104
10.3   A Definition of Game UX... 105

11 Usability   109

11.1   Usability Heuristics in Software and Video Games.........................110
11.2   Seven Usability Pillars for Game UX...115
    11.2.1   Signs and Feedback...115
    11.2.2   Clarity 117
    11.2.3   Form Follows Function 123
    11.2.4   Consistency 125
    11.2.5   Minimum Workload... 127
    11.2.6   Error Prevention and Error Recovery.................... 129
    11.2.7   Flexibility...131

12 Engage-Ability   135

12.1   Three Engage-Ability Pillars for Game UX 135
12.2   Motivation...137
     12.2.1   Intrinsic Motivation: Competence,
             Autonomy, Relatedness 138
     12.2.2   Extrinsic Motivation, Learned Needs, and Rewards 149
     12.2.3   Individual Needs and Implicit Motives 151
12.3   Emotion...153
     12.3.1   Game Feel...153
     12.3.2   Discovery, Novelty, and Surprises 160
12.4   Game Flow 161
     12.4.1   Difficulty Curve: Challenge and Pacing 163
     12.4.2   Learning Curve and Onboarding.......................................167

13 Design Thinking   173

13.1   Iterative Cycle..175
13.2   Affordances..178
13.3   Onboarding Plan 180

14 Game User Research   185

14.1   The Scientific Method 185
14.2   User Research Methodologies and Tools 187
     14.2.1   UX Tests... 190
     14.2.2   Surveys... 195
     14.2.3   Heuristic Evaluations 196
     14.2.4   Rapid Internal Tests 197
     14.2.5   Personas 197
     14.2.6   Analytics... 198
14.3   Final User Research Tips 198

15 Game Analytics   199

15.1   The Wonders and Dangers of Telemetry... 200
     15.1.1   Statistical Fallacies and Other Data Limitations............. 200
     15.1.2   Cognitive Biases and Other Human Limitations........... 202
15.2   UX and Analytics 204
     15.2.1   Defining Hypotheses and Exploratory Questions 205
     15.2.2   Defining Metrics 207

16 UX Strategy   209

16.1   UX at the Project Team Level 210
16.2   UX in the Production Pipeline 210
     16.2.1   Conception..211
     16.2.2   Preproduction...211
     16.2.3   Production...213

   16.2.4 Alpha 213
   16.2.5 Beta/Live 213
  16.3 UX at the Studio Level 213

17 Concluding Remarks   219

  17.1 Key Takeaways 220
  17.2 Playful Learning (or Game-Based Learning) 222
    17.2.1 Making Educational Games Engaging 223
    17.2.2 Making Game-Based Learning Truly Educational......... 224
  17.3 "Serious Games" and "Gamification" 225
  17.4 Tips for Students Interested in Game UX 226
  17.5 Parting Words 227

Acknowledgments   229

References   233

Index   245

Foreword

"Oh, no way! Oh my god. Oh no…"

I looked up to see Felix, the lead tester on the alpha version of Wizardry 8, staring at his computer in absolute horror. It wasn't a crash or some terrible bug that had caused his reaction, but rather a character named Zant, a harsh leader of an even harsher group of insect-like creatures known as the T'Rang. He'd just ordered the extermination of Felix's entire party of six characters, but that wasn't the thing that upset Felix. Rather, he was horrified that Zant had discovered his treachery, and worse, Zant seemed genuinely hurt by it.

Only a few days before, I was watching Felix play. He was doing something I thought was impossible: playing for both sides of a bitter divide. Not only had Felix been working for the T'Rang, he'd also been working for their sworn enemy, the Umpani. Somehow, he had managed to make it quite far in the game oblivious to the fact that this wasn't something I intended (or even considered). However, his experience—and more importantly, his motivation to resolve the differences between the Umpani and the T'Rang—led me to create a path forward for him. As Felix told me a few days before, the Umpani and the T'Rang had a shared enemy, even stronger than the two. He felt sure that if he could just get the two together that their collective forces could defeat their common enemy. Felix was incredibly emotionally invested in an outcome that didn't even exist, and he was motivated to see his non-existent solution through. I didn't tell him it wasn't possible. Instead, I made it so.

Felix's surprise when Zant discovered his betrayal, the remorse he felt when he read Zant's words ("I have trusted in you the secrets of our empire. That trust is never easily earned.") and his subsequent sadness when he was completely locked out of any future T'Rang involvement were sobering. It could have gone the other way, though. Replaying the game, he was indeed able to forge that alliance.

"I can't believe that happened," he told me.

It remains one of my most vivid memories as a game designer, and certainly one of his most impactful moments of play. It came to be because of a player-centric approach to game design. Then, fewer than 20 years into my career, it taught me that I had more to learn from players and how they played my games than they had to learn from me. I didn't have a book like this one then nor had I seen Celia's excellent lectures on UX, usability and engage-ability. I had Felix, but he taught me a lot.

During those years and in the years that followed, I have also seen players throw up their hands in frustration when they felt overloaded with information or couldn't figure out how to make a game do something they were sure it could actually do. I've seen players miss whole sections of gameplay because its clues were poorly telegraphed or watched them struggle with learning curves that were designed for designers who already knew how to do it and not the players who would have benefited from learning by doing, particularly those that might be new to playing such a game. Among these many memories, one specific memory stands out. Having served on a variety of "game of the year" award committees, I fought for a game I considered just beautiful—art, design, audio, story, code—a game loved by so, so many players. It was defeated by the committee not because of the things that its team had carefully crafted, but rather the quirkiness of its controls. It was like putting a poor steering wheel on a Ferrari. It was incredible to look at and to experience if you could just control the damned thing. I still love that game, but its Game of the Year award is on someone else's shelf.

And that's the thing with games—they *are* their interface and intercept—that point at which the game meets the mind of the player and where the actual experience of play really happens. In my talks and with other designers, I often use the example of a beautiful meal. Sometimes, I am torturous and have an actual delectable edible present or an image of something I know the audience is sure to go for. Looking at the food, it's easy to compliment the chef, the plating, the quality of the ingredients and even the ambience of the restaurant. But in the end? It's all down to these little, bumpy taste buds. Without passing through our interface, there is no satisfaction, only frustration.

As an industry, we have learned much about the value of UX in our 40+ years. From our earliest origins of teaching through death. ("You have died. I hope that taught you a lesson.") to our experiments with different endless control schemes, the UX of games has undeniably evolved. Much of our evolution has been through our own trial and error, "doing what they did" and first-party codification. Prior to Celia's work, however, which by now is well known and regarded within the game industry, I have yet to find anything which seeks to explain how the gamer's brain works in such a profoundly deep, clear and helpful way as *The Gamer's Brain*. I am at work on a commercial game as I write this, and this book changed my thinking and improved my designs by offering insights into the brain, the player and their motivations, among many other things. *The Gamer's Brain* has tremendous potential to make us better designers and game developers. I hope it makes your game, your research and your play more meaningful, too.

Brenda Romero
Game Designer, Romero Games
Galway, Ireland. May 29, 2017

Author

Celia Hodent is recognized as a leader in the application of user experience and psychology in video game design and in the development of UX strategy and process in game studios. She holds a PhD in psychology from the University of Paris Descartes-Sorbonne, France, where she specialized in cognitive development. In 2005, Celia stepped aside from academic research to work with an educational toy manufacturer, VTech, and then entered the video game industry. She has worked at Ubisoft Paris, Ubisoft Montreal, LucasArts, and Epic Games to help guide the studios, and their projects, toward improved user experience practices. Celia's approach is to use cognitive science knowledge and the scientific method to concretely solve design problems and make sure the player experience is always enjoyable and engaging, while reaching business goals. Celia is also the founder and curator of the Game UX Summit, which was launched in Durham, NC, in May 2016, hosted by Epic Games. She has worked on many projects across multiple platforms (PC, console, mobile, and VR), including the *Tom Clancy's Rainbow Six* franchise, *Star Wars: 1313*, *Paragon*, *Fortnite*, and *Spyjinx*.

Why You Should Care about the Gamer's Brain

1.1 Disclaimer:
     The "Neuro-Hype" Trap

1.2 What This Book Is
     about and Who It Is for

Have you ever wondered how magicians trick you? How they seem to defy the rules of physics or read your mind? I'm not going to give away magicians' secrets but, in reality, magicians and mentalists have a good understanding of human cognition, such as perception, attention, and memory. They learn to take advantage of brain loopholes, and when they master certain practices (such as "misdirection"—whereby the attention of the audience is distracted to deceive their senses), they succeed in tricking us (Kuhn and Martinez 2012). For me, a video game is also a type of magic: When it's done well, players suspend their disbelief, and they enter a state of flow. Understanding the gamer's brain will provide you with tools and guidelines to help you craft the magical experience you intend for your audience. And it is an even more important tool to master today as video games represent an increasingly growing competitive market.

In 2015, the revenues from the video game industry reached a whopping $91 billion worldwide and $23.5 billion in the United States alone (according to the Essential Facts 2016 report from the Entertainment Software Association). Although these numbers are encouraging, they are hiding a harsh truth: Making good video games that are successful is actually very hard. There are thousands of games that are now easily, in some cases freely, accessible with a click (or a tap on a touchscreen), and the competition is fierce. The video game industry is volatile.

Video game studios, including established ones, are regularly hit with closures and layoffs. Small indie projects as well as AAA projects with large development budgets fail—even those made by industry veterans with considerable marketing and publishing support. The game industry, in the business of manufacturing fun, often struggles to accomplish its goal. Furthermore, even the games that are successful on their release may not sustain their audience's engagement over time.

This book is designed to provide you with an overview of how to identify the ingredients that contribute to the enduring magic of video games and the most common barriers to enjoyment and engagement. Although no recipe for success currently exists (and probably never will), identifying the ingredients and barriers drawn from scientific knowledge and game development best practices should help you increase the likelihood that your game will be more successful and enjoyable. To attain these goals, you need some knowledge and a methodology. The knowledge comes from neuroscience, which pertains to understanding how the brain perceives and processes information as well as retains it. The methodology comes from the user experience (UX) discipline, which offers guidelines and a procedure. UX and neuroscience combined will help you make the best decisions for your game faster and remain aware of the trade-offs you need to make to achieve your goal. It will help you stay true to your design and artistic goals and offer the game experience you intend for your audience. It will also hopefully help you meet your business goals, allowing you to sustain your passion and providing you with enough funds to keep making magic.

Anticipating how players will understand and interact with your game is very important. It's not an easy task, but it is somehow easier than to acknowledge another very important element: your own biases as a human being and a developer. We humans like to believe that we mostly make decisions based on logic and rational analysis. However, numerous studies in psychology, as well as behavioral economics, have shown that the brain can actually be quite irrational and that our decisions are heavily influenced by many biases (see, e.g., Ariely 2008; Kahneman 2011). Creating and shipping a game is all about making countless decisions. As a game developer, this raises difficulties that you must take into account if you and your team want to make the right decisions all throughout the development process and ultimately achieve your goals. This is why you need to understand the gamer's brain—and your own—in order to increase the likelihood of shipping the game you intended to create while also giving it the best chance to succeed.

1.1 Disclaimer: The "Neuro-Hype" Trap

There is a relatively new and increasing interest in the use of scientific knowledge and methodology in the video game industry—particularly related to neuroscience. This can be seen as a reflection of a broader public and business interest in anything using the word "brain" or the prefix "neuro" (such as "neuromarketing" or "neuroeconomics"). Articles allegedly explaining "your brain on dopamine," "how to rewire your brain for success," or "the role of oxytocin in persuasion" flood our news and social media feeds. Let me put it bluntly: Most of the clickbait neuro-articles that are circulating nowadays are at worst outright false and at best a gross simplification of how the brain—a very complex and fascinating organ— works (so much so, in fact, that neuroscientists consider these articles to be "neurotrash," "neurobullshit," or "neurobollocks," depending on how exasperated they are with seeing their complex field being oversimplified to sell ad space or products that are supposedly enhanced by "brain knowledge"). The reason why these clickbait articles and companies have been invading our lives recently is because their narrative works. Who doesn't want to know the simple magic trick that will improve our lives, accomplish our endeavors, or run our businesses better? This phenomenon was not born with the neuroscience hype though. For example, who can resist the "five secret foods you need to start—or stop—eating to lose 20 pounds in two weeks"? The sad truth, however, is that there is no magic pill that can make you lose weight. You need to pay attention to what you eat every day and exercise regularly. This is what science tells us about losing weight. It involves hard work, sweat, and sacrifices. And even then, depending on how lucky you were in the DNA and environment lottery, you could still have additional difficulty losing weight. You have to admit that this narrative is far less compelling than the clickbait smoke-and-mirrors one! Often, we do not like the more complex explanation, or we choose not to believe it because it implies more effort. We prefer to fool ourselves with inefficient but more seducing solutions. The same rule applies to neuroscience. If you do not want to be fooled or fool yourself, you have to remember that our brain is biased, emotional, irrational, and yet it is extremely complex. To paraphrase professor of psychology Steven Pinker in his book, *How the Mind Works* (1997), the problems that our brains are solving as we make it through our day-to-day lives are far more challenging than sending humans to the moon or sequencing our genome. So, as seducing as it may be, do not believe the hype—especially when it promises you a lot with little to no efforts; that is, unless you prefer to comfort yourself by believing in convenient lies, but if you did you would have probably stopped reading this book already.

The same is true for making games. There is no magic pill you can swallow, nor is there any known long-lasting recipe for success, especially if you are trying to innovate. Analyzing what made a game or a company successful in hindsight is always much easier than predicting which game will be successful, which one will fail, and which one will become the new *Minecraft* (originally published by Mojang) or *Pokémon Go* (Niantic) phenomenon. This book will not try to convince you that I have a magic wand that will solve all your development problems. However, it will give you some quality and time-tested ingredients that will help you make your own successful recipe, if you are ready to put in the effort it will take (and the pain, too, because analyzing the game you are lovingly crafting will be painful). Still up for the challenge?

Since you are still reading, I will now admit that I used the terms "neuroscience" and "brain" in the title of this book to surf on the neuro-trend. I did so only to grab your attention so I can deliver sound scientific knowledge that can help you develop your game more efficiently, while also helping you detect and ignore the neuro-nonsense trying to seduce you. We have about 100 billion neurons, each of which can be connected up to 10,000 of other neurons. That makes a lot of synaptic connections, and we have yet to clearly understand how neural circuits impact our behavior or our emotion—not to mention the influence of hormones and neurotransmitters (chemical messengers transmitting signals between neurons), for example. Neuroscience, the study of the nervous system, is a very complex discipline. Most of the things I will talk about in this book actually have more to do with "cognitive science," the discipline that studies mental processes such as perception, memory, attention, learning, reasoning, and problem-solving. Cognitive science knowledge is directly applicable to designing games because all these mental processes are involved as players are playing these games. User experience, the discipline concerned with the experience users are having overall as they interact with a product or a game, relies heavily on cognitive science knowledge.

1.2 What This Book Is about and Who It Is for

Discovering a video game, learning about it, mastering it, enjoying it: It all happens in the brain. As a game developer, you can achieve your design goals—as well as your business goals—more efficiently by understanding the brain's basic mechanisms, which are also the foundation of UX principles. This book is not about telling you how to design a game, hampering your creativity, or dumbing down your game (see the main UX misconceptions in Chapter 10), it is about helping you achieve your objectives faster by understanding the mechanisms at work when someone interacts with your game. Part of the content of this book comes from my background in cognitive psychology (Part I) and part comes from my experience working with development teams at Ubisoft, LucasArts, and Epic Games (Part II).

Overall, this book is an introduction to game user experience and cognitive science as applied to video games and is accessible to anyone interested in these topics; it is *not* a specialized handbook dedicated to UX experts. This book is intended for a broad professional and student game developer audience. Part I is even appropriate for anyone interested in how the brain works as related to playing video games. Therefore, all disciplines should be able to find some useful information. However, creative directors, game directors, designers (game designers, user interface [UI] designers, etc.), programmers (mostly gameplay and UI programmers), and artists should probably be the most concerned audience because the content of this book is more directly applicable to their everyday challenges. Professional game UX practitioners (interaction designers, user researchers, UX managers, etc.) should already know many of the concepts tackled in this book, although I do hope it will provide them with some good reminders, as well as tips to develop UX maturity in a studio. The content of this book should also be valuable to UX practitioners not familiar with the game industry that are interested in learning about it. Upper management, producers, and support teams overall (quality assurance [QA], analytics, marketing, business intelligence, etc.) should gain some perspective regarding the importance of considering user experience in shipping a more engaging game faster. Lastly, the main purpose of this book is not to deep dive into each of the subjects tackled, it is mostly to provide a thorough overview about game user experience in order to facilitate collaboration and communication across the whole studio. Along the way, I'm also hoping to be a good advocate for players.

This book is organized in two parts. Part I (Chapters 2 through 9) focuses on our current understanding of the brain and on cognitive science findings, while Part II (Chapters 10 through 17) focuses on the user experience mindset and practice and how to implement this in game development, which constitutes a UX framework for video games. We will discuss perception (Chapter 3), memory (Chapter 4), attention (Chapter 5), motivation (Chapter 6), emotion (Chapter 7), and learning principles (Chapter 8), which make up the main knowledge you need to have in order to understand how the brain works, what our human capabilities and limitations are, and what this implies when designing a game. Chapter 9 will offer a takeaway about the gamer's brain. In Part II, we will start by giving an overview of game user experience (Chapter 10), discussing its history, debunking the main misconceptions, and outlining a definition. To offer a compelling user experience, two components are critical: "usability," or ease of use of a product (Chapter 11), and "engage-ability," or how engaging the game is (Chapter 12). For each component, we will discuss the main pillars that can make a game both usable and engaging. Chapter 13 will discuss user experience through the lens of design thinking. Chapter 14 will describe the main tool used to measure and improve user experience: user research. In Chapter 15, another tool for user experience, analytics, will be touched on. Chapter 16 proposes some tips for building up a UX strategy in a studio, and we will conclude with key takeaways, overall tips, and some thoughts about educational video games and "gamification" in Chapter 17.

Throughout this book, I will use many examples from commercial games to illustrate a best practice or a UX issue. All the games mentioned are those that I have either worked on or have played extensively because I really enjoyed them. So please note that, when I'm highlighting a UX issue with one of these games, I am certainly not making a value judgment. I am well aware that making games is hard and that no game offers perfect user experience when considering UX best practices.

PART I
Understanding the Brain

2

Overview about the Brain

2.1   Brain and Mind Myths
2.2   Cognitive Biases
2.3   Mental Models and
       the Player-Centered
       Approach

2.4   How the Brain Works,
       in a Nutshell

2.1 Brain and Mind Myths

The human brain began evolving well before any hominids walked the Earth and has further evolved over thousands of generations as our ancestors survived the harsh life in the African savanna. However, our modern life is very different from prehistoric times, and we face many problems that are new for our brain in terms of the relatively slow scale of evolution. Therefore, understanding the wonders and limitations of our brain as it navigates the complexity of the modern world is useful for improving our decision-making on a daily basis. And this is what we're going to talk about all throughout the first part of this book. I will mostly limit myself to describing what should be the most useful things to know in the context of game development though, so if you are curious about the subject as applied to broader situations, you will find some useful tips in the book *Mind Hacks* (2005) from cognitive scientist Tom Stafford and engineer Matt Webb.

Even though we are only scratching the surface of the brain's mysteries, fascinating discoveries about how it works have been made in the past century. They are, however, sadly tempered by countless myths that pollute our media. I won't go through all of these myths because other authors have already covered them in wonderful detail (e.g., Lilienfeld *et al.* 2010 and Jarrett 2015), but I will briefly describe the ones that are the most relevant to video game development and which I believe you need to know about before we go any further.

2.1.1 "We Only Use 10% of Our Brains"

It is very tempting to believe that we have untapped brain powers that can be unleashed by anyone who has the key. (I've heard that some companies will give it to you in exchange for money.) In reality, even doing something as simple as clenching your fists takes more than 10% of your brain to execute, and modern brain imagery shows activity throughout the entire brain whenever we do something—and even when we don't do anything. The brain does, however, have the capacity to reorganize itself, such as when you learn to play a musical instrument or after a brain injury. The fact that the brain manifests such flexibility is a wonder by itself and offers you massive amounts of potential to learn new knowledge and skills; so, don't be too disappointed that you are already using much more than 10% of your brain. You would be in a very sad state if you weren't.

2.1.2 "Right-Brained People Are More Creative than Left-Brained People"

"Develop your right brain to unleash your creativity!" as the story goes. It is true that both hemispheres of our brain are different and are not necessarily used equally when we accomplish certain tasks, but the "left-brain right-brain" distinction is mostly false. For example, you might have learned that language is mostly dominated by left hemisphere activity. Well, generally speaking, the left hemisphere is in fact *relatively* better at generating words and applying grammatical rules while the right hemisphere is *relatively* better at analyzing prosody (speech intonation). However, for any given activity, both hemispheres work together in harmony. Suggesting that the left hemisphere is the logical one while the right hemisphere is the creative one is a gross and inaccurate simplification. Both hemispheres are connected through the corpus callosum, a large pathway of nerves that allows both hemispheres to share information. So even if you were tempted to enhance your creativity by stimulating your right hemisphere, it would be nearly impossible to accomplish such a discriminatory thing—unless you are a split-brain patient with a severed corpus callosum and you artificially received input only through the left side of your body (or through the left side of your fixation point in the case of vision). In that very specific case, information would then be processed only by your right hemisphere. There are actually neuropsychology labs that do test split-brain patients that way, but you have to admit that this is far from the seducing right-brain story lines some people would like you to believe. Don't worry though; it wouldn't be useful anyway given that there is no scientific evidence that the hemispheres have "creative" or "logical" specializations. So we can stop romanticizing our right (or left) hemisphere and be one again, whether you are aspiring to be more creative or more logical.

2.1.3 "Men and Women Have Different Brains"

We love to find simple reasons that would explain our differences, don't we? It is admittedly difficult for a man and a woman to make their romantic relationship survive the tumults of life. So let's blame it on some neurological differences to ease our cognitive dissonance instead of blaming it on our own mistakes and lack of empathy! But you know what? Homosexual couples probably have the same difficulties as heterosexual couples do. (I only say "probably" because I do not have any statistics to back my claim, but I'm ready to take a bet on this one.) It is true that the average female brain is not exactly the same as the average male brain when we compile the brain imagery of many people, but they are much more similar than they are different. In fact, there usually is a greater difference among the brains of people of the same sex than between the sexes. No, males and females do not come from different planets, not even rhetorically. There is no scientific evidence, for example, that women can multitask better than men or that they are "prewired" to master language whereas men are "prewired" to master math or park a car. Even if there are *some* differences in brain wiring and *some* behavioral differences between men and women, we cannot link the neurological differences to the behavioral ones when considering cognitive skills. Most of our cognitive differences—such as our performance in science or language—are likely due to our level of practice of a particular skill and to the cultural environment (stereotypes) and social pressure we develop within.

2.1.4 Learning Styles and Teaching Styles

You might believe that you have a preferred learning style and that you will learn better if teaching occurs within that style. For example, you might think that you learn better when taught with visual information rather than verbal information because you are a visual learner. One of the issues with the concept of learning styles is that it's not necessarily easy to measure what is one's preferred learning style. Another issue is that the criteria determining what sort of learning style we are talking about are often all over the place. Are you a right-brained person? An analytic person? A visual person? The idea for training programs is, of course, to find a classification that will resonate with you. You're unsure if you're a left-brained person? How about matching the teaching style with your score on the Myers-Briggs Personality Test? By the way, the Myers-Briggs test is not a scientifically validated test (quite the contrary), so you can play with it if you find it fun, but please do not use it for any important purpose such as hiring. One last issue with the concept of learning styles is that there is actually no solid scientific evidence that you will learn something better if the teaching style matches your learning style preference (assuming you know what your preferred learning style is). Research has shown that, although people differ in their aptitudes for different kinds of thinking and for processing different types of information, there is no indication that the application of learning styles actually enhances learning. Furthermore, some studies have even contradicted the idea that instruction is more effective when the teaching style matches the preferred learning style (Pashler *et al.* 2008), and the concept of learning styles can in some cases even be damaging. However, there *are* ways to design a teaching environment that can facilitate learning, which I will describe throughout this book. One of the most important things is to make the teaching meaningful and to repeat the teaching in different contexts and activities. However, and despite their broad appeal and adoption, "learning styles" themselves have not been found to be a suitable concept for improving learning.

2.1.5 "Video Games Are Rewiring Your Brain and Digital Natives Are Wired Differently"

Your neural networks are constantly rearranging themselves depending on the environment and your interaction with it. This is why all the articles that you see that say something like, "Such and such (say, the Internet) is rewiring your brain" are simply dramatic ways of stating the obvious because pretty much everything you do, perceive, or think about will "rewire" your brain—watching a movie, reflecting on the latest article you read, practicing piano, and so on. Rewiring is not even the right term to use because the brain is not hardwired in the first place. The brain—even if it does have computational powers—is not a computer. Our brain is plastic; it constantly changes throughout our life (although it becomes less plastic as we age), and new synaptic connections are created while others are lost. There is also a tendency to consider "digital natives"—a term coined by Marc Prensky (2001) to describe the millennial generation who grew up with digital technology such as the Internet and video games—as being wired differently than older generations (who are sometimes also called "digital immigrants"). Although we are all wired a bit differently depending on our environment and our interaction with it that does not mean that there are cognitive or behavioral differences between the millennials and previous generations. For example, it's not because millennials are used to texting while doing other activities such as reading that they are better at multitasking than other generations. They are not (see Bowman *et al.* 2010) and that's because their brains function overall like any other *Homo sapiens sapiens* on the planet today or back in prehistoric times; therefore, they face the same limitations. (See Chapter 5 in which I describe the limitations of human attention.) What is true though is that millennials, and every other generation younger or older, have different expectations and a different mental model for the products they are interacting with, such as a video game. However, anyone—millennial or otherwise—who has spent countless hours playing shooter games will not have the same expectations or mental model as someone who prefers to spend their time playing *Minecraft*. Therefore, again, the reality is much more nuanced than the clickbait titles would like us to think.

2.2 Cognitive Biases

As if dealing with brain myths was not enough, we also need to be aware of how our brains might hinder our own objectivity and capabilities for rational decision-making. To explain what these *cognitive biases* are, let me use the more

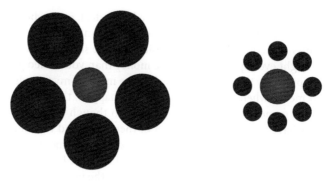

Figure 2.1

Optical illusion.

familiar example of optical illusions. In the illusion presented in Figure 2.1, the two central purple circles have the same size—although we perceive the central circle on the left as being smaller than the one on the right because of their relative sizes compared to the other circles surrounding them. Well, the same principle applies to cognitive biases. Cognitive biases—or cognitive illusions—are patterns of thought that bias our judgment and our decision-making. Just like optical illusions, they are very difficult to avoid even if we are aware of them. The groundbreaking psychologists Amos Tversky and Daniel Kahneman were the first ones to study cognitive biases (see Tversky and Kahneman 1974, and Kahneman 2011). Specifically, they demonstrated that the human mind uses shortcuts of intuitive thinking (heuristics or rules of thumb in judgment) that result in making predictable mistakes in our reasoning. Professor of psychology and behavioral economics Dan Ariely in his book, *Predictably Irrational* (2008), went into more detail on how cognitive biases impact our everyday lives, inducing systematic errors in our reasoning and in our financial decision-making. For example, "anchoring" is a cognitive bias that is somewhat comparable to the optical illusion presented in Figure 2.1: We have a tendency to rely on previous information (the anchor—such as the size of the circles surrounding the purple central circle in the optical illusion) to make a judgment about a new piece of information by comparing one to the other. Marketers use anchoring to influence our decisions. For example: You see a video game blockbuster on sale for $29 with an initial price of $59 next to it. In that case, the $59 price tag represents the anchor (often emphasized by a strikethrough effect applied to it) to which you compare the current price. This makes you recognize that it is a good deal, and this might sway you into buying this title over another one at the same price of $29 but that is not on sale. Even though the cost is the same, the game that is not on sale might seem less interesting because it doesn't make you feel that you are saving money ($30) compared to the game on sale. Similarly, the same price of $29 can appear less of a good deal if there are other blockbusters on sale for $19 and, therefore, representing even better deals. Maybe you will end up buying a game that you were less interested in just because it offered a better deal, or maybe you will buy more games instead of the one(s) you were initially interested in because you just cannot miss this compelling opportunity to make such a good purchase. In the end, you might even spend much more money than your video game budget allows. This is probably the main reason why I see many of my friends complaining on social media whenever some *Steam* sales happen; they just cannot help buying all those games at such a great price, even though they know they will probably never have the time to play most of them. We tend to compare things to one another to make decisions, and it influences our judgment. The worst part is that we are mostly unaware of being influenced by these biases. I'm not going to list them all here because there are too many, but the product manager Buster Benson and the engineer John Manoogian created the chart shown in Figure 2.2 in an effort to sort and categorize the cognitive biases listed on the dedicated Wikipedia page (see Benson 2016).

Whenever relevant, I will mention specific cognitive biases throughout this book. The chart can look scary and discouraging, but it is quite useful to keep these biases in mind to avoid making too many bad decisions. It is also useful to be mindful that, no matter how aware of these biases you are, you will fall prey to

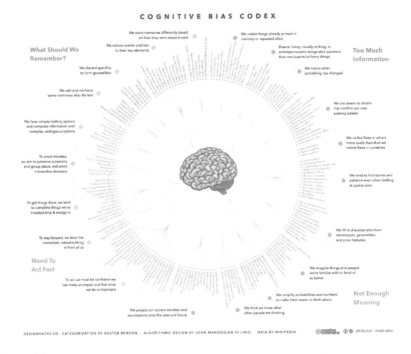

Figure 2.2

Cognitive Bias Codex, designed by John Manoogian III (jm3) and organized by Buster Benson. (From John Manoogian III and Buster Benson, *Cognitive Bias Codex*, Designhacks.co, Chatsworth, California. With permission.)

them from time to time. Try to recognize these traits in yourself and others, even in hindsight. It will make you understand yourself, others, and people's mistakes better—unless you are really attached to the "ostrich effect" and prefer to keep your head buried in the sand. We are all human, with human limitations.

Daniel Kahneman, who received the Nobel Prize in Economic Sciences in 2002, explains in his book, *Thinking, Fast and Slow* (Kahneman 2011), that two modes of thought (System 1 and System 2) influence our mental life. System 1 is fast, instinctive, and emotional thinking. System 2 is much slower, deliberate, and logical, and it involves effortful mental activities such as complex computations. Both systems are active whenever we are awake, and they influence one another. Cognitive biases occur mostly because System 1 operates automatically and is prone to errors of intuitive thoughts and because System 2 might not be aware that these errors are being made. In my opinion, one of the most important cognitive biases to take into account when developing a game is the "curse of knowledge." It is very hard for us to ignore the knowledge we have about something (say, the video game we are developing) and to accurately predict how someone else, who is ignorant about it, will perceive and understand it. This is the main reason why it is critical to regularly test your game's user experience (i.e., UX test) with participants representing your target audience and who do not know anything about it (e.g., playtest, usability test, etc.; see Chapter 14). It is also the reason why game developers, while watching these tests behind one-way mirrors, can become very depressed when they see a participant doing something they find "weird" or "irrational." "Can't he see that he needs to click on the big flashing ability to unleash his powerful ultimate?? I don't understand how he cannot see it, it's so obvious!!" No, it's actually not obvious. It is only obvious to the game developer who already knows where to look, what information is relevant to the current situation, and where to direct attentional resources to be effective. The new player discovering your game does not necessarily know any of this, even if they are expert gamers in the genre. You will have to teach them, which is what we will see in Part II of this book. Now that we have faced brain myths and cognitive biases, let's talk about the cognitive processes that take place in the mind of a person interacting with a product.

2.3 Mental Models and the Player-Centered Approach

Experiencing and enjoying a video game happens in the player's mind, but the experience is crafted by a—sometimes quite considerable—number of developers' minds and is implemented in a system with specific constraints. The difference between what developers originally had in mind, what was implemented given the system's constraints and production constraints, and what players experience in the end can be quite different. This is the reason why considering the gamer's mind and adopting a player-centered approach is key to offering a compelling user experience and to ensuring that what the developers intended is what the players will ultimately experience. In his seminal book, *The Design of Everyday Things*, Donald Norman (2013) explains how designers and end users

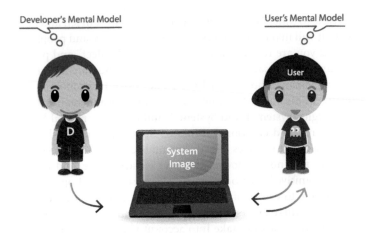

Figure 2.3

Mental models. (Inspired by Norman, D. A. (2013). *The Design of Everyday Things, Revised and Expanded Edition*. New York: Basic Books.)

invoke different mental models, as illustrated in Figure 2.3. A system (such as a PC video game) is designed and implemented based on the developers' mental model of what the system should entail and how it should function. They have to tweak their vision of the game to comply with the limitations of the system (e.g., the rendering features supported by the engine they are using) as well as its requirements (e.g., a virtual reality game must run at a minimum of 90 frames per second to avoid making people simulation sick). Players enter the scene with their prior knowledge and expectations and will develop their own mental model of how *they* think the game works through their interaction with the system image—the part of the system with which they interact and which they perceive. The main objective of user experience and a player-centered approach is to make sure that the user's mental model matches the one developers had intended. To do so, just like developers need to comply with the system limitations and requirements, they also need to comply with the capabilities and limitations of the human brain, and this is why you need to know how the brain works.

2.4 How the Brain Works, in a Nutshell

Pretty much anything you do in life is a learning experience for your brain: watching a movie, finding your bearings, meeting new people, listening to an argument, seeing an advertisement, interacting with a new tool or gadget, and so on. Playing a video game is not any different, and this is why knowing how the brain learns can help developers craft a better experience for their audience. Although learning to play and master a game happens all throughout the game experience, the newest elements are learned during the tutorial—or the onboarding part of the game—so this constitutes one of the biggest hurdles to overcome for players.

First, you have to keep in mind that there is only so much workload the brain can tolerate: The brain consumes about 20% of the body's energy although it only represents 2% of a person's weight. The workload that your game imposes on your audience's brain must therefore be carefully weighed (as much as it can be given that there is no precise measurement for cognitive load) and dedicated to the core experience and challenges you want to offer, not in figuring out, for example, menus, controls, or icons (unless this challenge is by design). Defining your core pillars—what is important for your players to learn and master—and staying focused on them is therefore critical to help you define where you want the player to be challenged. You then need to understand the basics of learning principles to efficiently teach these core elements. The brain is a very complex organ, and it still remains mysterious for the most part. Nonetheless, with the understanding of the learning process explained here, you will be able to determine why players have difficulty grasping or remembering some elements in your game. This will enable you to fix issues efficiently and even to anticipate them. Note that the mind is a product of the brain (and the body); therefore, both are intertwined. Cognitive scientists currently debate the subtleties between mind and brain, but I won't go down that rabbit hole. I consider the brain to be the organ enabling the mind (i.e., mental processes); thus, I will often use one term or the other interchangeably.

Figure 2.4 represents a very simplified chart showing how the brain learns and processes information. Although the brain is not a computer and does not

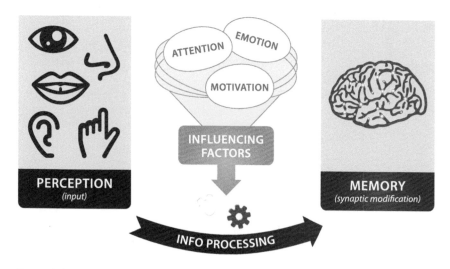

Figure 2.4

A very simplified chart of how the brain learns and processes information.

really have compartments dedicated to a specific function, this chart is a way to boil it down to the essential concepts you need to know as a game developer. Information processing usually starts with the perception of an input and eventually ends with modifications in memory via synaptic modifications in the brain. So, it starts with your senses. We do not have only five senses: sight, hearing, touch, smell, and taste. Rather, we have many other senses, such as those that allow us to perceive a change in temperature, pain, or balance. For example, proprioception is the sense of our body in space that allows us to easily touch our nose with our eyes closed (unless we're inebriated). From a sensory perception to a change in memory, a complex process is happening that is influenced by a myriad of factors. Some of these factors are physiological: You will not learn something as efficiently if you are tired, in pain, or hungry, for example. Your level of attention and the emotions elicited during information processing will also impact the quality of learning, and these are highly dependent on environmental factors (level of noise in the environment, the way the information is organized, and so on). In an effort to boil this down to the essential knowledge you need in order to design video games, the next chapters will focus on perception, attention, memory, motivation, and emotion as if they were independent buckets. However, keep in mind that this is a very simplified version of what is actually going on in the brain. In reality, these cognitive processes are intertwined and do not occur strictly one after the other. And, if I wanted to be perfectly accurate, I should not even say that the brain "processes information" because it does not work like a computer; although getting into this subtlety would probably be overkill for the purposes of this book.

3

Perception

3.1   How Perception Works
3.2   Limitations of Human
      Perception

3.3   Application to Games

3.1 How Perception Works

Perception is not a passive window to the environment; it is instead a subjective construct of the mind. It all starts with the senses at a physiological level: The energy emitted or reflected by an object is stimulating sensory receptor cells. Let's take vision as an example, although the basic process is similar for the other senses. When you look up at clear skies at night to enjoy some stargazing, the stimuli received by the receptor cells are all about physics: orientation, spatial frequency, brightness, and so on. Then, the brain processes the sensory information to make sense of it, and that process is perception (see Figure 3.1). For example, the brightest stars will be grouped into a shape that is meaningful to the individual viewing it (e.g., a saucepan). The brain is a powerful pattern recognizer, which allows us to swiftly create mental representations of the world and see meaningful shapes in our environment, sometimes mistakenly. The last step of information processing allows an access to semantics, to cognition. If you know which constellation appears to have the shape of a saucepan, then you will recognize that you are gazing at Ursa Major, the Big Dipper. At this point, information has reached your cognition. Although it could seem intuitive for this process to be bottom-up (first sensation, then perception, and lastly cognition), it is

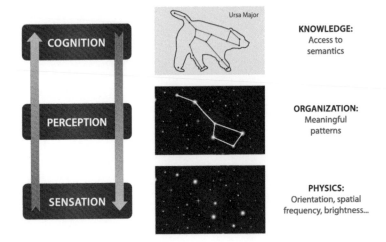

Figure 3.1

Perception is part of a three-level process.

actually very often top-down, which means that your cognition (your knowledge and expectations about the world) will have an impact on your perception of it. Perception is therefore highly subjective because it is influenced by your past and present experiences.

We do not perceive the world as it is in reality; we instead perceive a representation of it. This concept could seem suboptimal—to perceive a "reality" that isn't objectively "real"—but it actually helps us survive. We need to react very quickly to our environment, especially when predators are around. So, if we were taking too long to recognize the shape of a lion (especially because input from the three-dimensional world is inherently hard to disambiguate based on the two-dimensional image of it on the retina), we would be dead before we could decide to either fight or take flight. The brain associates a meaningful pattern with the sensory stimuli as fast as possible, even if it means creating false positives (what you perceive to be a crocodile sneakily swimming toward you is in reality a floating log); but it's better to be safe than sorry (or dead). This is the reason why our perception is flawed (or blessed, depending on your perspective) by perceptual illusions.

3.2 Limitations of Human Perception

Most of us take perception for granted; yet the process is complex and uses considerable resources. For example, about one-third of the cerebral cortex is dedicated to vision processing, directly or indirectly. Yet our perception has great limitations that need to be taken into account. As explained earlier, our perception is influenced by our cognition; therefore, it is subjective. One won't necessarily perceive what someone else perceives in the same way. Take Figure 3.2 as an example. What do you perceive? Some random blocks of color stripes? Or *Street*

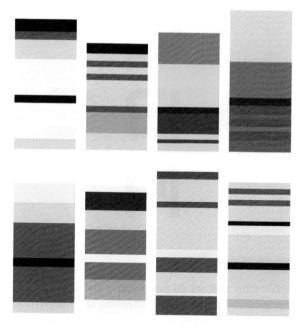

Figure 3.2

Street Fighter—Abstract Edition (2010), by Ashley Browning. (Courtesy of Ashley Browning.)

Fighter characters? Depending on your past experience with that video game and your emotional connection to it, you may perceive the image differently than if you have never played the game or had little exposure to it. When I show this image at video game conferences, roughly half of the crowd perceives Capcom's *Street Fighter* characters, which could seem to be a small proportion given the specialized audience. Imagine then how a less homogeneous population could perceive a given input. Some research has even suggested that language might have some influence on perception and cognition (see, e.g., Whorf 1956, and Hodent *et al.* 2005). Also, if you are among the 8% of the male population (or 0.5% of the female population) who has some sort of color blindness, you perceive Figure 3.2 very differently than most people, and you are likely feeling excluded by this example. (I apologize for that!) As game developers, we need to account for the perceptions of all of our audience, not only the small part of the audience who perceives the environment exactly the same way we do.

Perception is influenced by prior knowledge. (For example, you perceive Figure 3.2 differently whether you played *Street Fighter* extensively or not.) But this is not the only factor that will impact your information processing. For example, context has an impact, too. In Figure 3.3, you are more likely to perceive the middle element as a "B" if you look at the horizontal line, and as a "13" if you look at the vertical line. The same stimulus can therefore be perceived differently depending on the context of which it is a part.

Figure 3.3

Role of context in perception.

These examples show that we do not perceive the world as it is; instead, our brains construct mental images of it. Perception is subjective, and it is influenced by our personal experience, expectations, and even our culture, in some cases. It is therefore important to keep that characteristic of perception in mind when designing the visual and auditory inputs for a video game because what you perceive as a designer, a programmer, or as an artist is not necessarily what your audience will perceive. For example, the save icon (usually illustrated with a floppy disk) is a symbol that does not have any meaning for younger generations who have never interacted with a floppy disk. For them, the functionality expressed by this icon will have to be learned, whereas the older generations who used computers in the last decades of the twentieth century already have a strong mental representation of it.

Marketing can also bias our perception and trick us into choosing a drink that we don't necessarily prefer in reality, while we believe we have free will and make our decisions uninfluenced. Shocking, I know. If you enjoy drinking colas, which between Coke and Pepsi do you prefer? Well, an interesting research study (McClure *et al.* 2004) suggests that your preference is likely influenced. The researchers first asked participants which between Coke and Pepsi they preferred, then gave them a series of taste tests to verify what they actually preferred after they drank samples of each. In some cases, participants drank from unlabeled cups, so they didn't know which one contained Coke and which contained Pepsi. In this blind test condition, participants did not have a clear preference for one or the other even if they had previously declared they had a preference. In another condition, one cup was unlabeled while the other was labeled Coke. Participants were told that the unlabeled cup could either contain Coke or Pepsi, although in reality both cups always contained Coke. (Experimenters can be perfidious in the name of science.) In that case, when asked about their preference, participants showed a strong bias to prefer the cup labeled Coke. Brand knowledge, in the case of Coke, biases our preference decisions. Moreover, when looking at brain scans [functional magnetic resonance imaging (fMRI)] it appears that the delivery of brand-cued Coke activated relatively more regions of the brain that have been found to modify behavior based on emotion and affect (the dorsolateral prefrontal cortex and the hippocampus). In contrast, in the blind test condition where the participants didn't know what brand they were drinking, their preference judgment was solely based on sensory information (relative activity in the ventromedial prefrontal cortex). These results suggest the influence of cultural information—put differently, the power of marketing on people's mind.

Besides these individual differences, perception also has more common limitations that affect us all in the same way. I have no doubt that you know many optical illusions and maybe some auditory ones, such as the Shepard tone that makes you perceive a sound as being continually ascending or descending when in reality it consists of a superposition of a set of tones carefully arranged. If you have played *Super Mario 64* (Nintendo), you might remember the Shepard tone used as you climb up the endless staircase. Another particularity of our visual perception is that our visual acuity is very sharp at the center of our gaze, our fovea, but decreases rapidly as the distance from the fovea increases. In other terms, our central vision is very sharp whereas our peripheral vision is pretty weak, which has direct implications with heads-up displays (HUDs) in games, for example. You cannot expect players who typically gaze at the center of the screen to grasp precisely whatever is popping up in their peripheral vision. They might be able to see something popping in (although not necessarily, as we will see when describing the attention limitations), but it will take them a visual saccade (a movement of the focal vision point) to fixate on the animating elements to precisely perceive what they are. Figure 3.4 demonstrates the variation in acuity

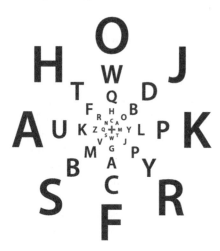

Figure 3.4

Visual acuity. (Adapted from Anstis, S. M. (1974). Letter: A chart demonstrating variations in acuity with retinal position. *Vision Research*, 14, 589–592.)

with the retinal position of certain elements. If you stare at the central cross, the letters need to be increasingly bigger the farther away they are from the fovea to be equally legible (Anstis 1974). Now, I am not saying that you need to necessarily increase the size of the elements on your HUD, I am only pointing out that the information you display in peripheral vision might not be seen precisely (or may not be perceived at all) by players, so it should be simple enough for them to clearly identify and understand.

All in all, perception is a wonderful system, but it has many flaws and limitations that you must be aware of when designing your game. It is particularly central to game development because the experience of your game starts with how your audience is going to perceive it. Therefore, you want to make sure that what they perceive is what you intended them to perceive.

3.3 Application to Games

The main characteristics and limitations of human perception that you need to remember are the following:

- Perception is a construct of the mind.
- We do not perceive reality as it is; we build a mental representation of it.
- This mental representation is influenced by our cognition.
- Perception is subjective; therefore, we might not all perceive a given input the same way.
- Our perception is influenced by our prior knowledge and experience, our expectations and goals, and by the current environmental context.
- Our perception is biased by perceptual illusions that affect us all according to the same principles.

From these characteristics, here are a few applications you can use to design your game more effectively.

3.3.1 Know Your Audience

One of the first applications of the aforementioned list to games entails that you need to have a good understanding of your target audience. Perception is subjective and is influenced by prior knowledge and expectations. Therefore, your audience might not perceive the overall visual and audio cues, the HUD, and the user interface (UI) in the exact same way as the developers designing them do. Also, depending on who your target audience is, they might have different prior knowledge and expectations about the type of game you are creating that will impact their perception of it. An interesting example from the game *No Man's Sky* (Hello Games) can be used to illustrate this point. When this game was released in 2016, it started with a completely white screen on which you could see the word "Initialise…" Underneath it, if you were playing on a PC, you would see the letter E circled. The game developers expected players to perceive this visual cue (sign) as an invitation to start the game by holding down the E key.

(As soon as players pressed the E key, a progression circle would travel clockwise around the circled E on the screen until the circle was complete; then the game would start.) Well, many players (including veteran game developers and hardcore gamers) stayed stuck on that very first screen because they did not understand they had to do something. Most of the players who encountered this issue, according to the posts I've read on social media, thought they simply had to wait for the game to load, and they assumed the game was freezing on them. I believe what happened here is that, first of all, avid gamers have an expectation that a game map needs to load, so they might not have perceived the visual cue "Initialise..." as a sign inviting them to accomplish an action but as an informative sign from the system notifying them that the map (or something) was loading (initializing) and that they needed to wait. This is reinforced by the fact that suspension points ("...") are used as a common visual cue informing players that some content is loading. Second of all (although I do not have access to Hello Games' analytics data), I'm guessing that PC gamers were more often stuck on that screen than console gamers because the "hold button" action is common on consoles but not as common on PCs. Therefore, it is not expected to be a valid action on a PC. The Sony PlayStation 4 (or PS4) version of the game, instead of having a circled E underneath the word "Initialise..." had a circled square button, which is a more commonly used symbol to signify that players have to press the square button. The button on the PS4 controller is indeed round, whereas the E key on a PC keyboard is square, which could have also further confused PC players. This example is a perfect illustration of how players' prior knowledge and expectations as well as platform context can influence gamers' perception, leading them to incorrectly understand relatively simple information. Note that you might get away with frictions like these if people have to pay to play your game because they are committed to go past the opening screen, at the very least. If your game is free to play, however, you had better make sure that no unnecessary frictions (i.e., points of confusion) are impairing the players' ability to play your game because, in the case of being free to play, your game does not benefit from a prior commitment (purchase) and players are therefore less likely to persist if they encounter issues.

So, how can you know your audience? Well, if you are an indie developer, ask yourself who will likely play your game. What visual and audio cues and symbols are they used to (because some depend on the game genre)? What platform are they usually playing on? And so on. Thinking about the audience you want may help you possibly anticipate some usability issues due to perception biases. If you are working in a video game studio that has its own marketing department, I encourage you to chat with the consumer/marketing insights representative to get some valuable information about market segmentation. In some studios, they use a *persona* method to identify a fictional character personifying the goals, preferences, expectations, and behaviors of the target audience. This user-centered method allows the game development team as well as the marketing and publishing teams to be aligned regarding who the core player hypothetically will be. It also helps to keep in mind who is the user you are designing for more specifically, as opposed to trying to remember a cold and abstract market segmentation. (I will describe this tool in more detail in Chapter 14.) Overall, the better you understand your audience, the better you can anticipate how they will perceive the game you are designing.

3.3.2 Playtest Your Game Regularly and Test Your Iconography

Knowing your audience will certainly help you anticipate some issues but not all of them. It is very difficult to take a step back from our own mental model and perspective in order to try to put ourselves into the shoes of a new user who has a different mental model than we do. Even if you consider yourself to be very empathetic, you are still operating under the curse of knowledge bias, and you cannot possibly anticipate all the different ways a new player will perceive your game. You are too close to your game; you know too much about it; and there is no way for you to escape from this bias all by yourself. What you can do, though, is invite players from your target audience whom you do not know personally, and ideally, who do not know anything about your game, to play early versions of it. We will tackle in greater detail how to conduct playtests (a specific kind of UX test whereby participants play through the game with minimum guidance from user researchers) in Chapter 14, but keep in mind that you will discover many issues you had no idea players would encounter simply by watching people play your game. Another thing you can do very early on to fix perception issues related to your HUD and UI is to test the most important icons and symbols you are using by asking people in a survey to describe what they believe the icons illustrate and what functionality they believe they represent in the game. This can be done very early in development with minimal effort, and I will explain this methodology in Chapter 11 when describing the *form follows function* pillar.

3.3.3 Use Gestalt Principles of Perception

A lot of perception biases are common to everyone. To address these, you can use the Gestalt laws of perception to guide your UI design. Gestalt theories of perception were developed by German psychologists in the 1920s. *Gestalt* means configuration in German and *gestaltism* provides useful principles (see Wertheimer 1923) that account for how the human mind organizes the environment, which can be used more specifically to improve the organization of the user interface (UI) and heads-up display (HUD). In his book, *Designing with the Mind in Mind*, Johnson (2010) gives examples of how to use Gestalt principles in software design. Here, I will describe only the most useful principles for video game UI and HUD design: figure/ground, multistability, closure, proximity, similarity, and symmetry.

- **Figure/Ground**
  The figure/ground principle is illustrated in the below figure: Our mind discriminates between a foreground (the figure), which is usually the center of our attention, and a background (ground). In this

illustration, figure/ground ambiguity is used so you can either perceive a vase or two faces. Unless a figure/ground ambiguity is intentional and has a specific purpose in your game, you should try to avoid it in your iconography.

Figure/ground principle

- **Multistability**
  Another example of an ambiguity you want to avoid is multistability. Look at the below figure. What do you perceive, a duck or a rabbit? Again, some icons can be ambiguous—although the designer who created them might not realize this is the case. I remember when we tested some icons at LucasArts for a game in progress (a first-person shooter); the designer created an icon depicting a radar cone with dots representing radar-identified objects. However, when asked to describe the icon, some participants saw a pepperoni pizza slice instead. Once a pizza slice is seen, it becomes very difficult to perceive the icon differently, so the designer had to iterate on this icon to avoid such ambiguity.

Multistability: Is this a duck or a rabbit?

- **Closure**
  Closure is the Gestalt principle stating that we tend to see whole objects, not separated pieces (the whole is greater than the sum of its parts, as the Gestalt motto goes). For example, in the below figure, we tend to see a see a white triangle in the foreground although it is not complete (there isn't

any triangle in fact). We have a tendency to close open figures, which explains why negative space works so well in art. It can, of course, also be used in video games.

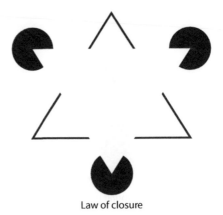

Law of closure

- **Symmetry**
  The principle of symmetry explains that we organize input based on its symmetry. For example, in the below figure, we group similar brackets, "[" and "]," and braces (the curly brackets, or accolades), "{" and "}," with each other because of their symmetry. However, we could group them by how close they are to each other, resulting in four groups (i.e., one bracket alone on each end and two groups made of one bracket and one accolade), which is likely not what you perceive here. This principle allows us to perceive three-dimensional elements depicted in two dimensions, such as the drawing of a cube.

Law of symmetry

- **Similarity**
  The principle of similarity refers to the fact that elements that have the same characteristics, such as color or shape, will be grouped together. For example, in the below figure, you are likely to perceive one group of dots on the left. However, at the top right, you probably perceive columns of circles and squares, whereas at the bottom right, you probably perceive rows of circles and squares. These differences occur because your mind organizes the circles and the squares together since they look similar. It's this principle that helps us understand icons on a map. For example, the blue waves are grouped together to represent water, the brown triangles are grouped together to represent a mountain range, and so on.

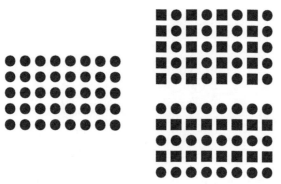

Law of similarity

- **Proximity**

  The principle of proximity states that elements that are closer to one another are perceived as being part of the same group. For example, in the below figure, the dots on the left are perceived as being part of one group but, on the right, three separate groups of dots are perceived because of the added empty space.

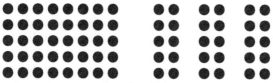

Law of proximity

This principle of proximity is particularly useful when organizing menus without adding lines or arrows to segment space and suggest an orientation. However, this simple law of proximity is often not respected in game menus or HUDs, which can add some friction for players who are trying to make sense of the interface the first time they discover it. Let's take the example of *Far Cry 4*, a first-person shooter game developed by Ubisoft. In the front-end menu, the "skills" tab allows players to spend skill points, as illustrated in Figure 3.5. In this game, there are two sets of skills that you can buy to become more power-ful: offensive skills (the tiger, on the left) or defensive skills (the elephant, on the right). The first time players discover this interface they might believe that the skills can be bought one after the other on the vertical axis. After all, many skill trees in games with role-playing elements behave that way; you unlock them bottom-up or top-down. Furthermore, the skill circles are closer to each other on the vertical axis, which may make players more likely to group them verti-cally. However, that's not how the skills work here. You can buy the tiger skills from right to left and the elephant skills from left to right. If you look more closely, you might see small arrows indicating what path you need to take to unlock skills. This might be a small detail but, by using the Gestalt principle of

Figure 3.5

Far Cry 4 (Ubisoft), skills menu. (Courtesy of Ubisoft Entertainment, © 2014. All Rights Reserved.)

proximity, this unusual skill tree could be understood much more intuitively by players. Let's focus on the elephant skills—the ones on the right. If you only consider the shapes, the pattern is illustrated in Figure 3.6a. As previously mentioned, the circles are closer to one another on the vertical axis, which means that we have a tendency to perceive them as columns, not lines, despite the subtle arrows. By applying the principle of proximity, as shown in Figure 3.6b, we can help players to quickly grasp how to unlock the skills (from left to right) simply

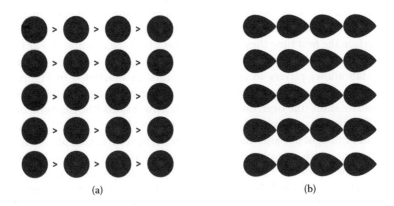

(a)　　　　　　　　　　　　　　　(b)

Figure 3.6

(a) *Far Cry 4* skill tree pattern (b) Applying Gestalt principles to make the skill tree pattern more easily readable.

by placing the dots closer to one another on the horizontal axis and by changing their shape a little bit to infer an orientation. It takes up the exact same space in the interface, and we can remove the subtle arrows that are no longer necessary. This illustrates how you can help players understand an interface more intuitively just by applying Gestalt laws.

3.3.4 Use Affordances

Researchers have suggested that there are two major functions in the visual perception system that fulfills different purposes (Goodale and Milner 1992): a system used to identify objects ("what") and a system used for visually guided actions ("how"). The "what" system codes the information very quickly and is object-centered, or allocentric, which allows us to identify what we are looking at and perceive spatial relationships. The "how" system is a slower system that codes information relative to the person's perspective, which can be referred to as egocentric, and allows us to use the objects surrounding us, such as grabbing our keys on the counter or catching a ball (see Figure 3.7).

One feature of the "how" egocentric system allows us to identify the potential use of objects—in other words, to perceive object affordances (Gibson 1979). For example, a handle on a door affords grasping and pulling while a plate on a door affords pushing. This is the reason why the forms (the shapes) of all the elements in your game (in the interface but also in every other element of art from character design to environment design) are very important because they can help players understand the functionality of these elements and how they work (see Chapter 11 and the *form follows function* pillar). For example, an icon designed with a drop shadow or gradients affords clicking because it mimics the depth of a button in real life (this is called "physical skeuomorphism"). We will see the different types of affordances in greater detail in Chapter 13. Just keep in mind that what the elements of a game look like is not just about style and therefore must be

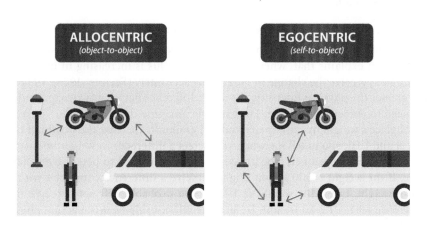

Figure 3.7

Allocentric versus egocentric.

carefully considered. This doesn't only impact art direction; it also deeply affects how intuitive (or usable) your game will be.

3.3.5 Understand Visual Imagery and Mental Rotation

Visual imagery allows us to construct a mental representation of an object. For example, if you close your eyes and imagine the map of the country you live in, this constitutes a mental representation of this country that is different from what you actually perceive when you look at Google Maps. Visual imagery also allows us to anticipate the transformation or movement of an object. For example, when you play a game of *Tetris* (originally created by game designer Alexey Pajitnov), you can anticipate how you can place the next shape (named "tetromino") by mentally rotating it. The funny thing is that, when we mentally rotate an object, it takes us proportionally more time the more we need to rotate it (Shepard and Metzler 1971). For example, if you need to mentally rotate a tetromino by 180 degrees to anticipate if it can fit in an empty space in your game, it will take you more time than if you only need to rotate it by 90 degrees to find a good-fitting spot (nearly twice as much time—although you won't probably realize it). One of the most direct applications of this phenomenon in video games has to do with maps and minimaps. Just like on your phone, a map in a game can be either allocentric (always orientated in the same way—usually using cardinal points, with North pointing up) or egocentric (orientated depending on where the user is standing; if you are facing South, South will be pointing up on your map). In a game with a first-person or third-person camera (as opposed to a top-down camera), having a map that is allocentric, and therefore not relative to the player, will take more time to use because players then need to rotate it mentally to navigate. This might seem like a small detail but, depending on the type of game you are developing, having an egocentric map or minimap can remove considerable friction (the friction being in this case extra cognitive load caused by the necessity of a mental rotation).

3.3.6 Be Aware of the Weber–Fechner Bias

The last example of perception bias I will talk about here is the Weber–Fechner bias, which explains that, when a physical stimulus is increasing in intensity, we do not perceive the change in magnitude accurately (Fechner 1966). In fact, the greater the physical intensity, the more difference between two magnitudes we need to detect a difference. For example, imagine that I blindfold you and that I place a weight in your open hand. If I gradually increase the weight of the object and I ask you to tell me when you detect a difference in weight intensity, the heavier the object gets, the greater increase you need to perceive a difference. If the weight is 100 g, you might perceive a difference compared with a 200-g weight; but if the weight is 1.1 kg, you probably will not perceive the difference with a 1.2-kg weight. In fact, the relationship between actual physical stimulus intensity and its *perceived* intensity is logarithmic, not linear, as illustrated in Figure 3.8. This bias, or law, has a direct impact on games having analog controls, such as those using the analog controller sticks or those tilt

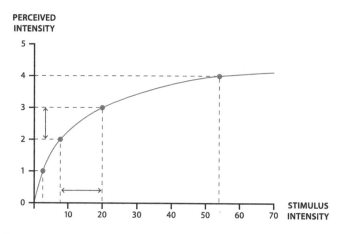

Figure 3.8

The Weber–Fechner law.

controls using a gyroscope sensor. The intended change in movement intensity players want to execute (expected outcome) will not be linear in relation to the actual force they *perceive* they need to apply, so gameplay programmers will have to fine-tune the analog response, keeping the Weber–Fechner law in mind. If your game requires twitch skills, it will also be important to conduct UX tests with players having to perform specific tasks in specifically designed "testing rooms" (sometimes called "gym levels") in order to measure on average what force players apply to the controller to reach a certain goal (for console games). For example, you could ask players to aim at pop-up targets as fast as possible while you vary the distance between two targets. You will then be able to verify the amplitude by which players sway the analog stick to reach the next target depending on its distance from the previous one. If players have, on average, a tendency to go past the target and correct their trajectory, it means that the controls are too sensitive for this particular task. If players have a tendency to stop pushing the stick too early before reaching the target, it means that the controls are too stiff for this particular task. Fine-tuning the controls (input parameters) has a very important impact on game feel (see Swink 2009), which we will address in Chapter 12.

Another impact of the Weber–Fechner bias is that gains with a threshold (such as experience points to level up in role-playing games, for example) will feel less rewarding the farther away the next step is. For example, at Level 1, the experience bar of your avatar is typically smaller (or fills up faster) than at Level 30, so you need more experience points (XP) to gain a level. Therefore, players will need a logarithmic increase of XP to feel the same progress pace all throughout the game. A linear increase of XP would be perceived as progressing more slowly as players level up. Depending on the intended perception you want players to have, it will impact how you will need to fine-tune progression (linearly or logarithmically).

4

Memory

4.1   How Memory Works   4.3   Application to Games
4.2   Limitations of Human
      Memory

4.1 How Memory Works

Remembering something—say, your e-mail box password—implies retrieving information that was previously encoded and stored. Memory is not only the process of storing information, it encompasses these three steps: encoding, storage, and retrieval. A popular architectural model of memory in psychology, called the multistore model (Atkinson and Shiffrin 1968), suggests that human memory has three components: sensory stores, short-term store, and long-term store (see Figure 4.1). Before I describe each of these stores, or memory types, keep in mind that they are functional components (as opposed to physical brain areas) and that, as always with the brain, memory is more complex than this simple breakdown; the components are not necessarily independent from one another, nor are they necessarily separated in a clear-cut way. Information processing does not necessarily go from sensory to short-term to long-term memory in this serial order. Many researchers have challenged and refined this model since it was first outlined; yet it is good enough for the purposes of this book. The only nuance I will mention when describing the model concerns the short-term memory because it was later replaced by the concept of working memory, which is a more relevant concept when considering video games.

Multistore Model of Memory (Adapted from Atkinson, R.C., & Shiffrin, R.M., 1968, Human memory: A Proposed System and its Control Processes, *in* K.W. Spence & J.T. Spence (Eds.), *The Psychology of Learning and Motivation*, Vol. 2, Academic Press, New York, pp. 89–195.)

4.1.1 Sensory Memory

According to the multistore model, information is first stored very briefly (for less than a second to a few seconds at most) in one of the sensory stores, depending on the modality—the iconic memory for visual information or the echoic memory for auditory information. (There are other sensory stores but they haven't had as much attention from researchers so far.) Sensory memory is therefore usually considered as being part of perception, not memory, but as I previously said, mental processes are not strictly separated into independent modules. Persistence of vision is an example of an expression of iconic memory and allows you to see a continuous animation even though only 24 images per second are displayed. However, if the information is not attended to, it will be lost very quickly, within a second. The change blindness phenomenon illustrates this visual sensory memory limitation beautifully. Take a picture of an outside scene and make a copy in which you modify one salient element—for example, move one tree a little bit or remove a prominent shadow. If you present both pictures one after the other with a flicker between the two images and make them loop indefinitely, you have your change blindness test material ready. For example, you show image A (the original one) for less than a second, then you add an 80-ms blank (called a "flicker"), then you show the altered image A' for the same time as A, then another 80-ms blank, then image A again, and so on. The flicker forces you to rely on your sensory memory to compare the two images. If you ask people to identify the change between the two images, it will actually take them quite some time. We are very often blind to salient changes occurring in a visual scene (Rensink *et al.* 1997). Until you *draw attention* to the specific element that is changing from one image to the other, you stay blind to that change, and that's because the information retained in sensory memory is ephemeral. If you remove the flicker between the two images, then the change is much easier to spot because it stands out as being the only "moving" element when you alternate indefinitely two images that only have one difference. (If you want to try it yourself, I invite you to visit the Web page of University of British Columbia psychologist Ron Rensink: http://www.cs.ubc.ca/~rensink/flicker/.) The change blindness phenomenon illustrates the critical role of attention to detect changes. The somehow amusing catch about this phenomenon is the change blindness *blindness*: We do not realize that we are very often blind to salient changes, and we even overestimate our ability to detect changes. What this means for games is that, even if you make a very clear and significant change in your front-end menu to, for example, promote some new content, your players may not necessarily notice the change. Another example would be that the player has unlocked an ability enabling a new element on the heads-up display (HUD): The player might take some time to realize that the HUD has changed. So, if the new content or the change is really important for your game, you might want to draw attention to it very explicitly—for example, by making the element blink every now and then and adding sound effects when relevant.

Although paying attention to an element is critical to perceive it changing, change blindness can still occur for attended objects. In a study conducted by Simons and Levin (1998), an experimenter interrupts random people on the street to ask for directions. The pedestrian starts giving directions to the experimenter but is briefly interrupted by two people passing between them carrying a door. As they pass by, one of the door carriers surreptitiously swaps roles with the experimenter and continues the conversation with the pedestrian as if nothing has happened. About half of the participants failed to detect that they were talking to a different person after the occlusion happened. (You can see a video from this "door" study at: https://www.youtube.com/watch?v=FWSxSQsspiQ.) This surprising effect has been replicated in various situations, and it emphasizes that attention is undoubtedly important yet not always sufficient to accurately process what is going on in our environment. It can be argued though that participants in these studies actually did not pay attention to their interlocutor enough because they were distracted by some other tasks (i.e., giving directions). However, at the very least, these studies emphasize that superficial attention is often not enough to notice changes.

4.1.2 Short-Term Memory

If the information that is very briefly stored in the sensory memory gets some attention, it can be processed in short-term memory. Short-term memory has a very limited capacity in time (less than a minute) and space (referring to the number of items that can be stored in short-term memory at the same time). You might have heard of the concept of the magical number seven, plus or minus two, which was considered the short-term memory span (Miller 1956). This refers to the number of items that someone can recall without errors immediately after encoding them. For example, if I present you with a list of 20 words to remember and I give you one minute to memorize them, you will likely be able to recall five to nine words (seven more or less two). The remembered words are usually the first ones and the last ones on the list, corresponding to the elements that were processed first and last during the encoding exercise. This is called the primacy effect and the recency effect, and these are important to take into account for marketing trailers. For example, the important information should be presented at the very beginning of the video and/or at the very end to have more of a chance of being remembered.

So, short-term memory can retain around seven items. What constitutes an "item" is the largest meaningful unit: letters, words, digits, numbers, and so on. Consider the following digits:

$$1 - 7 - 8 - 9 - 3 - 1 - 4 - 1 - 6 - 1 - 4 - 9 - 2$$

These are 13 items, which can be very hard to remember unless you can group them into larger meaningful chunks:

$$1789 - 3.1416 - 1492$$

Now, these constitute three meaningful items: the year of the French Revolution (or the year the first American president, George Washington, was elected), an approximation of pi, and the year Christopher Columbus reportedly discovered America. This concept of the magic number seven to understand short-term memory is widely popular, but there's a twist: It's usually only valid if you try to remember items by rote learning without processing any other information, which is pretty rare in our everyday life. Here's one example of when you could use your short-term memory: Imagine you are visiting your parents' home (or grandparents') and you need to connect your smartphone to their Wi-Fi. Because they are not particularly tech savvy, their Wi-Fi password is the default long list of digits and letters displayed on the modem. Imagine now that your phone is charging away from the modem and you're too lazy to go find a pen and paper to write down the password. So, you need to try to encode the password and retain this information long enough to get to your phone and type it in. Well, in that very specific case, you would use your short-term memory and probably repeat the string of characters in your head (or even out loud) until you feel you can retain it for the time it takes you rush to your phone (assuming the password is within seven more or less two characters). If you have ever experienced a similar situation, you might have noticed that, if someone talks to you at any moment during this whole process, or if anything distracts your attention, you will likely forget the password, except maybe for the first and/or last characters. This is because of the primacy and recency effects I mentioned earlier. Short-term memory only accounts for information that we store temporarily without doing much else, which doesn't happen very often. This is why the concept of short-term memory needed to be replaced by one accounting for our more complex everyday life and, in our case, for our information processing when playing a video game: that is, working memory.

4.1.3 Working Memory

Working memory (WM) is a short-term memory that allows us to temporarily store *and* process information (Baddeley and Hitch 1974). For example, if I asked you to mentally calculate 876 + 758, it would likely require you to keep the numbers in short-term storage in addition to processing them. Another example would be if I asked you to read the section about short-term memory again out loud and you had to remember the last word of every sentence (which is a task similar to the one originally designed by Daneman and Carpenter (1980) to measure WM capacity). In our everyday life, WM is usually the memory system that helps us accomplish our tasks. It turns out that it is severely limited in capacity: An adult can hold about three to four items in WM simultaneously, and this number can be even lower in some cases. Stress and anxiety, for example, have been identified as negatively impacting the WM capacity (Eysenck *et al.* 2007). Children also have a lower WM span.

WM accomplishes executive functions and complex cognitive tasks. It has an important role in controlled attention and reasoning, so you need to account for its limitations. WM is composed of a central executive component supervising two "slave systems" responsible for short-term maintenance of information: a visuospatial sketchpad and a phonological loop. The phonological loop stores all information relative to language while the visuospatial sketchpad stores all visual and spatial information. Imagine this task: You have to underline all the verbs in an unfamiliar text while singing the lyrics of a song. This task is pretty demanding for WM because the phonological loop needs to deal with two phonological tasks (underlying verbs and generating lyrics) competing for attentional resources. When I ask developers to accomplish this task in my user experience training sessions, they usually stop singing every now and then or sing some gibberish, miss some verbs, falsely identify a word as being a verb, and more importantly, they usually have no idea what the text is about when I ask them after the task is over. This is just too much information to process for WM. Now, if I ask them to sing the lyrics of a song while drawing a picture, it's usually easier for them to do this; that's because the phonological loop is dealing with the language task (singing) while the visual sketchpad is dealing with the visuomotor task (drawing). While it may be easier, completing two tasks soliciting both slave systems is still less efficient than completing one task at a time, depending on how much attentional resources each task demands. When none of the tasks are demanding (say, chewing gum while walking), it's usually fine. When at least one of the tasks becomes more demanding, trying to multitask usually leads to less efficiency or results in making more mistakes in *both* tasks. Take the example of driving while listening to music. Imagine that you are driving your car on the way home from work. You are an expert driver and you know the road by heart. You can in that condition easily listen to music and even sing along while you drive. No big deal. Now imagine that there is some construction work on the way forcing you to follow a route that is completely new to you. It's very likely that you will then stop singing to direct your attention to the unfamiliar navigation task. You might even turn the volume of your radio down to help your focus. We are not good at all at multitasking and, again, we are often unaware of it. Our brain has limited attentional resources, which are critical to processing information in WM and therefore have a direct impact on how well we will retain information in long-term memory. The limitations of our attention will be tackled in more detail in Chapter 5.

The interesting thing about WM in terms of retention of information is that the deeper the information is processed in WM the better the long-term retention (Craik and Lockhart 1972). For example, Craik and Tulving (1975) tested the impact of level of processing on incidental learning. Participants were presented with a list of words and for each they had to either decide if the word was in capital letters (shallow structural processing, fast to complete), decide if the word rhymed with a target word (medium phonemic processing), or decide if the word could fit the blank in a sentence (deep, semantic processing, longer to complete). Participants had to answer "yes" or "no" for each question, and they did not know that their memory would be tested afterward (incidental learning); they were instead informed that the experiment concerned perception and speed of reaction. Once the task was over, they took a recognition test: They were given a sheet containing the 60 words used in the task plus 120 similar words used as distractors, and they were asked to check all the words they remembered having seen in the task. Results showed that the number of words correctly recognized (i.e., remembered) could be as much as about four times higher in the deep processing condition (when participants had to decide if the word could fit a sentence) compared to the shallow one (when they had to decide if the word was in uppercase). More specifically, recognition performance increased from 15% for case decisions to 81% for sentence decision when the answer to the question during the first task was "yes" (interestingly, recognition of "no" words also increased, but less severely, from 19% to 49%). The level of processing therefore has a dramatic impact on incidental learning and retention. This means that all the important features that your player must remember should be taught in a situation where they have to process the information deeply, which usually requires more cognitive resources and takes more time than processing information superficially. This is why learning by doing is generally more efficient than learning by reading a tutorial text because when you act, when you accomplish a task, it requires a deeper level of processing in WM. Although it depends, of course, on the complexity of the task, but simply pressing a button to acknowledge reading a tutorial text does not require a deep level of processing.

4.1.4 Long-Term Memory

Long-term memory is a system that allows us to store all kinds of information—from the movements you need to make to drive a car to facts like your cell phone number. Contrary to sensory and working memories that we know have strong limitations, long-term memory has no known limits in time and space. This means that it could potentially store an unlimited number of information for an unlimited time, sometimes even for a lifetime—*potentially*. In reality, we forget information all the time, but we'll get to memory lapses in a moment. Long-term memory has two main components that store different types of information: explicit memory and implicit memory.

Explicit memory refers to all information that you can describe, that can be declared (explicit memory is often also called "declarative memory"), and that you explicitly know you know. It includes information such as the capitals of European countries, the name of your parents, the first video game you played, the last movie you watched, your favorite book, the places you went on vacation, the date of birth of your loved ones, the discussion you had with your colleagues yesterday, the languages you speak, and so on. It's the memory for facts (semantic) and events (episodic). In contrast, implicit memory (also called procedural memory) refers to all non-declarative information that is tied to action. It's information that you cannot easily describe and that does not involve conscious recollection—for example, how to play the guitar, how to ride a bike, how to drive a car, or what is the sequence of buttons you need to press to execute your favorite *Street Fighter* combo move. In a nutshell, the explicit memory stores knowledge while implicit memory stores how we do things, and they are associated with different brain regions. Thus, amnesic patients with a damaged hippocampus—the brain region partly responsible for explicit memory—can still learn new motor skills such as a new drawing technique (procedural learning in implicit memory), although they would not remember that any of the lessons ever took place (explicit declarative memory).

Implicit memory is involved in priming and in conditional responses, both of which can be interesting to use in video games. Priming is the effect whereby a response to a stimulus is influenced by the exposure of another stimulus presented right beforehand. For example, if I asked you to determine whether a stimulus is an existing word (e.g., BUTTER) or a nonword (e.g., SMUKE), which is called a lexical decision task, your response time in deciding that BUTTER is indeed a word would be faster if you read the word BREAD right before, which represents a semantic prime (Schvaneveldt and Meyer 1973). The priming effect can even work in some cases when the previous word is masked (presented too fast to be attended) and therefore is not consciously perceived by participants. (Remember, when a stimulus is presented too fast for you to fully pay attention to it, it stays transitorily in sensory memory.) That's probably the most impressive and scientifically validated effect of subliminal influence. I know; it's less exciting than imagining that a subliminal input could make us do things we did not really want to do! Subliminal priming is, in reality, very limited, such as in the example I used earlier, so we cannot suggest marketers can stealthily influence us with subliminal messaging. To be fair, they do not need to because they can simply exploit our cognitive biases—so it's up to you to learn how to identify when this happens. To go back to game development, you could think of using a priming effect to facilitate or hinder your players' reaction time in shooting an enemy, for example. If you make something flash close to the area where an enemy appears right afterward, it will constitute a perceptual priming that will draw players' attention to the specific area and therefore prepare them to react to the enemy. If, on the contrary, you draw attention to the opposite corner of the screen right before the enemy enters the scene, this will likely increase players' reaction time.

The other interesting characteristic of implicit memory is its implication for conditional responses. Conditioning is a form of implicit learning by which two stimuli are associated. Just like how Pavlov's dogs were conditioned to salivate when hearing a bell ring because this sound was usually followed by food presentation, you can be conditioned to react to a specific stimulus. If you have played *Metal Gear Solid* (Konami), you may have been conditioned to have an emotional and behavioral response when you hear the alert sound effect because you have learned over time that this sound signals an imminent danger. (For those of you who haven't played *Metal Gear Solid*, the alert sound can be heard every time an enemy notices you.) We will describe conditioning in more detail in Chapter 8. Some researchers have suggested that implicit learning is more robust than explicit learning (Reber 1989) mainly because it seems to last longer than explicit knowledge. As the saying goes, you never forget how to ride a bike! However, as you have probably guessed by now, it's not exactly true. We do forget implicit learning. Try to play an action-packed game relying on twitch gameplay after putting it down for a while; you need to retrain your "muscle memory" (procedural memory) to get back in shape. Taking advantage of implicit learning can still be very powerful because learning is happening mostly incidentally and, in some cases, can indeed be more robust than explicit learning, especially when it concerns "muscle memory" and when that learning has some emotional content such as in the *Metal Gear Solid* example.

4.2 Limitations of Human Memory

Human memory is a fascinating system allowing us to individually discover and learn as well as to develop a culture and progress together as a society. However, our memory has many limitations of which game developers must be mindful to avoid common pitfalls. The most obvious limitation of our memory is memory lapse. We are all pretty aware that we constantly forget information, yet I frequently observe developers acting surprised while watching a playtest session when they see players forgetting about a feature they learned to use just minutes before. In the late eighteenth century, Herman Ebbinghaus, a German psychologist, was the first to experimentally study the boundaries of our memory (Ebbinghaus 1885). He established the now famous forgetting curve, as presented in Figure 4.2. To come up with that curve, Ebbinghaus actually tested himself. He memorized a long list of nonsensical syllables (e.g., "WID," "LEV," "ZOF," etc.) and measured how many of these he could recall as time passed by. The results are pretty dramatic: After only 20 minutes, about 40% of the content learned was already forgotten and, after a day, nearly 70% of the content learned was forgotten. Several researchers with a more standardized approach later replicated these results, and the forgetting curve remains generally valid today. Think of it as the worst-case scenario for your players' memory. This forgetting curve is obtained when people have to memorize non-meaningful content for no real purpose and with no mnemonic techniques of any kind. Hopefully, it won't be that bad in the context of learning how to play and master a game where the material should be meaningful and reinforced by the game.

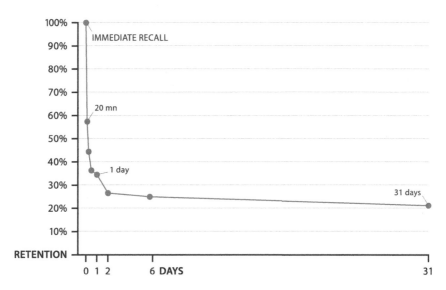

Figure 4.2

Forgetting curve. (Adapted from Ebbinghaus, H., 1885, *Über das Gedächtnis*, Dunker, Leipzig, *Translated* Ebbinghaus, H., 1913/1885, *Memory: A Contribution to Experimental Psychology*, Ruger HA, Bussenius CE, translators, Teachers College, Columbia University, New York.)

If the material to learn is meaningful and if the environment helps in the memorizing of it, such as by repeating the material in different contexts and increasing the depth of processing, this will positively impact the rate that players forget it. We also know that some information is easier to remember than others. For example, recent information can be better preserved if associated with already well-known information; simple information is better preserved over complex information; organized information is better preserved than messy information; images are better remembered than their word counterparts; meaningful information is better preserved than nonmeaningful information, and so on. Therefore, you can try to associate new information with already familiar concepts, make sure to organize information clearly in menus and the HUD, use a well-designed iconography as much as you can (but be careful because it's sometimes more beneficial to add a word to the icon if the function it represents is not clear), make sure that what you teach players is always meaningful to them, and so on. However, you must keep in mind that players will undoubtedly forget many things about your game—from the controller mapping to their next objective.

Not only are we prone to forget information but also what we do remember is often distorted, especially when considering declarative memory (knowledge, facts, events). We can recall a memory that actually did not occur (false memory bias), or our memories can be biased and distorted by our cognition just like our perception is. In a study examining the reliability of eyewitness testimonies, Loftus and Palmer (1974) found that memories could be influenced by something as simple as how a question is framed. In this study, participants were shown video clips of different traffic accidents. In one condition, the question asked of them after they watched a video was "How fast were the cars going when they *hit* each other?" In another condition, the question asked was "How fast were the cars going when they *smashed* each other?"—only changing the verb describing the crash. I'm emphasizing the verbs "hit" and "smashed" to help you detect the difference between the two sentences, but in the study no particular font effect was used. The results showed that, in the condition where the verb "smashed" was used, the participants estimated the speed of the cars being faster (10.46 mph) than in the condition where the verb "hit" was used (8 mph), and this was a statistically significant finding. Moreover, a week later, the same participants were asked, without seeing the video again, if they remembered seeing any broken glass in the scene (there was none). About twice as many participants falsely remembered seeing broken glass in the "smashed" condition versus the "hit" condition. Simply using the verb "smashed," which conveys more intensity than the verb "hit," in a question had some influence on the participants' memory of the accident they watched. This is what we call a "leading question." The subtle impact that one word can have on our memories is both fascinating and concerning. This admittedly raises a lot of questions regarding the validity of eyewitness testimonies in a court, especially because they are among the greatest contributors to wrongful convictions (Pickel 2015). On another note (if you allow me to make a big leap here), it could maybe explain why Steve Jobs' keynotes were so appreciated. Whether Jobs was aware of memory biases or not, he was often using words such as "amazing," "incredible," and "gorgeous" when revealing new Apple products or features, which might have had some influence on how the audience remembered the content of the keynotes. In another study, this time conducted in Sweden by Lindholm and Christianson (1998), participants had to watch the video of a (simulated) crime being committed—a robbery during which the perpetrator seriously injured a cashier. After watching the video, participants were shown pictures of eight men and they had to try to identify who among them was the perpetrator of the crime. The results showed that participants—both Swedish and immigrant students—were twice as likely to mistakenly identify an immigrant rather than a Swede as being the crime perpetrator. Our memory biases can have some grim consequences in some cases, and it is our responsibility to keep these biases in mind to avoid injustice in our society. The impact is surely less dramatic for our subject matter, yet it means that, when you ask players to fill out surveys about your game, their answers are based on the (often biased) *memory* they have about their experience—not about how they *exactly* experienced the game. So, take it with a grain of salt and make sure to design your surveys in a way to avoid biasing answers as much as possible (more about surveys in Chapter 14).

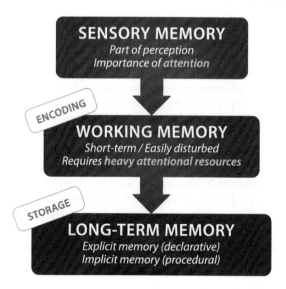

Figure 4.3

Overview of memory.

4.3 Application to Games

We saw earlier that our perception is a subjective *construct* of our mind. Not only do we not perceive the reality as it is, but our memory of it can also be distorted because memory is a process of *reconstruction*. The main characteristics and limitations of human memory that you need to remember are the following:

- Memory is a system that encodes, stores, and later retrieves information.
- It can be broken down into sensory memory (which is a part of perception), WM (heavily relying on attention to encode information and process retrieved information), and long-term memory (storage); see Figure 4.3.
- The level of processing happening in WM during the encoding phase has an impact on the quality of retention. The deeper the process, the better the retention.
- Long-term memory consists of explicit memory (declarative information) and implicit memory (procedural information).
- The forgetting curve illustrates the decline of memory retention in time.
- When the content learned is nonmeaningful and the information processing is shallow, the decline in long-term memory is worse.
- When we do remember information, our memories can be distorted and biased.

The main concern when it comes to video games is to make sure players will remember the critical information necessary to enjoy the game (e.g., game controls, mechanics, objectives, etc.). Given that memory is responsible for encoding, storing, and retrieving information, a memory lapse can be a result of an encoding deficit, a storage deficit, or a recall deficit (or a mix of these because the quality of encoding has an impact on storage). An encoding deficit happens when information is superficially encoded—because of a lack of attention or because of a lack of depth during information processing. To avoid it, it's critical to draw players' attention to the important information and to make them process it deeply. A storage deficit happens when information is correctly encoded but it weakens with time (forgetting curve). To avoid this deficit, it's important to reconsolidate (strengthen) memories, mainly by repeating in different contexts the content that players must remember. A recall deficit happens when information is available in memory but is momentarily inaccessible (e.g., the "tip of the tongue" phenomenon). To avoid recall deficit, you can give frequent reminders to players so they do not have to retrieve certain information stored in memory. In this section, I will exclusively focus on storage and recall deficits affecting long-term memory because we will tackle the encoding deficit in the next chapter about attention (upon which WM relies).

4.3.1 Spacing Effect and Level Design

When we learn about something—say, how to use a new ability in a game—the long-term memory for the event and its associated procedural information (finger movements to execute the action) is usually not instantaneously sealed in the brain unless it's already familiar information (e.g., it's the same kind of ability as in a game you have previously played). Instead, the memory for the event consolidates, or is reinforced, after each occurrence. This is the reason why repetition is crucial to learning. However, repetition should be spaced apart in time to have a greater impact on retention (see Paivio 1974; Toppino *et al.* 1991; Greene 2008). Every time information is repeated, its relative forgetting curve becomes less steep. What this means is that, to consolidate a teaching, you do not need to give a reminder at regular intervals. Instead, the more you repeat a teaching, the more you can space the reminders out, as shown in Figure 4.4. It also means that it's more efficient to distribute learning over time rather than teach too much at a given point (i.e., massed learning). There are likely a lot of things you need to teach your players, so it's better to make a plan for your onboarding. I will give an example of how to make an onboarding plan in Chapter 13. Keep in mind that you will need to distribute teaching the most complex features of your game over time. For example, to teach a complex mechanic, you might want to give a reminder quite soon after the first exposure. Then, you can introduce a second mechanic or feature while you keep consolidating the first teaching (see Figure 4.5), preferentially across various contexts. Nintendo games are often very efficient at introducing new mechanics while consolidating a previously taught mechanic, until both can be combined and another mechanic or a feature is introduced. Take *Super Mario Bros.,* for example. One of the first things you learn is the jumping mechanic (let's call it Teaching A). You first have to jump over an enemy (A), then you can jump to hit question blocks (A2), then you jump over obstacles (A3), and so on. The jumping mechanic is repeated in various contexts and gets increasingly difficult because you need to be more precise. At some point, you are introduced to the shooting mechanic (Teaching B), and you get to practice it by shooting a few enemies (B2); then you jump to hit some blocks and collect coins (A4). Another enemy comes by, a Koopa Troopa (the turtle). This enemy cannot be easily defeated by jumping on it, which is an affordance signified to the player by the turtle's shell (see the *form follows function* pillar tackled in Chapter 11). So it's better to shoot it (B3). And so on. At some point in the game, you might also need to shoot enemies while jumping, which is

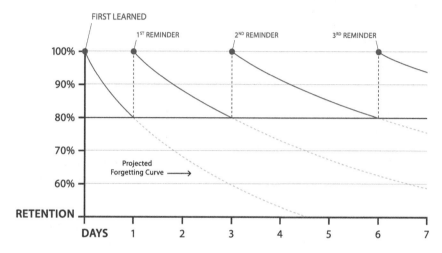

Figure 4.4

Spacing effect.

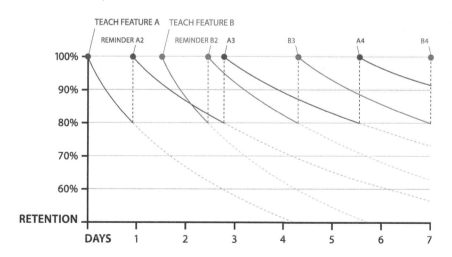

Figure 4.5

Spacing effect when teaching two features.

combining both mechanics. Depending on the type of game you are developing and the audience you are targeting (expert or novice), determining the onboarding plan will be more or less difficult. In any case, you need to think about tutorials as being a part of the level design. Learning to play and master a game is a substantial part of the experience. If you design the game without thinking about how to introduce the mechanics and features ahead of time, you will end up having to squeeze in all your tutorials at the beginning of the game, which is less efficient and also usually not appreciated by gamers.

4.3.2 Reminders

Playing a video game is an activity often happening across several days or more. If your game has enough content, it will likely not all be consumed in one go. Players will launch the game and maybe play for a few hours. If a player has significantly progressed during their first game session, the system has also likely increased in difficulty accordingly to keep the challenge at the right level (not too easy, not too hard—see Chapter 12 and the section about gameflow). At some point, players will inevitably put the game down to go on with their lives. If they do pick up the game again, the time that has elapsed since their first game session is unknown and could range from a few hours to a few days or more. When the player finally resumes the game, the system does not usually take into account how much time has passed. During that time, the forgetting curve occurred and some amount of information learned during the first game session was inexorably lost; the memory loss increases with the time elapsed. What happens then is that there can be some discrepancy between the player's skill level and the challenge level reached at the end of the last game session. Players might have forgotten about some game mechanics, controls, or objectives, but they can also feel downgraded because they now need to catch up with the system (see Figure 4.6). One of the things you can do is to provide reminders when players resume the game. Interestingly, the action-adventure game *Alan Wake* (Remedy Entertainment) gave a reminder about the story when the game was resumed in the same way that TV shows provide a summary of the previous episodes. However, reminders about the game mechanics and controls will be the most important ones because a game is an interactive experience and it needs input from players to unfold. If your system allows for it, you can think of adding dynamic tutorial tips that can pop up if players don't perform the required action for a certain amount of time. These tutorial tips, although not the best method during information encoding, can act as reminders to consolidate previously learned information. You could also make sure to always display the important information on-screen to prevent players from having to retrieve that information. For example, in the open world action-adventure game *Assassin's Creed Syndicate* (Ubisoft), the HUD always provides a contextual mapping of the controls (see Figure 4.7). This allows players to know exactly what actions they can accomplish at all times (e.g., "shoot," "counter," "stun," etc.) but also how to execute them because the information is displayed in such a way as to mirror the four face buttons of a console controller. They never have to remember this information; this HUD design alone reduces players' memory load and prevents any storage or recall deficit (at least for the control mapping of these actions). Similarly, in the action-building game *Fortnite* (Epic Games), every time the player comes near a searchable object, the key that needs to be pressed to search it pops up in the user interface (Figure 4.8).

So, you cannot assume that because players successfully went through your tutorials they will remember forever the things they have learned. Players have busy lives, and they might abandon your game for a while because a blockbuster was just released or maybe because they need to reduce their gaming habit for a few weeks to concentrate on their finals. If you do not provide reminders in your game to allow your players to get back to speed after they were away for some

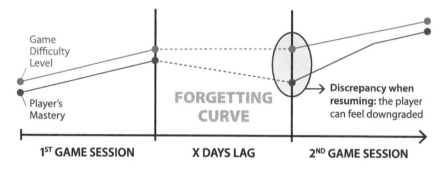

Figure 4.6

An example of the forgetting curve applied to games.

Figure 4.7

Assassin's Creed Syndicate (Ubisoft). (Courtesy of Ubisoft Entertainment, © 2015. All Rights Reserved.)

Figure 4.8

Fortnite Beta © 2017, Epic Games, Inc. (Courtesy of Epic Games, Inc., Cary, NC.)

time, you increase the likelihood that it will demand too much effort of them to catch up and increase the likelihood that they will churn for good. That's one of the reasons why many free-to-play games have introduced a daily chest feature to encourage players to come back every day. Not only does it keep players engaged with your game because they have a reason to come back daily, but it also increases the likelihood that they will play for a little while because they are already logged in—thus consolidating the memories and learning tied to the game.

Overall, what you need to keep in mind here is that, no matter how hard you will try, players will forget some amount of information. So you need to list all the things that players will have to learn and remember in your game (which I call putting together the onboarding plan) so you can prioritize it. The top elements on your list are the ones that you will want to teach deeply and provide reminders for. The elements at the bottom of your list should probably be implemented in a way that it's not critical if players forget about them or, whenever possible, you should offer memory aids for them. For example, if your game is not about the challenge of remembering the button you need to press to accomplish certain actions, consider displaying that information at all times, such as in the *Assassin's Creed* example. You likely won't be able to craft the perfect learning experience for your game, so define what is critical to the game experience and focus on it.

5

Attention

5.1   How Attention Works
5.2   Limitations of Human Attention

5.3   Application to Games

5.1 How Attention Works

Our senses are continuously assailed by multiple inputs from our environment. Attention allows us to concentrate our processing resources onto selected inputs. We use attention to process what we perceive around us and to accomplish every single task of our busy days. In fact, when we do not pay enough attention to what we are doing that often is when mistakes occur. Maybe your coffee mug fell on the floor this morning because you didn't really pay attention to where you were putting it down (as it turned out, not entirely on the table). Our attention can be active or passive. In the case of active attention, it is a controlled and top-down process by which you direct your attention to a certain goal, such as checking the e-mails on your phone. Passive attention is a bottom-up process whereby the environment triggers an attentional response from you. For example, imagine you are walking down a corridor at work and someone behind you calls your name, which draws your attention and makes you turn around to focus on the person calling out to you. Your attention can also be focused or divided. When your attention is focused (which is also called "selective attention"), it acts like a spotlight that selects a certain element of your environment to process while keeping the rest in the dark. The "cocktail party effect" (Cherry 1953) is an example of focused attention: When you are having a conversation with someone in the midst of a loud party, you can focus specifically on what that person is saying while all other conversations are filtered out. By contrast, your attention is divided when you try to focus on two or more elements at the same time (which is more commonly called "multitasking"). For example, your active, top-down, and selective attention allows you to fully focus on what your boss is telling you at a work party. At some point, you hear your name mentioned in a nearby conversation: Your passive, bottom-up, attention triggers you to now also listen to this other conversation because you are curious to know what these people are saying about you. Because you do not want to be rude to your boss, you still try to listen to what she is telling you at the same time, which is a case of divided attention (multitasking). It can be extremely difficult to process two sources of information at the same time. In fact, what happens in that case is that you "flip-flop" your focus from one conversation to the other, hoping to fill in the gaps of what you are missing. If you do not remember the limitations of working memory that we tackled in the previous chapter, let me take this opportunity to offer you a reminder (so that your forgetting curve for that memory can be smoothed out a little bit): This example is a case of working memory directing attentional resources to the phonological loop system because it has two language-processing tasks to complete by itself. This kind of situations triggers a "processing bottleneck," seriously limiting our ability to process both tasks properly.

Just like perception and memory, attention can be influenced by prior knowledge and expertise. For example, musicians showed better performance than nonmusicians in following a melody when random distractor notes were added to the tune (Marozeau *et al.* 2010). This suggests that expert gamers will probably have less difficulty than occasional gamers in staying focused on the relevant information conveyed in a game while filtering out irrelevant information (e.g., following an enemy while various distracting visual and sound effects are happening as explosions are generated to keep the scene exciting). Given that attention has a critical impact on learning, it is a key component to account for in user experience. The human brain has very restricted attentional resources—although we are mostly unaware of them—so there are plenty of limitations to consider.

5.2 Limitations of Human Attention

One of the most important limitations to remember is that our attentional resources are extremely scarce. We are the most efficient when we direct our full attention to one task only. Anytime we divide our attention and try to multitask, we increase our processing times and our likelihood of making mistakes. According to the cognitive load theory, the more demanding a task is for working memory (e.g., if it's complex or new), the more attentional resources are required and the more distraction will have disruptive effects and will likely be perceived as irritating (Lavie 2005). Also, learning can be hindered if it requires attentional resources that exceed the working memory limits (Sweller 1994), so it's particularly important to mind the cognitive load (i.e., the attentional resources required to achieve a task) during the tutorials and onboarding part of your game. Indeed, this is when cognitive load can be particularly substantial because processing new tasks demands relatively more resources than processing a familiar task. Moreover, if cognitive overload occurs, it will obstruct the learning process. So, not only could your players feel overwhelmed, but they could also fail to learn the important mechanics and systems that you are trying to teach them.

Excessive cognitive load can happen when we process one very demanding task (e.g., a complex mental calculation), but it happens more frequently when we divide our attention in an attempt to multitask. The reason being that multitasking requires not only the attentional resources required to accomplish each task but also resources for the executive control necessary to coordinate and manage the tasks. This phenomenon is called "underadditivity" and was demonstrated by several neuroimaging studies. Consider, for example, a task consisting of listening to sentences (processed by the phonological loop, if you remember the characteristics of working memory) and another task consisting of mentally rotating objects (processed by the visual sketchpad). An fMRI (functional magnetic resonance imaging) study found that the sum of brain activation in the regions associated with the described tasks (language processing and mental rotation) is substantially less when both tasks are performed concurrently as compared to the sum of brain activation in each region when the tasks are performed separately (Just *et al.* 2001). Moreover, the decrease of brain activity was found to be greater than 50% in the case of the language-processing task. These results roughly mean that we have a certain total amount of attentional resources that we can "dispatch" to process information and accomplish tasks. When we multitask, we first need to subtract some attentional resources required to coordinate the different tasks (executive control). Then, the attentional resources left can be divided among the tasks. Our attentional resources are therefore hampered when we try to multitask, and this is why we usually take more time to accomplish each task in a multitasking condition than if we do one task after the other. Practice can have a dramatic positive effect on multitasking performance (as well as monotasking performance) because some processes can become automatic when practiced long enough. For example, when you are in the process of learning how to drive, it takes all of your attentional resources. A novice driver will therefore have much more difficulty managing tasks in addition to driving, such as conversing with a friend. After driving is practiced long enough, its process becomes automatic and therefore requires much less attentional resources and little to no executive control.

Another element that can increase cognitive load is when you have to inhibit distractors to be able to focus on the relevant information to accomplish a task. The famous "Stroop effect" illustrates that phenomenon. Named after the psychologist who designed the task revealing the effect, the Stroop effect shows interference in information processing when irrelevant information has to be inhibited (filtered out) to be able to direct attention to relevant information. The task consists of naming the color of the ink used with a series of color words. For example, the word GREEN would be written with blue ink, and the task of

RED   BLUE   GREEN

Figure 5.1

Example of material used in the Stroop task.

the participants is to say "blue" (see Figure 5.1). Sometimes the color would match the color word but sometimes not. In the case when the color does not match the color word, it takes participants more time to name the color of the ink, and they can also make more mistakes. What probably happens in the mismatch condition is that the executive control (coordinating attentional resources) has first to inhibit an automatic response, which is to read a word—at least in the case of expert-reader adults—before directing attentional resources to detect the color of the ink and name it (see Houdé and Borst 2015). Distracting stimuli, especially when they directly conflict with a given task, will add some more workload that can hinder the speed and/or the quality of the process.

The most surprising thing about cognitive load and divided attention is that not only are we bad at handling it, but we also believe otherwise. Multitasking in particular is often praised in the workplace. We are expected to check our e-mails frequently, for example, instead of deeply focusing on our tasks and checking our e-mails later. Instant messaging, social media, and the ambient noise from open spaces can also divide our attention and are now the norm in most offices, especially in game studios. If you add the fact that game developers have a tendency to "crunch" (do overtime), knowing that tiredness and stress also have a negative impact on performance, I'd say that we are adding a lot of unnecessary hurdles to our already strenuous endeavor (making successful and fun games, that is). What it means for your players, though, is that you must be careful not to put them into demanding multitasking situations that would overwhelm them (unless it is specifically what the challenge of the game is about), especially when they are learning about the game. Sustained attention also cannot last forever; our working memory becomes fatigued quite rapidly. Our sustained attention capability varies depending on many variables, such as motivation to do the task, complexity of the task, individual differences, and so on, but it's generally a good practice to offer breathing moments for the player's brain. For example, if you are using cutscenes in your game, it would probably be more beneficial to avoid using them at the beginning of a game session (when working memory is still fresh and attentional resources can be utilized to interact with the game); play them instead after players have had to sustain their attention for some time, to offer working memory a break.

There is one last curiosity of the mind that I would like to bring to your attention here, called "inattentional blindness." When we are focused on a task, we can be completely blind to unexpected events happening right in front of us. Remember, attention works like a spotlight; therefore, it filters out what is not the focus of our attention. However, this phenomenon can still be truly surprising. The most striking and popular example of a study demonstrating inattentional blindness is the one conducted by researchers Simons and Chabris (1999). They asked participants to watch a video of two teams of three people passing basketballs to each other. One team had white T-shirts and the other team had black T-shirts. Participants were asked to count how many passes the team in white made. Most participants did not have difficulty accomplishing the task. However, as they were focused on counting the basketball passes, about half of the participants failed to notice a person in a gorilla suit walking in and out of the scene thumping his chest. (You can watch the video used in the study on this Web page: http://www.simonslab.com/videos.html. Although, now that you know the trick, you probably won't fall for it.) This startling phenomenon illustrates the important role of attention in perception (and, subsequently, in memory). It also further illustrates the considerable limitations of our attentional resources and explains why car accidents often occur because of drivers' insufficient attention (e.g., mind wandering) or distracted attention (i.e., checking a new text message) and why augmented reality technology such as Google Glass (requesting its wearer to divide their attention between the environment and the Glass interface) is particularly challenging. For game design, it means that it is not enough to send visual or audio cues to the player to inform them about something important. Indeed, there is a good chance that they won't even perceive the cues if they are deeply focused on a task (say, killing zombies). Furthermore, several studies have demonstrated that working memory load increases inattentional blindness, so the more inputs there are to process and the more complex information is, the less players will be able to pay attention to some new or surprising event happening at the same time. It is your responsibility to mind players' cognitive load and to find ways to draw their attention and/or to ensure through player input that important information was attended and processed. You cannot blame it on players if they did not process elements you simply displayed at some point in the user interface. Similarly to magicians who are *misdirecting* an audience's attention to perform a magic trick, you need to understand human attention to *direct players' focus* on what you want them to process.

5.3 Application to Games

Attention is key to learning and to information processing. It has a major impact on what we perceive in our environment at any given time and on the level of processing dedicated to the perceived input (or to the mental representation), therefore greatly impacting the quality of retention in long-term memory. "Memory is often a product of attention," as Castel *et al.* (2015) pointed out. A person's level of attention is also indicative of their *engagement* in an activity, which is an important concept for video games. The main characteristics and limitations of human memory that you need to remember are the following:

- Attention can be focused (selective attention) or divided (multitasking).
- Selective attention works like a spotlight: We direct attentional resources on a particular element while the rest is filtered out.

- A side effect of selective attention is the phenomenon of "inattentional blindness" whereby unattended elements are not consciously perceived, even unexpected or surprising ones.
- Attentional resources are extremely scarce.
- Cognitive load theory suggests that the more attentional resources are required to accomplish a task, the more distraction will have disruptive effects and the more likely learning will be hindered.
- An unfamiliar task (that needs to be learned) requires much more attentional resources than a familiar one.
- The brain is terrible at multitasking (divided attention has a negative impact on performance), yet we are mostly unaware of it.

The applications to video games are pretty simple in theory yet very difficult in practice: You must direct players' attention to relevant information while minding their cognitive load to avoid overwhelming their working memory. The main reason why it's difficult to apply is because we currently have extremely limited ways to measure the cognitive load of a player at a given time (with our current technology, putting players in a brain scanner while they playtest your game would be overkill while not necessarily helpful). When we conduct UX tests (e.g., usability tests), we mostly make educated guesses based on eye-tracking data (do players direct their gaze to certain elements, which can indicate—although not necessarily—where their attention is directed), behavioral data (how fast and how well players accomplish certain tasks), and survey answers (what do players remember and can they explain what they had to do). The other reason why adjusting the cognitive load is difficult is because it's impossible to precisely anticipate the load of a given task: it not only depends on the complexity of the task itself but also on players' prior knowledge, familiarity with the game mechanics and systems, and other factors such as how tired they are that day. For example, frequent action video game players seem to have enhanced visual selective attention as compared to non-gamers (Green and Bavelier 2003). We therefore have to make educated guesses when we put together our onboarding plan (see Chapter 13): We evaluate the difficulty of each teaching depending on its complexity and uniqueness to the game and depending on the prior knowledge and level of expertise we expect our target audience to have (which is one of the reasons why it's important to clearly know for whom you are designing the game). For example, when putting together the *Fortnite* onboarding plan, we anticipated that the shooting mechanic would be fairly easy to grasp for our core audience while we anticipated the building mechanic specific to *Fortnite* would be more unfamiliar to players and require more effort to learn (because it works differently than the *Minecraft* building mechanic). Therefore, we could anticipate that learning all the subtleties of the building mechanic would require a good amount of attentional resources and consequently would require some specific tutorial missions.

Overall, you want to prevent dividing and distracting players' attention while they are processing and learning some important elements of your game. Here are a few examples of what you should try to avoid:

- Avoid displaying tutorial tips about some important mechanic while players are focused on another task (e.g., displaying information about how to heal while players are getting attacked by enemies and therefore are fully directing their attention to dealing with them).
- Avoid displaying important tutorial text while at the same time a non-player character engages in a monologue (unless the non-player character says the same thing as what is displayed on the screen).
- Avoid relying on only one sensory modality to convey important information. (Make sure that there are always at least a visual cue and an audio cue.)
- Avoid using a pop-up text that disappears automatically after a defined delay to convey some important information (you cannot guarantee that the player will see the information or process it so, if you cannot leave the information until the player executes the action because of engine limitation, at the very least make it so the player has to acknowledge reading the text by pressing a button).
- Avoid designing the onboarding in such a way that a core gameplay loop or a complex mechanic will be superficially processed by players (e.g., explaining the building mechanic in *Fortnite* only through tutorial text instead of crafting the level design to put the players in a situation where they will have to learn about the building mechanic subtleties by doing certain tasks).
- Avoid flooding the player with too much information (e.g., adding too many tips on a loading screen might discourage players from processing them).

Just like a magician, you need to learn how to manipulate your audience's attention to lead them toward the experience you have intended. You can draw attention through perception by using the salience effect: An element is usually detected better if it contrasts well with the rest of the environment—for example, using a red element in a black-and-white environment, a flashing/moving element if the rest of the scene is still (although a player's camera movement can make detection of a moving element more difficult), a louder sound, and so on. Of course, if your players' attention is deeply focused on something else, it might not be enough. Another important factor in getting people's attention is to get them *motivated* to pay attention, which is what we will talk about next.

6

Motivation

6.1 Implicit Motivation and Biological Drives

6.2 Environmental-Shaped Motivation and Learned Drives

6.3 Intrinsic Motivation and Cognitive Needs

6.4 Personality and Individual Needs

6.5 Application to Games

6.6 Quick Note on the Importance of Meaning

Motivation is paramount for survival because it directs our behavior to satisfy drives and desires. Without motivation, there can be no behavior, no action. You need to be motivated to find food and water to survive the day, and you need to be sexually motivated to pass on genes, to only mention our physiological drives. In fact, mice that cannot produce dopamine—a brain chemical involved with our ability to want something—just sit there all day and eventually die of hunger because they do not seek out food (Palmiter 2008). Therefore, it has been theorized that cognition, emotion, and social interaction could all have emerged to sustain motivation (see Baumeister 2016). Research on motivation is relatively young, and academic debates are still very vigorous. Countless theories have been proposed to explain human motivation, but a solid meta-analysis is still missing that makes sense of it all. There is no current consensus or a unified theory of human motivation that can account for all our drives and behaviors in a clear mapping. To be honest, it took me quite some time to figure out how I could organize this chapter in order to give a good enough overview about human motivation while *trying* not to oversimplify things too much. I propose to break down the various and complex mechanisms of motivation in the following four types, which all interact with one another (inspired by Lieury 2015):

- Implicit motivation and biological drives
- Environmental-shaped motivation and learned drives
- Intrinsic motivation and cognitive needs
- Personality and individual needs

This categorization is not necessarily a standard mapping of motivation; but then again, there is no widely agreed-upon classification as I'm typing these words. This is just my personal attempt at making sense of this complex mechanism while communicating it as clearly as possible. What is important to understand is that these motivation types are not independent. They all closely interact to influence our perception, feelings, cognition, and behavior. Also, these motivations do not have a specific hierarchy, contrary to what psychologist Abraham Maslow's well-known motivation theory suggested (Maslow 1943). Maslow theorized that humans fulfill needs in a certain priority, and he organized these needs in a now famous pyramid, with the most basic needs at the bottom. According to Maslow, at the base of the pyramid stand physiological needs (e.g., food, water, sex), then come safety needs (e.g., security, family), then belonging needs (e.g., friendship, family), then esteem needs (e.g., achievement, confidence), and lastly, self-actualization needs (e.g., problem-solving, creativity). However, Maslow's theory of needs was greatly criticized for its hierarchical construction (see Wahba and Bridwell 1983) given that our "lower" needs (e.g., sex) do not always take precedence over "higher ones" (e.g., moral ideals), which is somewhat reassuring.

6.1 Implicit Motivation and Biological Drives

If I told you now that I would like to drink a glass of red wine (some Bordeaux, if you please), I would be expressing a self-attributed motive that I have control over because my goal is admittedly not to quench my thirst (I drink water for that). In contrast, implicit motivation consists of spontaneous processes and physiological events, such as hormone release, the primary goal of which is to keep an internal balance (scientists refer to this as homeostasis). It cannot be controlled in the sense that you cannot control which biochemicals are being released in your brain. Biological drives are very basic needs that we share with other mammals. For example, hunger, thirst, need for sleep, pain avoidance, and sex are powerful innate physiological motives aimed to satisfy our biological drives. They are regulated for the most part by the hypothalamus, which is part of the limbic system. It controls the pituitary gland (hypophysis), an endocrine gland that in turn regulates all the other endocrine glands that are producing hormones. For example, in the presence of a predator, sensory information is gathered, dispatched, and interpreted by other systems and ultimately reaches the hypothalamus, which activates a fight-or-flight response by regulating the release of hormones such as epinephrine, norepinephrine, or cortisol that will modify our heart rate and increase our awareness (to focus our scarce attentional resources on this urgent matter). Without going too much into complex details, the important information to remember is that many of our actions are coordinated by the release of biochemicals in our brains. These are what we call *impulses*.

Other implicit motives can also influence our *social* behavior. Three of these implicit drives have been studied in more detail: the power motive, the achievement motive, and the affiliation motive. Depending on how strong these drives are within us, how they influence the pleasure we feel from certain situations will vary, which in turn will influence our behavior. The power drive influences one's motivation to dominate others; the affiliation drive influences one's motivation for close and harmonious social relationships; and the achievement motive influences one's motivation to improve on a task (see Schultheiss 2008, for an overview). For example, in contrast with individuals low in achievement, achievement-motivated individuals will have a tendency to prefer solving challenging tasks. One might hypothesize that *tea-bagging*—a curious behavior whereby a human player expresses its domination over another human player after slaying them, by crouching up and down on the player's dead avatar—could be more satisfying for power-motivated individuals. Who knows?

This is not to say that we are the slaves to our biochemicals and unconscious brain processes. If that was the case, we would not be able to control our impulses, which would not be very efficient given that we have survived as a species thanks to our social structures, which are governed by behavioral rules to follow. (For example, rapists and murderers normally go to jail for hurting fellow human beings.) However, implicit motivation and physiological drives do play an important role even in the other levels of motivation, such as in intrinsic motivation. This has an even more direct impact on learned needs, which are the ones we will tackle next.

6.2 Environmental-Shaped Motivation and Learned Drives

6.2.1 Extrinsic Motivation: Of Carrots and Sticks

The behaviorist approach studies how the environment shapes motivation. We implicitly learn to associate a stimulus to reinforcement, either rewarding or aversive, which we commonly call "conditioning" or "instrumental learning." (I will explain the behavioral learning principle underlying conditioning in more detail in Chapter 8.) According to Hull's law, motivation is the sum of "need" and "reinforcement" (Hull 1943). Said differently, we are influenced by the reward value of a given behavior in satisfying a need and by our probability of success in obtaining the reward. For example, if we are hungry (i.e., need), we are going to seek food (i.e., motivation). As we eat, we feel satiation satisfaction, which is a type of reward (i.e., positive reinforcement). Rewards from our environment act like positive reinforcers that induce change in our behavior by increasing the frequency of the behavior that led to the reward gain. In contrast, punishments from the environment will shape our motivation by inducing a reduction of the frequency of a behavior that resulted in punishment (e.g., you do not touch a hot frying pan to avoid getting burnt and feeling pain). The absence of an expected reward can also act as a punishment: If you work toward an incentive but ultimately don't get it, it will be felt as a punishment, and you will be less likely to repeat that behavior in the future.

Learned drives, just like all behavior, are greatly under the influence of hormones and neurotransmitters (chemicals released across synapses, which is how a signal is transmitted from one neuron to another), although not in the way the clickbait pop science articles would like you to believe. Dopamine, cortisol, oxytocin, testosterone, adrenaline, norepinephrine (noradrenaline), endorphins, and so on impact our mental states, how we feel, what we do, and our perception of rewards. For example, testosterone has been found to increase concerns about social status (van Honk *et al.* 2016), and endorphins have been found to impact our enjoyment (liking) of something. So we could say that motivation is "wanting" but can be sustained by "liking." You might have heard of the term "brain-reward circuitry," which is an oversimplified way of describing a person's response to natural rewards from the environment. It is what influences us to "want" (i.e., impacts our desires) and "like" (i.e., impacts our enjoyment), as well as impacting our behavioral learning via reinforcement (conditioning). Most of the time it happens unconsciously, even in the case of liking, which means that implicit "liking" reactions can happen without a conscious feeling of pleasure. It is, of course, not as simple as there being a "reward center" in our brain. Rather, numerous brain systems and corresponding neurotransmitters are involved in the brain-reward circuitry—such as the amygdala, the hippocampus, the prefrontal cortex, endorphins (opioids), and dopamine. The amygdala, for example, in connection with the hippocampus, helps us memorize the association of a particular stimulus and whether experiencing it was rewarding or aversive. Thus, if such a stimulus is encountered again, we can make the decision to engage with it or not. In sum, environmental-shaped motivation is powered by reward for engagement behavior, by punishment for avoidance behavior, and by our memory of the experience. This is why it is called a *learned* drive.

There are many things in life that we do not want to do (i.e., intrinsically) but that we do anyway because we have learned that accomplishing these tasks will bring us direct or indirect rewards of value, such as food, housing, or entertainment (Vroom 1964). Money is an indirect reward used to gain these things of value because we can exchange it for a steak, a one-month lease, or a movie ticket (unless you value money for the sake of it). Numerous studies have shown that incentives promote effort and performance (e.g., Jenkins *et al.* 1998). In certain situations, the amount of compensation can even directly impact our level of effort in performing a task. For example, students asked to drag and drop as many circles as possible onto an area of a computer screen performed better when they were given a medium incentive ($4 in cash) than when they were given a low incentive ($0.10) (Heyman and Ariely 2004). As we will see in more detail in the intrinsic motivation section, some types of incentives are more efficient than others, with rewards that are perceived as controlling (such as money, in some cases) being less efficient overall. However, there is some evidence that the brain-reward circuitry is activated during reward anticipation and reward delivery, with the activation being stronger with monetary reward than with a verbal reward (Kirsch *et al.* 2003).

6.2.2. Continuous and Intermittent Rewards

A major factor influencing the perceived value of a reward is uncertainty in terms of the perceived chance of receiving the reward. Uncertainty itself can be influenced by personality: People who are risk-averse will perceive an uncertain reward (i.e., you are not sure you will get it) as less valuable compared to people who are risk-seekers (see Schultz 2009). However, there is strong evidence that rewards given in an *intermittent* fashion (e.g., a certain action is sometimes rewarded) have a greater impact on behavior than those given *continuously* (e.g., a certain action is always rewarded). In his experiments on rats, psychologist B. F. Skinner found that those who were given a reward (i.e., food pellet) each time they pressed a lever would eventually abandon the task if the reward stopped coming on schedule. In the case when the reward was not given each time the lever was pressed, but instead was given on a variable-ratio schedule (i.e., every 1 to 20 presses), the rats were much more hooked on their task. This phenomenon is what makes slot machines so addictive. These machines are, in fact, designed as "Skinner boxes" and rely on the principles of operant conditioning with an unpredictable intermittent reward (Schüll 2012). If you are planning to gamble, I strongly recommend you define in advance how much money you will spend on a casino experience; otherwise, you will likely get hooked and lose much more money than you would like.

Intermittent rewards are particularly interesting for video games, and they are, in fact, often used. These rewards can be intermittent based on time (i.e., interval) or on behavior (i.e., ratio), and they can be given expectedly (at a fixed interval or ratio) or unexpectedly (at an uncertain interval or ratio). In games, for example, a reward given at a fixed interval would be the daily reward that you can get by logging in every day. Another example would be in games like *Clash of Clans* (Supercell) in which you need to wait a certain amount of time for your buildings to be constructed. An example of a reward given at a variable interval would be mobs in massively multiplayer online games (also known as MMORPGs) such as *World of Warcraft* (Blizzard), which can spawn in a certain area although players do not know exactly when; it's unpredictable. A reward given when a specific ability is unlocked in a skill tree is an example of a fixed ratio reward. Players know exactly how many actions (i.e., behavior) they need to do in order to receive the reward. Progression bars could also be considered as fixed ratio rewards because players know exactly how many experience points they need to earn to level up. However, the actions rewarded by experience points are not as predictable, and players cannot usually precisely anticipate how many experience points they will get for each of their actions (e.g., killing an enemy). Lastly, as mentioned earlier, variable ratio examples are things that look like slot machines. Card packs, chests, loot crates, and so on are all examples in which players do not know if they are going to receive the reward they want as they open their loot. It's gambling. Each type of intermittent reward has a different impact on the response rate, as illustrated in Figure 6.1 in an approximate and stereotypical way. After a fixed reward

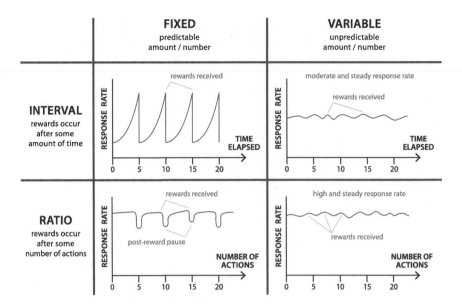

Figure 6.1

Different types of intermittent rewards and their approximate impact on behavior.

is given, there is usually a pause in the behavior: Once we have what we wanted and we know when the next window of opportunity will happen (either based on time or our actions), we stop doing the behavior that grants the reward for a little while (i.e., there is a pause in the response rate). A fixed reward that stops coming on schedule can often lead to a fast response extinction, which means that when an expected reward does not come, we usually stop working toward getting it. By contrast, variable rewards overall usually lead to a more steady response rate, which is understandable because we do not exactly know when the reward will happen. Rewards based on one's actions (i.e., ratio) usually have a higher response rate than those based on time (i.e., interval). Lastly, rewards given on a variable ratio schedule usually lead to the highest and most steady response rate of all.

Our addiction to checking our e-mails or social media notifications might be caused by variable-ratio/interval schedules of reinforcement (as proposed by Ariely 2008). Each time we refresh our applications on our phone, maybe we will discover some "likes" on our latest post (social recognition is important to humans), or maybe we will discover a message that feels rewarding (e.g., a con-gratulatory e-mail from your boss, a loving text message from your significant other, etc.). Just like with slot machines, we get junk most of the time we check our phones; but every now and then we are unpredictably rewarded with something we really care about, and that's what feels compelling.

Rewards are powerful in shaping our motivation and our behavior. We learn to associate certain stimuli with specific rewards through conditioning, thus forming expectations that impact our motivation for doing (or not doing) certain tasks.

Learned needs rely heavily on implicit systems, which make them quite powerful in shaping our behavior. That being said, an important body of research suggests that specific types of rewards, linked to intrinsic motivation, can be in certain circumstances even more powerful than extrinsic rewards.

6.3 Intrinsic Motivation and Cognitive Needs

In the second half of the twentieth century, the behavioral approach to motivation started being challenged—in the sense that it was becoming clear that this approach could not account for all human behavior. Indeed, humans (and some animals) engage in many activities independent of the provision of extrinsic rewards. This is called intrinsic motivation. We are intrinsically motivated when we engage in a task for its own sake, when the task is not a means to an end. If you are a sports car aficionado, you might want to go for a drive with your brand new car just for the pleasure of riding it. In contrast, we are extrinsically motivated when we accomplish a certain task in order to gain a benefit that is external to the task itself. For example, you need to drive your car in order to go see the latest *Star Wars* movie at the theater. Your motivation to drive in that case is extrinsic because it is instrumental in obtaining an extrinsic reward that does not have anything to do with driving (i.e., watching the movie). Recent research has tried to measure the impact of each motivation on our performance and our well-being, but few have studied their interactive impact so far (Cerasoli *et al.* 2014). This means that it's not currently clear how intrinsic motivation and extrinsic rewards are interacting and how this interaction impacts performance of a given task. Some research has shown that extrinsic incentives can reduce intrinsic motivation in some cases. For example, schoolchildren that were rewarded for drawing (which children usually do for the intrinsic value) were less likely to draw spontaneously later on compared to children who were not extrinsically rewarded (Lepper *et al.* 1973). The interesting subtlety is that the children who received a surprise reward for drawing were not seen drawing less often later on. Therefore, when we expect to receive a reward for an activity we were initially intrinsically motivated to do, the extrinsic reward can actually have undermining effects on intrinsic motivation.

6.3.1 Undermining Effect of Extrinsic Incentives

We often accomplish certain activities for no external incentive at all—just for the pleasure of the activity itself. Play is probably the most suitable example of an intrinsically motivating activity because it is autotelic by essence; it contains its own purpose. Some research has found that when we are intrinsically motivated to do a certain activity or a task, we perform better at it (Deci 1975). Some people can spend countless hours efficiently harvesting and building in *Minecraft* just because they love doing so. A more surprising finding, however, is that when an extrinsic incentive is offered to reward a task we are intrinsically motivated to do, it can undermine our subsequent intrinsic motivation for the activity. Let's say that you like playing *Minecraft* for its own sake but that I now offer you a dollar for every hour you play it. If this external incentive is later removed, it is possible that you might be less motivated to play the game afterward; thus, you might play less often than before an external reward was introduced and removed.

This reduction of time doing an activity after an undermining effect of external reward occurred is sometimes called the "overjustification effect." When you start gaining an extrinsic reward for an activity you were initially intrinsically motivated to perform, you might subsequently misattribute the reason why you are engaged in the activity. You could initially identify that you had no reason other than the pleasure of the activity itself to engage with it. But now that an external reward has been introduced, you might misattribute that the reason why you are engaged in this activity is for gaining the reward. Thus, when the extrinsic reward is no longer available, you could fail to consider again the intrinsic reasons for engaging in the activity. This is particularly damaging for education. Learning can be intrinsically motivating. In fact, our "brain-reward circuitry" is active when we learn because our survival depends on how well we remember about the goodies and dangers in our environment. So adding extrinsic rewards to learning (i.e., grades) can have a dramatic effect. However, this phenomenon might not be as clear-cut given that, depending on the context of the research, the overjustification effect is not always found. For example, the undermining effect of extrinsic rewards is usually confirmed only when individuals initially find an activity interesting and when the reward is perceived as external to the activity (especially in the case of monetary rewards). Another example concerns creativity: When the task is creative, primarily extrinsic motivation to complete it will undermine creativity (Amabile 1996). However, Hennessey and Amabile (2010) later suggested that rewards can enhance intrinsic motivation and creativity when they provide useful information in a supportive way, when they confirm competence, or when they enable people to do something that they were already intrinsically motivated to do. These examples illustrate the fact that we currently do not have definitive answers as to when exactly intrinsic motivation can predict performance, what role extrinsic rewards have, and which between intrinsic motivation and extrinsic reward matters the most.

6.3.2 Self-Determination Theory

Self-determination theory (SDT) currently is the dominant framework for the study of intrinsic motivation (Deci and Ryan 1985; Ryan and Deci 2000). It posits that three innate psychological needs are at the basis of intrinsic motivation: competence, autonomy, and relatedness. The need for *competence* is about a desire to be in control and to master the environment. We thrive when we are optimally challenged; we seek opportunities to acquire new skills and abilities, to get better at them, and to receive positive feedback reinforcing our sense of progression. The need for *autonomy* concerns the sense of meaningful choice, self-expression, and free will. It concerns the feeling of a sense of agency and volition when accomplishing a task. The need for *relatedness* refers primarily to the need to feel affiliated with others. It has been suggested that the undermining effect of extrinsic rewards would take place when they thwart these three needs.

Some self-determination theorists have moved away from the extrinsic/intrinsic motivation dichotomy to focus instead on the distinction between autonomous (self-determined) and controlled (not self-determined) motivation (see Gerhart and Fang 2015). The incentive type of reward would thus have a different impact on intrinsic motivation depending on whether it rewards engagement (incentive given for simply engaging in a task), completion (reward for completing a task), or performance (reward for attaining a certain level of achievement). To these task-contingent rewards we must add noncontingent incentives that are not at all related to any particular behavior. The hypothesis is that the more the incentives are trying to *control* an individual, the more they will have an undermining effect on intrinsic motivation because they thwart the satisfaction of the need for autonomy. Thus, performance-contingent rewards that are given specifically for matching some standard of excellence are likely to be experienced as the most controlling. However, because they can also act as a feedback on competence, the negative effect of the control can be counteracted by the expression of a sense of progression (when there is such progression). Rewards that are task-contingent but that are given simply for completing a task might be felt as less controlling, but they also do not offer any perceived increase of competence and could therefore ultimately be the worst kind of all as far as intrinsic motivation is concerned. Per that classification, a performance-contingent pay (monetary incentive) would not undermine intrinsic motivation if the financial incentive was valued as important for other goals. All in all, it's not particularly easy to anticipate which rewards in what conditions will hamper intrinsic motivation. It is nonetheless an interesting concept to keep in mind when designing rewards in your game; your best guess is to at least provide feedback on players' progression.

6.3.3 The Theory of Flow

Flow refers to a state of enjoyment when one is totally engaged and immersed in an intrinsically motivating activity. It describes the optimal experience whereby a "person's body or mind is stretched to its limits in a voluntary effort to accomplish something difficult and worthwhile" (Csikszentmihalyi 1990, p. 3). For psychologist Mihaly Csikszentmihalyi, flow is the secret to happiness; he found that people are the happiest when they experience this sense of optimal experience. Flow doesn't happen by random chance. We have to meaningfully work to make it happen, and such an experience is not necessarily pleasant at the time it occurs. If you are learning to play the guitar, for example (and you are intrinsically motivated to learn), you will go through painful moments when your fingers ache—or even bleed—or when a particular tune you want to play is hard to nail. However, once the obstacle is overcome and you can observe your progress, you feel really good about it. This moment during which you are deeply immersed in overcoming a challenge that is not too easy or too hard is flow. You can become so immersed that you could lose track of time and disregard your need for food, water, or sleep (which is further evidence that needs are not hierarchical as Maslow theorized). The state of flow is intrinsically rewarding, but it also enhances learning processes because when you are in that state, all attention is concentrated on the task; you are zoning out. Your spouse could be talking to you, but you wouldn't even perceive what's happening outside of your zone (and that's because of inattentional blindness, if you remember Chapter 5 about attention).

To reach that state of flow, you need to attempt tasks that require skills and are challenging yet that you have a chance to complete. The task must have clear goals and unambiguous feedback on how performance is progressing toward the goals. You must be able to fully concentrate on the task, which means that distractors must be avoided before reaching the flow zone. (But once you're in the zone, it's easier to stay focused unless some external event ends up moving you away from the zone.) You also need a sense of control over your actions—a sense that you can master your own fate. Lastly, the task has to be *meaningful* to you so that you can reach the state of optimal experience.

This concept of flow is an interesting one to apply to video game development, especially regarding the difficulty curve a game should have. It constitutes one of the user experience framework pillars (*game flow*) I am utilizing to help guide developers in crafting a more engaging experience (see Chapter 12).

6.4 Personality and Individual Needs

Although a lot of our behavior can be explained by mental processes that affect us all in similar ways, individual differences exist and have an impact on what we find intrinsically motivating at a cognitive level. We saw earlier that implicit drives can influence behavior differently depending on how strong these drives are within individuals: the power motive, the achievement motive, and the affiliation motive (see Section 6.1 on implicit motivation). Another interesting difference, this time at a cognitive level, could impact motivation—whether you believe that intelligence is fixed (predetermined early on) or changeable (i.e., effort can enhance intelligence). People who believe that intelligence is fixed may tend to choose performance goals (i.e., they seek to obtain positive judgment on their performance) over learning goals (i.e., increased competence), perhaps because they feel that challenging learning goals involve the risk of failure, which would pose the threat of revealing incompetency. By contrast, people who believe (more accurately) that intelligence is malleable seem to prefer learning goals to performance ones (Dweck and Leggett 1988). This result (although debated) could be particularly interesting because it implies that children would engage more in learning activities if they understood that being smart is not a state but a process. As you must know by now if you didn't already, the brain is constantly evolving; thus, we can work to get better at nearly anything. In fact, even IQ scores are not fixed. This is why psychologists usually recommend that you do not celebrate your child's accomplishments by telling them they are smart (e.g., "you did it, you're so smart!") but instead by acknowledging the effort they put into the challenge to overcome it (e.g., "you worked hard on this and your efforts paid off, well done!").

More generally, when we talk about individual differences, we mainly think about personality. Many models about personality have been developed in the past few decades. However, in an attempt to be concise and to stay focused on what can be applicable to game development, I will only talk about the one that has been the most widely and robustly examined: the "Big Five" personality traits (also known as the five-factor model). These personality traits have been identified using a statistical technique called factor analysis, which finds patterns and clusters of correlated variables within a large mass of data. Research on the Big Five has included studies across diverse populations over decades of life spans, which is what makes the data so robust. The five factors have been defined as openness to experience (O), conscientiousness (C), extraversion (E), agreeableness (A), and neuroticism (N) and are often referred to by the acronym OCEAN. These broad traits encapsulate most personality differences. Individuals are measured against each trait to define their personality. For example, individuals with a high score in extraversion are outgoing and enthusiastic, whereas low scorers are aloof and quiet. Here is a quick breakdown of the different traits:

- **Openness to experience**
  This trait outlines how inventive and curious we are. Low-scorer individuals are practical and conventional, whereas high scorers are creative and imaginative.
- **Conscientiousness**
  This trait outlines how efficient and organized we are. Low-scorer individuals are spontaneous and careless, whereas high scorers are organized and self-directed.
- **Extraversion**
  This trait outlines how outgoing and energetic we are. Low-scorer individuals are reserved and quiet, whereas high scorers are outgoing and enthusiastic.
- **Agreeableness**
  This trait outlines how friendly and compassionate we are. Low-scorer individuals are suspicious and hostile, whereas high scorers are trusting and empathetic.
- **Neuroticism**
  This trait outlines how sensitive and nervous we are. Low-scorer individuals are emotionally stable, whereas high scorers are prone to anger and anxiety.

Although the OCEAN model has some limitations (notably, it is not accurate in predicting behavior) and does not explain all of human personality, it is the most robust model we currently have. It is certainly interesting to keep in mind to account for human motivation. For example, an individual who scores high in openness might be more motivated to accomplish a creative task than a low scorer. It was also recently suggested that the five-factor model might align with gaming motivations (Yee 2016), with a high score in extraversion correlating with a high score in social play on the gaming scale, for example. These findings are still too recent to be considered reliable, but they represent an interesting path to explore.

6.5 Application to Games

Without motivation there is no behavior, and increased motivation seems to enhance attention, which we know is critical to learning and memory. Research on motivation has shown that extrinsic rewards can boost performance and intrinsic motivation can boost performance, but that extrinsic reward can reduce intrinsic motivation once the reward is removed. It all depends on the subtle context differences of the tasks and on how autonomy-controlling the rewards feel. At the very least, the impact of intrinsic and extrinsic motivation is not clear and neither is how both interact. Debates are still raging about the practical value of intrinsic motivation theories (see Cerasoli *et al.* 2014), but here is what you need to remember regarding the current state of our knowledge on motivation:

- Any reward is better than no reward at all.
- Performance for tasks that are straightforward and highly repetitive can be improved by extrinsic rewards. In that context, the reward needs to be salient and its value needs to increase with the amount of effort the task requires.
- Performance for tasks that are complex and require concentration, investment, or creativity can be improved by intrinsic motivation.
- When the task involves creativity, teamwork, ethical behavior, or when quality is valued, extrinsic rewards should *not* be salient.
- Although research findings suggest that it seems consistently beneficial to help people find their tasks intrinsically rewarding, extrinsic rewards can also play a positive role.
- To help people find their tasks intrinsically rewarding, aim to satisfy the needs for competence, autonomy, and relatedness (SDT). Focusing on the meaning and purpose of the task is also important.
- Flow is the optimal experience of intrinsic motivation, and it can be reached when accomplishing meaningful and challenging tasks having clear goals that are not too easy or too hard.
- Implicit motives and personality have an impact on individual needs. The Big Five model of personality (OCEAN) currently presents the most interesting and robust application in apprehending individual needs.

Human motivation subtleties are admittedly hard to grasp, yet motivation is very important to understand in order to engage players with your game. However, the brain, already eating up a lot of the body's resources, tends to seek minimum workload. This is why motivation actually constitutes an important pillar in the user experience framework, which I will describe in greater detail in Part II (see Chapter 12 about "engage-ability").

Keep in mind though that we are only barely scratching the surface of motivation, and many variables can impact it differently depending on the context in which they occur. Another interesting point to emphasize is that a phenomenon called *cognitive dissonance* can also impact motivation in a surprising way.

Leon Festinger (1957) theorized that, when we hold two or more inconsistent elements of knowledge (i.e., a dissonance between cognitions), we feel discomfort and are motivated to reduce the inconsistency to stop feeling that state of dissonance. For example, one can smoke while understanding that smoking is bad for one's health, which creates a cognitive dissonance. This can motivate individuals to post-rationalize a behavior in order to reconcile inconsistent elements—for example, by thinking that smoking is so enjoyable that it's worth the risk. The classic illustration used to describe cognitive dissonance is the fable *The Fox and the Grapes* from the Ancient Greek storyteller Aesop. In the story, a fox spots high-ranging grapes that look delicious. The fox tries to reach the grapes but because he keeps failing he finally decides that the grapes are probably sour and therefore not worth eating anyway. Very often, we post-rationalize our decisions or failures to avoid feeling a cognitive dissonance. I would argue that players that are confronted with hurdles and failures with a game might stop playing and decide that the game is stupid and not worth playing anyway. Because you cannot blame this behavior on the player (they do not owe you anything and the user is always right), you need to blame it on your design and iterate accordingly. It might be tough to do; you probably put all your heart in developing the game, so it's understandable to feel pain when you realize players don't understand its greatness. But beware of your own cognitive dissonance, which might influence you into dismissing your audience in order to ease your internal conflict.

6.6 Quick Note on the Importance of Meaning

According to Katie Salen and Eric Zimmerman (2004, p. 332), "Although there are always some extrinsic reasons to play, there are always intrinsic motivations as well. In playing a game, part of the incentive is simply to play—and often, it is the prime motivator." Understanding motivation is not simple, and its application to games is not obvious. Playing video games is indeed an autotelic activity that we usually are intrinsically motivated to do and the in-game rewards are also intrinsic to the game most of the time, except maybe for free-to-play games offering in-game currencies tied to real money or massive online games that have a player-driven economy (e.g., *Eve Online* developed by CCP Games). In this context, it's difficult to clearly establish guidelines as to how to motivate players to play your game and keep them engaged. However, what seems to be the most important thing to remember when you design your game onboarding, missions, and rewards is *meaning*.

Meaning is about having a sense of purpose, value, and impact, sometimes bigger than the self (Ariely 2016a). It helps us to engage in a long-term relationship or to be more efficient at a task, for example. When you design a tutorial to teach the player about an important feature, ask yourself why the player will care about it, what meaning this feature has for them. By doing so, you will find ways to place the player in a situation where learning about this feature or mechanic will be meaningful to them to progress (competence), to feel a sense of volition (autonomy), or to connect with others in the game (relatedness). Same goes with the rewards and all the goals you are setting for your players. Why is the reward they will get for slaying 30 zombies meaningful to them? Will it make them feel more awesome? I will describe in detail how to use this sense of meaning ("why") in the motivation section in Chapter 12. Another way to increase the meaning of an activity, to make its purpose bigger than the self, is to affiliate the player with a certain group. This is why being part of a guild or a clan is particularly motivating in games because then you do not just accomplish great things for yourself, but you also contribute to your team. It's the same principle in games that have factions, such as *For Honor* (Ubisoft) or *Pokémon Go* (Niantic). Players choose the faction they want to fight for, and their actions meaningfully impact their faction. One last example would be the game *Noby Boy* (Bandai Namco). In this game, players control the character "Boy," who could stretch his body, and they accumulated points depending on how much they stretched Boy during a game. These points could then be submitted online and be added cumulatively across all players to stretch the character "Girl" into the solar system. For example, it took seven years to *Noby* players to make Girl reach Pluto from Earth. Contributing to a purpose greater than the self is usually very compelling and therefore positively impacts one's motivation to accomplish a task.

7

Emotion

7.1   When Emotion Guides   7.3 Application to Games
       Our Cognition
7.2   When Emotion
       "Tricks" Us

We know that emotions influence our perception, cognition, and behavior, but defining what emotion is exactly is not an easy task. Simply put, emotion is a state of physiological arousal, and it can also involve the cognition related to this state of arousal (Schachter and Singer 1962)—what we commonly call a "feeling." For example, a rapid heart rate accompanied by muscle tension and sweaty palms is a physiological state (an "emotion") that can be linked to the *feeling* of being scared when we are in presence of a predator. We often talk about our emotions by primarily focusing on conscious experiences: "I'm *happy* at the thought of reuniting with my significant other after a long trip," or "I'm *angry* because the game we have just released has tons of bugs and our audience is complaining," or "I'm *sad* when I'm thinking about all the populations displaced as war is raging in many parts of the world." However, emotion is generated at a physiological level by different systems that have evolved for different purposes (see LeDoux 1996).

At its core, we could say that emotion is what evolution has found to motivate and guide us; it is helping us select the adapted behavior to survive or to breed in an often hostile environment. In that sense, emotion is fundamentally about motivation (i.e., to motivate us to behave in a certain way). For example, anxiety negatively impacts the breadth of our attention (Easterbrook 1959) and can ultimately lead to "tunnel vision" in highly stressful situations, which forces us to focus our attention. For example, if you're trapped in a building that is on fire, tunnel vision will make you focus on finding the exit signs, not on carefully scanning your environment. We know how limited our attentional resources are, so having an emergency system that helps us focus on what we need to do to survive in case of immediate danger is quite appropriate. Discrete emotions have adaptive functions that facilitate change, adjustment, and coping. For example, "interest" (or curiosity) is the mechanism supporting selective attention. Joy heightens openness to experience and signals readiness for friendly interaction in a social context. Sadness slows the cognitive and motor systems and can be useful in carefully looking for a source of trouble. Anger mobilizes and sustains energy at high levels that can lead to aggressive behavior. Fear, of course, motivates escaping from a dangerous situation—and the list goes on (see Izard and Ackerman 2000).

Emotion clearly influences our mind and guides our behavior. On the other hand, our perception and cognition can also induce and influence emotion. According to the appraisal theory, for example, our evaluation of an event elicits an emotional response based on that evaluation. This response can therefore be different among individuals (Lazarus 1991). Imagine this situation: You are behind a one-way mirror watching a few players discovering the game you are developing and a camera captures their facial expressions as they play. You focus your attention more specifically on their facial expressions only to realize that the participants all look as if they are terribly bored, which raises your anxiety. You perceive this as a sign that your game is awful! Next to you, the user researcher responsible for the test is, in contrast, pretty happy because it seems that not only did players not encounter any critical user experience issues, but they appear immersed in the game, which their (very neutral) facial expressions seem to indicate. The same event (players' facial expressions) can trigger different emotions in different people, depending on their appraisal of the situation. This is the reason why I usually avoid highlighting players' facial expressions in a playtest; it's rarely reliably indicative of players' appreciation of the game, while it can raise anxiety among game developers. The study of facial expressions is nonetheless interesting in the sense that all humans have at least five facial expressions (or six, depending on the theorists) that can be recognized worldwide as expressions of specific feelings. Professor of psychology Paul Ekman (1972) has identified six basic emotions having universal facial expressions: fear, anger, disgust, sadness, happiness, and surprise. Although these expressions seem universal, it appears that some people are less expressive than others and that cultural environment has some impact on facial expressions. For example, when American and Japanese participants in a study were asked to individually and privately watch stress-inducing films (while being surreptitiously recorded), the analysis of their facial expressions revealed that both populations expressed negative emotions similarly and at the same points in time. However, as soon as an experimenter in a white coat entered the room, Japanese participants masked negative expressions with positive expressions more often than did their American counterparts, suggesting that, even though they were likely feeling the same basic emotions as they watched the films, the Japanese participants more readily controlled their associated facial expressions when in the presence of another person (Ekman 1999). Relying on facial expressions to interpret how players are feeling about your game could thus be hazardous, unless you can measure micro-expressions and can carefully design an appropriate experimental protocol. But that usually is not the case in game development.

Emotion can exist without cognition, can happen before cognition, and can also be influenced by cognition. Although the relationship between cognition and emotion is extremely complex (like the rest of the mind), I propose to examine here what we (barely) know about the impact of emotion on our cognition—for good or ill. Again, the idea is not to precisely identify what originates from emotion and what originates from cognition, or to accurately assess our current understanding of how emotional systems work and interact with cognition, but more to depict a very broad picture that can help you achieve your design goals.

7.1 When Emotion Guides Our Cognition

Emotions are critical to learning and survival because they guide us through our interactions with the environment. There is some debate as to whether emotion comes first and causes motivation (e.g., fear causes us to flee), or if motivation comes first and emotion provides feedback about motivationally relevant events (e.g., feeling happy after satisfying a need). Given that motivation is what we need to survive (how we behave in a certain way to find food or avoid predators), there are some captivating arguments for primacy of motivation. From this viewpoint, cognition, social interaction, and emotion all serve motivation (Baumeister 2016). This debate is, however, a little off-topic for the purpose of this book. First or second, what is important to remember is that emotion guides us and therefore has an efficient impact on our behavior and our reasoning to help us survive. In that sense, emotions have adaptive functions.

7.1.1 The Influence of the Limbic System

Imagine that you are working at your desk and a sudden loud bang occurs behind you. You are likely going to swiftly turn around to identify the source of the noise and determine if it is a threat. You are going to feel fear and sense your heart pounding, and your awareness will rise. Because selective attention is critical in processing information (as we saw in Chapter 4), this rise in awareness will sharpen your perception, support your working memory demands, and will subsequently lead to a better long-term memory of the event. Your muscles will receive a surge of energy and get ready to be put in motion—just in case you need to run for your life. This whole process is largely facilitated by the brain's limbic system.

Currently, there is no definitive agreement among researchers regarding exactly what structures are involved in the limbic system. Some even suggest that the limbic system, defined as the system for emotions, does not exist (LeDoux 1996). However, most researchers agree that emotion involves (but is not limited to) the hypothalamus, the hippocampus, and the amygdala; all of these are brain areas that we consider part of the limbic system. If we were to describe very approximately what happens in the brain in case of a fight-or-flight situation, we could say that the senses convey outside world information to the cortical areas as well as to the subcortical areas, such as the thalamus. The thalamus acts like a "hub" and relays information to other areas, including the hypothalamus and the amygdala. The hypothalamus regulates endocrine glands that in turn produce hormones such as adrenaline (also called epinephrine), noradrenaline (norepinephrine), or cortisol that will modify your heart rate, pupil dilation, blood-glucose level, and blood pressure to raise your awareness and tense your muscles, for example. The amygdala, along with the hippocampus, identifies the input and the situation, comparing it to older events stored in memory, and helps store this new event. It is usually accepted that our recollection of information is greater when it has some emotional weight and is correlated with greater amygdala activity. However, it has been suggested that the notion of "flashbulb memory" (in the sense of a sort of vivid "snapshot" the brain would take when a highly emotional event happens) is probably exaggerated. We might remember more accurately one or two central elements related to a highly emotional event, but it seems that we are merely more *confident* in the accuracy of our memory of the event as a whole, which might be just as distorted as usual (see Chapter 4 about memory). In any case, the limbic system has some regulatory control over cortical areas that impacts our cognition (such as changing breadth of attention and directing attention) and, in turn, our behavior.

7.1.2 The Somatic Markers Theory

Did you ever experience some sort of visceral feelings that influenced your behavior? For example, remember that time when you kept procrastinating in the completion of a task although the deadline was inexorably approaching. (You know what I'm talking about.) As you were sitting on your couch, contemplating playing a game of *Overwatch* instead of working on a book about the gamer's brain (just one game, I promise!), didn't you feel some sort of weight, or knots, in your stomach? Maybe this feeling even motivated you to finally work on your task so that this uncomfortable feeling would go away? What about the much more positive feeling you felt once you finished what you had to do? Didn't it feel just like a "weight was taken off your shoulders"? Neuroscientist Antonio Damasio describes these emotions as being *somatic markers* forcing your attention on the negative (or positive) outcome that may occur following a certain behavior (Damasio 1994). Somatic markers, therefore, lead you to reject those options with negative outcomes so you can make the right decision for longer-term benefits. Admittedly, it doesn't work all the time because we do not avoid all bad choices, even when we clearly feel these somatic markers pounding. Hell, we might even drink a glass of rum to numb these feelings so we can more easily ignore them (and get excited instead by making the "play of the game" in that *Overwatch* match you decided to play after all). For Damasio, "gut feelings" and "intuition" originate from these somatic markers. Thus, the quality of your intuitions depends on how well you have reasoned and what decisions you have taken in the past in relation to the emotions that preceded and followed certain events, which would explain why the intuitions of highly experienced and successful professionals are not of the same quality as those of nonexperts in a specific situation.

According to the somatic markers hypothesis, emotions have an important role in decision-making. In fact, patients who have a defect in emotion and feeling due to a damaged prefrontal cortex also are insensitive to future consequences (they take more risks) and are impaired in making value-based decisions, although they still have good reasoning skills overall. For example, these individuals would make a decision involving the offer of an immediate reward without caring about social norms or long-term effects; they could, for example, conduct business with their close friend's worst enemy because gaining a client is an immediate reward. They don't appreciate that losing a friend over such a situation is not worth it. Patients with bilateral lesions of the ventromedial prefrontal cortex can be jerks in that way. They have difficulty making moral judgments and understanding irony. Contrary to common belief, emotions do not necessarily prevent us from making a rational decision—quite the contrary. In many cases, emotions help us make a decision that has moral consequences or simply help us choose between two options (or more) that are similar in terms of cost/benefit. For example, we do not endlessly analyze whether eating Italian or Japanese food at lunch would be the best option when both have equal costs and benefits; we instead follow our instinct. ("I *feel* like eating Japanese today.") Humans are not computers; we do not engage in complex calculations each time we need to make a tricky decision. Given our limited attention and working memory capacities, we often just follow our guts. For Damasio, this gut feeling comes from somatic markers—emotions originating from bodily changes—influencing attention and working memory within the prefrontal cortex. That is not to say that emotions cannot influence us when making bad decisions, but this is not a black-or-white situation—as is often the case with our brain.

7.2 When Emotion "Tricks" Us

Emotions—especially fear—can make us react automatically to a stimulus, which usually helps us survive. If someone throws a plastic spider at you, you might react swiftly by swiping the fake spider off of you because of automatic responses governed by emotional systems. Better safe than sorry; it's more beneficial to avoid what looks like a threat even if we realize later on (through cognition) that it was not. However, in some cases, we need to inhibit automatic responses like these. Imagine that you are driving in a busy city. The light is green so you accelerate because the driver behind you seems in a hurry and is tailgating you. All of a sudden, you detect a kid running up to the curb as if she was about to cross the street right in front of you, but the kid stops at the intersection and waits for her turn to cross. You might have been ready to either hit the brakes or make a swift turn to avoid hurting the kid, which would be an automatic response to a danger. In that case, though, doing such a thing would likely provoke a crash with the cars around you. Such an outcome would be justified to avoid hurting a kid but not if the threat was a false alarm. This is one of the reasons why we are often wary of letting our emotions "take control," and we say we need to keep a cool head to accurately assess the risks in a situation and regulate automatic responses, if need be (which is seemingly managed by our prefrontal cortex). However, as LeDoux (1996) pointed out, it seems that the amygdala has a greater influence on the cortex than the cortex has on the amygdala, which explains why it might be difficult to go to sleep after watching a horror movie, even if we try to convince ourselves that our physiological arousal was provoked by fiction.

We experience emotions both from bottom-up processes involving perception and attention and from top-down processes involving prior knowledge, expectation, and judgment (appraisal) about a situation (Ochsner *et al.* 2009). For example, you might experience fear if you spot a copper snake in your basement (bottom-up process), and you might experience guilt if you forgot your spouse's birthday (top-down process). The interesting thing is that, once we are in a specific emotional state (originating from a bottom-up or top-down process), this emotion will impact our appreciation of a situation even if it is not related with what created the emotional state in the first place. Once we are emotionally aroused, we extend our emotional arousal to the whole experience and not only to the element that generated that emotional arousal. Moreover, we can often misattribute our arousal. In an experiment conducted by Dutton and Aron (1974), the researchers demonstrated that a physiological arousal created by fear of heights could be misattributed as a sexual arousal. In this study, male individuals were interviewed by an attractive woman while standing either on a non-fear-arousing bridge (sturdy bridge) or a fear-arousing bridge (suspension bridge over a canyon). They were asked to answer a projective test that consisted of making up narratives based on ambiguous pictures. After the interview, the woman experimenter gave them her phone number in case they had further questions (or so she told them). In the fear-arousing bridge condition, the subjects were significantly more likely to create stories with sexual content, and they were also more likely to attempt to contact the woman interviewer later on than in the non-fear-arousing bridge condition. The researchers interpreted these results as a misattribution of the physiological arousal from being on a high suspended bridge (related to fear) to a sexual arousal from being attracted to someone. Players might also be emotionally aroused by something unrelated to your game but misattribute their feelings to your game. For example, they might be frustrated by a poor framerate, long loading times, or by constant advertisement pop-ups and misattribute their frustration to the gameplay itself. Similarly, after winning a player-versus-player match and feeling happy about it, they will likely appreciate your game more than if they had lost. Once someone is in a particular emotional state, it will affect their perception. What is even more surprising is that this effect is also true in the case of a placebo arousal. For example, subjects who were given false information about their heart rate as they were looking at pictures of partially nude women later judged as more attractive the pictures that were associated with the falsely high heart rate feedback even though their actual heart rate was not getting faster at the time said pictures were presented to them, indicating that they were not actually aroused by the pictures (see Valins 1966).

Chefs know the food itself is not the only important element in our appreciation of a meal; presentation matters as well. In fact, when coffee condiments are presented in fancy containers, people appreciate the same coffee better than when the condiments are presented in Styrofoam cups (Ariely 2008). Heightened expectations (unless expectations are noticeably betrayed in the end) have a positive impact on appreciation. In a somewhat similar fashion, how information is framed has an impact on its perceived value, especially when the notion of loss is present. If I told you that by turning off instead of unplugging unused electronics at home you are losing about $100 a year, the information might have more impact on you than if I told you that you could win $100 a year by unplugging turned-off electronics. We perceive a loss as having more weight than a gain of comparable value. This phenomenon is called loss aversion (Kahneman and Tversky 1984); humans have a strong aversion to loss. For example, consider these proposals:

1. Would you accept a gamble that offers a 10% chance to win $95 and a 90% chance to lose $5?
2. Would you pay $5 to participate in a lottery that offers a 10% chance to win $100 and a 90% chance to win nothing?

Although both options offer an identical probability and value in money of gain and loss, people are more likely to accept the second proposal than the first one, merely because thinking of $5 as a payment is less painful than thinking of it as a loss (Kahneman 2011). Humans also have a strong emotional reaction to unfairness that can influence them in making decisions that will cost them. The ultimatum game is a compelling illustration of this phenomenon: This game is an economic experiment with two players. The first player receives a sum of money and is allowed to decide how to split the money with the other player. If the other player accepts Player 1's decision, the money is split accordingly between the two. If Player 2 rejects the decision, neither player receives any money. The results depend on the cultural environment but, overall, Player 2 has a tendency to refuse the split if treated unfairly. A fair split would be 50/50. If Player 1 decides to attribute significantly more money to himself or herself (the threshold varies but, e.g., a 70/30 split), Player 2 usually prefers to not make any gain rather than letting Player 1 be unfair (see Oosterbeek *et al.* 2004, for a meta-analysis). This reaction is not necessarily logical because gaining 30% of the money is better than gaining $0. Still, the feeling of unfairness is too strong to let the other participant go unpunished, even if it costs us. Another example is that you might feel happy about your salary until you discover that a colleague having the same experience and responsibilities as you (or worse, less!) has a better salary. Unfairness is a powerful emotional trigger. If you are interested in the history of civilizations, it is inequality more than poverty that has historically unleashed the most horrifying human violence. It's partly because of the untenable inequality between the rich and the poor that the Roman Empire collapsed. This is why is it critical for peace and a good balance in our global society to ensure that inequalities between the poorest and the richest do not become too great. Unfortunately, it seems that the forgetting curve is inexorable with regard to this history lesson.

It would be unfair to blame all of our irrational behavior on emotions. Humans commit a lot of systematic errors in reasoning and, as Daniel Kahneman (2011) stressed when summarizing the extensive research he conducted with Amos Tversky, "We traced these errors to the design of the machinery of cognition rather than to the corruption of thought by emotion." Nonetheless, emotions can bias us into making bad decisions or automatically reacting inadequately.

7.3 Application to Games

There are undoubtedly a lot of things that humans have to say about emotions. We talk about our feelings all the time. We want to be happy; we seek to feel specific emotions through a narrative fiction when we pick up a book, go see a movie, or play a game. We do not perceive the world in the same way whether we are madly in love or we are mourning a loved one who just passed away. I did not talk about the romanticized view of emotion—not because I do not think it is important (it certainly is!)—but simply because our understanding of the under-pinnings of emotion is still very precarious. Moreover, you probably don't need to get a reminder about the importance of storytelling and emotional attachment to characters in increasing one's engagement in an activity. I also did not specifi-cally discuss how to place people in certain situations so oxytocin—called the "love hormone" by some— would be released to improve social interactions. Nor did I mention how to trigger "dopamine shots" to get players hooked. The rea-son I did not mention any of this is mainly because these viewpoints are mostly simplified exaggerations compared to what we actually understand about the brain (see Lewis-Evans 2013, for an overview about dopamine and games). Sure, oxytocin is released when we hug someone (among many other situations) and dopamine is released when we want something, but that does not mean we clearly understand how it all works—far from it. As always, be suspicious when someone gives you an oversimplified explanation of something as complex as our mental processes, especially in relation to biochemicals. This is why I limited myself to a more "down-to-earth" exploration of emotion here. As far as our current knowl-edge of the brain is concerned, the following is the main information you need to remember about emotions:

- Emotion serves motivation, it guides us and (hopefully) keeps us alive.
- Emotion can enhance cognition by raising our awareness, sharpening our focus, and by making us react swiftly to certain situations, especially dangerous ones.
- Emotion can also impair reasoning by influencing our perception of a situation, our cognition, or our behavior.

- Cognition can influence emotion—for example, through our appraisal of a situation.
- Emotion can impair cognition by influencing our perception of a situation, our cognition, or our behavior.
- Presentation, expectation, loss aversion, and unfairness are examples of how emotion can bias our appreciation of a situation or our decision-making.
- Emotional arousal can be misattributed; we can wrongly identify the cause of an emotion we feel.
- Emotional arousal is extended to the whole situation not only the element causing the arousal.

One important application to games is that, of course, you must use emotions to guide and delight your players. Music can be used to signal players that they are safe or that they need to be aware of an imminent danger. (Many action games have different music when the player is in an exploration mode as compared to when enemies are about to attack, for example.) Sound effects can also be used to indicate threats, failures, and successes through conditioning (*The Legend of Zelda* series developed by Nintendo has compelling examples of rewarding sounds.) The art direction will have an impact on players' overall appreciation of the game, and that includes menu and user interface presentation. Game feel, the satisfaction felt through mere interaction with the system, will also have an impact. And so on. (Just like motivation, emotion is a pillar in the user experience framework described in Part II and therefore will be developed in more detail in Chapter 12 in terms of application to video games.)

Another important takeaway from our understanding of emotion is that you must be wary of all the feelings your game induces because they will likely have a dramatic impact on players' overall appreciation of your game, even if the feelings are not necessarily caused by the gameplay itself. Bad usability, for example, can create deep frustration that could be misattributed to the gameplay, leading players (in the worst-case scenario) to rage-quit. Something to consider when designing multiplayer competitive games more specifically is that the players who lose the match will often feel negative emotions that you must ensure won't be attributed to the game systems and, even more importantly, to some unfair treatment. Losing can already be a difficult pill to swallow, but feeling humiliated or believing that the game is unfair or unbalanced, is even more damaging. Even if the game is fair, if losing players don't understand why they have lost, that loss will likely feel unfair. In addition, it is important to address toxic behavior, whereby a small minority of uncivil players could spoil the game for a majority and thus impact retention. It also is critical to make sure your game is not perceived as "pay to win" because it will be considered as unfair in a competitive environment. Lastly, design your game in such a way that even unskilled players can feel they are good at something. For example, in *Clash of Clans* (Supercell), leader boards are categorized by league. There can be only one absolute best player in the world at a certain time, leaving everyone else disappointed, but, in *Clash of Clans*, you can always become the best player in your league, which brings positive emotions to a majority of players. Another example is *Overwatch* (Blizzard), which highlights one player after each match in the "play of the game." Even if you are not particularly good at that game, there is a chance that you performed one cool action during the match that will be recognized in this way, even if your team has lost. In this game, you also see statistics regarding your own achievements and how you improved compared to your past performance (instead of comparing your performance with that of other players'). Find ways to keep positive emotions flowing even if the outcome of a match is not a win. You may even try to help players regulate their negative emotions by using cognitive reappraisal (see Gross 2007). Because appraisal can modify how we feel about a situation, helping players to reappraise their negative feelings might have some benefits. For example, instead of letting them feel badly as they see in big red letters that their team has lost, you could emphasize that they might have lost this round but they could win the next or highlight what they did better than the winning team or that, despite losing, they performed better on some personal metric than they had before.

Now that we have covered a broad overview of the main mental processes as the brain is making sense of its environment, we can more easily understand what variables can impair or facilitate learning.

8

Learning Principles

8.1 Behavioral Psychology Principles

8.2 Cognitive Psychology Principles

8.3 Constructivist Principles

8.4 Application to Games: Learning by Doing with Meaning

Understanding the brain's limitations, how it processes information, and how it learns can guide us in designing the environment more efficiently to facilitate learning. Over the years, several learning approaches have been developed: the behavioral paradigm, the cognitive paradigm, and the constructivism paradigm. Each has its own merits, limitations, and principles. It is important to note that none of these paradigms and principles has been abandoned in favor of newly developed ones; instead, each paradigm focuses on a different aspect of learning.

8.1 Behavioral Psychology Principles

During the first half of the twentieth century, the approach on learning was dominated by behaviorists who focused on instrumental learning and extrinsic reinforcement (e.g., Thorndike 1913; Pavlov 1927; Skinner 1974). They did not account for, nor did they want to consider, what was happening inside the "black box" (i.e., our mental processes) as we learn; they instead focused on environmental events and observable behaviors—inputs and outputs. Behaviorists, therefore, looked at stimulus-response relationships and how the environment shapes learning. The learned association between a stimulus and a response is called conditioning, and it involves—for the most part—implicit learning and memory (unconscious and procedural). Here, we distinguish between classical conditioning (which happens passively) and operant conditioning (which requires an action from the individual).

8.1.1 Classical Conditioning

Classical conditioning refers to a learning process whereby two events (or stimuli) that closely follow each other become linked (associative learning) because they happen repeatedly over time, creating a conditioned response to the first stimulus as one anticipates the appearance of the second stimulus. The famous illustration of Pavlov and his dogs is an example of classical (or Pavlovian) conditioning. Each time Pavlov would give food to the dogs, he would ring a bell right beforehand. Over time, the dogs would learn to associate the bell with food and would develop a response conditioned by the bell: They would salivate when the bell was ringing, anticipating the appearance of food. Dogs naturally salivate in the presence of food, but what happened here is that the bell became a *conditioned* stimulus, which elicited a *conditioned response* (salivation) even before the appearance of food. Humans, just like dogs and other species, learn many behaviors through classical conditioning. For example, think about a lemon (or a lime, depending on which you prefer). You might start to salivate just at the mention of a lemon because you have, over time, associated this fruit with its sour taste and, in fact, lemons are natural salivary stimulants. So, if you suffer from dry mouth, think about biting into a lemon. To take another example from games, the "alert" sound effect in *Metal Gear Solid* (Konami) that is triggered each time an enemy notices you is a conditioned stimulus that elicits a conditioned response from players—an increase in awareness and fight-or-flight behavior. Another example would be the chimes sound effect associated with chests, glyphs, and the like in *Assassin's Creed 2* (Ubisoft). You end up implicitly associating the sound with a treasure until you hear the sound without seeing the treasure: The conditioned response is a raising of awareness and anticipation of reward.

8.1.2 Operant Conditioning

Operant conditioning, also called instrumental learning, is a process whereby rewards and punishments are used to modify a behavior. Research on operant conditioning was pioneered by Thorndike (1913) but later was greatly popularized by B. F. Skinner (see Skinner 1974). In a nutshell, operant conditioning is when you learn (through repetition) the connection between one event and the probability of another event occurring if you make the appropriate action. The typical apparatus that Skinner used to conduct his experiments was the operant conditioning chamber, now called a "Skinner box." An animal (usually a rat or a pigeon) would be isolated in the chamber, which contained a food dispenser and a lever. After a specific stimulus occurred (such as a light or a sound), if the subject animal—say a rat—pressed the lever, a food pellet would be delivered into the food dispenser. Just like in classical conditioning, there is a conditioned stimulus (sound) and a positive reinforcer (reward in the shape of food); but in the case of operant conditioning, the conditioned response implies an action from the rat (pressing a lever)—a change in behavior, so to speak. In some experiments, the Skinner box would also have an electrified floor that would deliver electric shocks (punishment) if the rat's response was incorrect or missing.

Over the numerous experiments Skinner conducted, he demonstrated a number of basic behavioral rules (see Alessi and Trollip 2001):

1. Positive reinforcement (reward) elicits an increase in the frequency of a behavior (obtaining the food pellet after pressing the lever encouraged the rat to press the lever more often).
2. Behavior that is followed by the withdrawal of a punishment (called negative reinforcement) also increases in frequency (i.e., pressing the lever to avoid receiving electric shocks).
3. Positive punishment elicits a decrease in the frequency of a behavior (getting electric shocks after pressing the lever encouraged the rat to avoid pressing the lever). Decrease in the frequency of a behavior can also be elicited by negative punishment, where something positive is removed rather than something unpleasant being added (e.g., pressing a button removing food from the cage).
4. When a behavior that was previously increased through reward delivery is no longer reinforced (the food pellets stop being delivered when the lever is pressed), the behavior decreases in frequency (extinction).
5. Behavior that is always rewarded increases rapidly in frequency but also extinguishes rapidly once the reward is removed.
6. Rewards that happen on a variable ratio schedule (after a random number of responses) are the most efficient in eliciting a behavior and are at the heart of gambling addiction in humans.

Instrumental learning certainly has a lot of merits and was largely used in the twentieth century in education, military, or work environments. However, it also has been widely criticized because this paradigm ignores important unobservable aspects of learning (such as attention or memory) and because behaviorism enthusiasts often overlooked undesirable side effects. For instance, punishments can induce stress or aggression and ultimately can be detrimental to learning (see, e.g., Galea *et al.* 2015, for the impact of punishment on retention for motor learning, and Vogel and Schwabe 2016, for the impact of stress in the classroom), not to mention that stress and anxiety can also damage someone's health (rat or human). This is something to remember when designing the onboarding of your game: It's important to give players negative feedback if they do not do what they need to do (miss their jump over the first ravine obstacle) but also to avoid punishing them as they learn (they die in their fall as opposed to being able to climb back up immediately and try again). Challenges are, of course, important in games, and I am not saying that your players should never die, but you need to be careful when players are learning a new mechanic, especially at the very beginning of the game when they aren't necessarily deeply engaged (even more so if playing your game is free).

8.2 Cognitive Psychology Principles

In the second half of the twentieth century, cognitive psychology became popular because psychologists really wanted to open the "black box" and start understanding what was happening in there. Cognitive psychology, as I'm sure you know now, places emphasis on mental processes such as perception, attention, memory, and motivation. Part I of this book is dedicated to cognitive psychology principles and focuses on how the brain processes information and learns and what factors come into play. Therefore, I will not describe these principles again in this section. The bottom line regarding cognitive psychology principles for learning is to take into account the mind limitations in order to design a more effective learning environment.

One thing I would like to bring to your attention here, though, is the question of transfer of learning. We often make the assumption that what was learned in a certain context can be easily transferable to another. It's the main assumption of all the so-called brain-training games that are flooding the marketplace: What was learned in a multimedia context will be transferred to real-life situations. The problem is that it's actually not often the case and represents a considerable challenge to overcome for those concerned with education (for an overview, see Blumberg 2014).

8.3 Constructivist Principles

The developmental psychologist Jean Piaget is one of the most well-known theorists of the constructivist theory; he tried to understand how children *construct* knowledge through their interactions with the environment (Piaget 1937). Although researchers experimenting with infants later suggested that children can learn a lot about their environment through perception, such as learning about the physical or numerical properties of objects (e.g., Baillargeon *et al.* 1985 or Wynn 1992), it does appear that manipulating the environment helps children think and learn (see, e.g., Levine *et al.* 1992). According to constructivist theorists, we learn by doing—by actively constructing our own knowledge, and the environment can act as a facilitator (or as an obstruction). The emphasis is therefore on the active process of learning, which makes sense if you remember how working memory functions: The deeper the level of information processing, the better the retention (Craik and Lockhart 1972). The learner is therefore encouraged to explore, discover, and experiment as long as immediate feedback informs them about their successes and failures (either from educators or a designed learning environment such as games). This approach also emphasizes the importance of purposeful learning (as opposed to force-fed teaching) or meaning.

Seymour Papert, a mathematician and educator inspired by Piaget's constructivist theory, held a *constructionist* approach to learning by which learning is more efficient when the learner can experiment with the material in a concrete and meaningful situation. And because Papert developed his theory from the 1960s onward, he could use computers in experiments. If you are as old as I am, you might remember the Logo computer language that let children program computers. Logo is often remembered for its use of turtle graphics that allowed

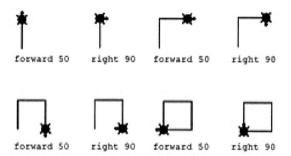

forward 50   right 90   forward 50   right 90

forward 50   right 90   forward 50   right 90

Figure 8.1

Logo Graphics Turtle © Logo Foundation. (Courtesy of Logo Foundation, New York City.)

controlling a virtual cursor (a "turtle") in a playful approach because the goal was to draw. Children had to find the way to teach the turtle to draw what they were interested in depicting, thereby experimenting with geometry. For example, if the children wanted to draw a house, they first needed to teach the turtle to draw a square shape. In the process, they would learn through their mistakes and successes the inherent characteristics of a square—such as that a square has four sides of equal length and four 90-degree angles. Thus, to draw a square, you needed to tell the turtle to "Repeat 4 [forward 50 right 90]," as shown in Figure 8.1. Geometry was made accessible to the child in a way that, "The knowledge is acquired for a recognizable personal purpose" because the "child does something with it" (Papert 1980, p. 21). And this example using simple geometry is only a shallow illustration of Papert's ideas and experiments. In sum, instead of thinking of a way for the computer to teach people (which is still sadly an approach that many developers use with "gamification" and "serious games"), Papert enabled *learning* by letting children teach the computer to do something *meaningful* for them.

This playful experimentation approach to learning and development somehow reflects the iterative process approach in design thinking. David Kelley, founder of IDEO Product Development (the product design and development firm behind Apple's first mouse) talks about "enlightened trial and error" as being a critical process in design (Kelley 2001). You want to fail faster to succeed sooner.

8.4 Application to Games: Learning by Doing with Meaning

To summarize, here are the most important characteristics about learning that you need to remember:

- Conditioning is a type of learning by association between a stimulus and a response that is repeated over time. When conditioning requires an action from the subject, it's called operant or instrumental conditioning. Reinforcement is critical in conditioning, especially positive reinforcement. Conditioning can be particularly powerful because it involves implicit learning.

- Rewards (positive reinforcers) that happen on a variable ratio schedule are the most efficient in eliciting and retaining engagement in a behavior.
- Cognitive psychology principles for learning take into account the mind limitations in order to design a more effective learning environment (perception, attention, memory, motivation, emotion).
- According to constructivist principles, we learn by doing—by actively constructing our own knowledge. The learning environment then acts as a facilitator or as an obstructer.
- The deeper the level of information processing when we construct knowledge, the better the retention.
- According to the constructionist approach, we learn better by doing—in context—with purpose (meaning).

If there is only one thing you had to remember about learning, it is: The most efficient way to teach something to someone, especially in the case of an interactive medium, is to let them learn by doing (in context) and with a purpose (meaning). This means that, to teach players about a game mechanic, it is much more efficient to place them in a situation where they need and are motivated to learn the new behavior (to progress or obtain a reward) than to simply freeze the game and display a tutorial text about said mechanic. For example, the first-person-shooter game *Blood Dragon* (Ubisoft) has hilarious tutorials because they mock bad tutorial practices. However, in this game, players learn most of the game mechanics and features in a learn-then-do situation through walls of tutorial texts that pause game play. (This is done on purpose to make hardcore players of such games laugh as they recognize how tutorials can sometimes be lousy.) Tutorial texts pop up one after the other, which makes it impossible to remember everything because of the massed learning effect. We learn better when the content is distributed over time. (You might remember the spacing effect in memory from Chapter 4.) High-budget games are moving increasingly away from a massed learn-then-do onboarding and more often use distributed learning by doing. However, the meaning of the learning is frequently weakly communicated, which has an impact on players' motivation to follow the instructions and, therefore, the attentional resources allocated to a task and, subsequently, the strength of the memory for it. For example, it's good to tell players to try their newly obtained grenades by tossing one, but it's not really meaningful if there is no threat at all and nothing to aim at. It's much better to place the player in a meaningful situation, or an emotional one, to teach them about something as long as the situation is not too stressful or overwhelming. For example, in *Fortnite* (Epic Games), we placed players in an underground cave at the very beginning of the experience; at some point, they have to learn how to build stairs if they want to get out and explore the world (and a chest is visible at ground level, which draws attention and hopefully gets players emotionally aroused a little bit as they anticipate what is in the chest), as shown in Figure 8.2. Another example is that we teach players to shoot in a situation with a little stress, although it is relatively safe: Zombies are behind a low wall, and players need to learn how to use a gun to shoot them. Because there is a threat due to the zombies attacking the wall (which looks like it might break), this helps players focus their attention on the task; but it's not stressful enough (zombies are not coming at players) to overwhelm them—hopefully. (Although it still might be a bit overwhelming for younger players because they are less tolerant of stress than adults.) Another example would be Nintendo's *Mario Galaxy* (and many other Mario games) where a player needs to chase a rabbit at the very beginning of the experience. The chasing rabbit situation has more than one purpose for game developers, but in terms of learning, it helps players become acquainted with the controls while navigating in a then-new three-dimensional space in a situation that has a little stress (the rabbit is taunting the player but is not a threat). Moreover, depending on a player's navigation skill level, they might take more or less time to catch the rabbit; but they will never get punished (die) if they don't succeed fast enough. In *Uncharted 2* (Naughty Dog), a player starts the game hanging at the bottom of a train suspended in the void; it is clearly meaningful to a player to learn the navigation mechanics in that situation to stay alive. The only issue I have with the opening of that game is that players are truly punished if they do not learn fast enough. They can die in that opening scene. One last example: In *World of Warcraft* (Blizzard), players learn how to swim only when they get a quest that requires them to go underwater.

Admittedly, it takes much more production effort to create meaningful learning-by-doing environments, but I would argue that learning to play the game is entirely part of the experience and should thus be considered as part of the level design. However, it would be idealistic to think that we have enough

Figure 8.2

Fortnite Beta © 2017, Epic Games, Inc. (Courtesy of Epic Games, Inc., Cary, NC.)

resources when developing a game to create such ideal learning situations (i.e., design a whole quest or map) for each and every teaching experience that needs to occur. We don't. We constantly run out of time and money, and we usually have to crunch to meet our deadlines, hopefully without sacrificing the quality of the game. This is why you must list and prioritize everything that you will need to teach your players and make an educated guess on the anticipated learning difficulty for each element (an original game mechanic will be harder to learn than common mechanics). As we will see in Chapter 13, such a prioritized list will help you plan the onboarding experience early on and design the related production tasks accordingly with the development team. It will be even more important to establish an onboarding plan for multiplayer games because the onboarding needs to be as short as possible while being as efficient as possible (so players aren't bored with your game even before being able to experience it fully in multiplayer mode). Unskilled players will likely have a negative experience if they get slaughtered in their first player versus player (PvP) match (and no, you cannot rely only on a balanced matchmaking to save the day).

Crafting a great user experience is not only about your audience learning to play and master your game, of course, but this is where the experience starts, and it constitutes a vast part of the journey. Understanding the mental processes underlying learning will also help you improve the usability of your game because it's all about removing unnecessary frictions (i.e., points of confusion) to make the experience more intuitive or, said differently, easier to learn.

9

Understanding the Brain

Takeaway

9.1   Perception   9.4   Motivation
9.2   Memory   9.5   Emotion
9.3   Attention   9.6   Learning Principles

Our brains contain about a hundred billion neurons, each of which is connected to up to 10,000 other neurons, which makes it immensely complex to study. What we do know is that although the brain processes information and has some computational characteristics, it is not at all like a computer. The brain does not really "process," "encode," or "store" information. Our brains are not as fast or reliable as computers, although computers are limited in connections whereas the brain has trillions of them. Our neural networks are not strictly separated into independent modules, each taking care of a specific mental "process." There are no isolated systems in the brain dedicated to perception, memory, or motivation. We do not carefully and objectively analyze our environment or memorize events perfectly. We construct information when we perceive and "encode" it, and we later reconstruct that information when we remember it. We tend to take short-cuts, jump to conclusions, use rules of thumb because it's good enough most of the time and it's more efficient than careful computing all the variables when our survival is depending on a very fast fight-or-flight decision, or at least it was back in the savanna. As Steven Pinker (1997) pointed out, it's not because our mind is the result of an adaptation designed by natural selection that the way we perceive, think, or feel is biologically adaptive. Moreover, the environment we are currently interacting with is very different from the ones that shaped the evolution of our brain. The human brain is undoubtedly a fascinating organ that allowed us to go to the moon as well as to design weapons of mass destruction. Yet, our brain has considerable limitations that will probably make it impossible for us to truly understand how it works—unless we get help from smart enough artificial intelligence, or "natural computation."

Although not accurate, the computer metaphor is useful to help our limited mind understand how the brain works. This is why we use terminology such as "process" or "storage"; it makes it easier to communicate the little we do know about the brain. However, remember that our brains have numerous limitations and that we are mostly unaware of them as we go about our daily lives. Worse, we constantly overestimate our capabilities. Players believe they do not need tutorials and they can figure out how to play by themselves, although they usually don't and will then likely blame their poor performance on your game and rage-quit. Similarly, you are likely overestimating your capabilities as a game developer. We tend to believe because we have experience or because our latest shipped game was a success that we know what players will be excited about and how to onboard them. The curse of knowledge bias, however, makes it nearly impossible for us to anticipate how a new player will perceive the game we know so well. Most of the time, we are just fooling ourselves simply because crafting a great user experience is a daunting task, and cognitive dissonance makes it more comfortable to keep our heads in the sand. "I don't need this psychology nonsense; I know how to make games." Maybe you do. But most of us will save time and considerable effort by minding the gamer's brain.

Here is what you need to remember, in a nutshell. Information "processing" and learning starts with the perception of a stimulus and will ultimately end with a synaptic modification—a change in memory. The level of attentional resources dedicated to the stimulus will likely determine the strength of the memory for it. Two other main factors will also have an impact on the quality of learning: motivation and emotion. Lastly, by applying learning principles (impacting the different factors), the whole "process" can be improved.

9.1 Perception

Perception is a subjective construct of the mind; we do not perceive the world as it is in reality, and we might not all perceive a given input the same way. Beyond optical illusions and Gestalt principles, perception is biased by our prior knowledge, the context in which we perceive an input, or our expectations. Applications to games are:

- First know your audience and their prior knowledge and expectations.
- Playtest your game regularly with your audience.
- Test your iconography.
- Use the Gestalt principles when applicable.
- Use affordances.
- Understand visual imagery and mental rotation.
- Be aware of the Weber–Fechner bias.

9.2 Memory

Memory implies retrieving (by reconstructing) information that was previously encoded and stored. It can be broken down into three components: sensory memory (part of perception), working memory, and long-term memory. Working memory is limited in space (about three items) and time (a few minutes), and it requires attentional resources. Working memory can be easily overwhelmed, especially during multitasking attempts. Long-term memory is composed of explicit memory (declarative) and implicit memory (procedural). It is impacted by the forgetting curve. Applications to games are:

- Reduce the memory load.
- Prioritize learning.
- Distribute learning over time (spacing effect).
- Repeat information.
- Give reminders.

9.3 Attention

Attention works like a spotlight selecting certain inputs to process while filtering out the rest, which can cause inattentional blindness. Attention has a critical impact on working memory and, by extension, on learning. Divided attention (multitasking) usually is not efficient because our attentional resources are extremely scarce. Applications to games are:

- Be a magician: Direct players' attention to the relevant elements.
- Avoid cognitive overload that could negatively overwhelm players.
- Avoid multitasking situations, especially when one of the tasks is important for onboarding.
- Avoid relying on one sensory modality only (e.g., vision) to convey important information.

9.4 Motivation

Motivation is at the origin of any behavior. There is no current unified theory of human motivation that can account for all our drives and behaviors. We nonetheless have attempted to break down motivation into four types: implicit motivation (biological drives), environmental-shaped motivation (learned drives), intrinsic motivation (cognitive needs), and personality (individual needs). Applications to games are (find more examples in Chapter 12):

- Provide clear goals and meaningful rewards to goals.
- Know the different types of rewards (continuous and intermittent) and the different types of intermittent rewards so you can anticipate the player behavior they should likely encourage.

- Use a variable ratio schedule to reward actions that are not tied to the completion of a goal (e.g., when opening a chest found in the game world).
- Use fixed ratio and interval schedules to reward habit formation and player strategy.
- To help players find their tasks intrinsically rewarding, aim to satisfy the needs for competence, autonomy, and relatedness (self-determination theory).
- Being in the flow zone, whereby a meaningful challenge is not too easy or too hard, is intrinsically motivating. Therefore, the game difficulty curve must follow this principle.
- Use OCEAN to apprehend individual needs.
- Focus on meaning to enhance motivation. Meaning is about having a sense of purpose, value, and impact, sometimes bigger than the self.

9.5 Emotion

Emotion is a state of physiological arousal that can be associated with a feeling. Emotion influences our perception and cognition and guides our behavior. It can enhance cognition, but it can also impair reasoning. Applications to games are as follows (find more examples in Chapter 12):

- Use emotions to guide and delight players.
- Avoid feelings of unfairness as much as possible.
- Polish your game feel.
- Avoid usability frustrations.

9.6 Learning principles

Several learning approaches have been developed: the behavioral paradigm, the cognitive paradigm, and the constructivism paradigm. The behavioral paradigm looks at the stimulus–response relationship and how environment shapes learning. There can be classical conditioning (passive associated learning) and operant conditioning (requiring an appropriate action). Rewards and punishments are paramount to conditioning. The cognitive paradigm places emphasis on mental processes and on human limitations. The constructivism paradigm posits that people construct knowledge through their interaction with the environment. Applications to games are as follows (find more examples in Chapter 12):

- Reward players appropriately.
- Avoid punishing players when they are learning about a new mechanic.
- Use cognitive science knowledge to create a learning environment that takes into account human capabilities and limitations in perception, attention, memory, motivation, and emotion.
- Make players learn by doing, in context, with purpose (meaning).
- Make players deeply process the important elements you need to teach them—the deeper the process, the better the retention.

PART II
A UX Framework
for Video Games

Game User Experience

Overview

10.1   A Short History of UX
10.2   Debunking UX
       Misconceptions

10.3   A Definition of
       Game UX

The user experience (UX) discipline is fairly new in the video game industry yet is getting increasingly more traction because it is now better understood and its benefits are better known. When I was working in the toy industry in the mid 2000s (developing educational games for infants, toddlers, and young children), satisfying those who were buying toys (parents) carried more weight than considering how educational and fun the experience of interacting with the products would be for the users (children). After all, the ones spending money for toys (adults) are usually not the ones using them. In 2008, I joined the video game industry and started to work at Ubisoft HQ (in France) as they became increasingly interested in understanding how cognitive science could help them create better games. At that time, playtest labs and user research was already part of the production cycle at Ubisoft; they were testing their games in development with external players to help identify issues and fix them before the games would launch. Although a few cognitive ergonomics specialists were working with designers and engineers to help them anticipate issues users could experience when interacting with the interface, the concept of user experience was not really a thing yet. There already was a clear understanding that a game needed to be easy to grasp (game usability) and fun, but this wasn't formalized. Of course, many developers and academics were individually introducing the new concepts of usability, playability, game flow, player enjoyment, or ingredients of fun, and some studios were more advanced than others, but there was no overarching definition of what a game user experience entails or a defined UX framework that could be integrated within the development process itself.

In 2017, user experience was formally introduced at the Game Developers Conference (the largest annual gathering for video game professionals) with the debut of the UX summit. Knowing that Don Norman popularized the concept of UX back in the 1990s (Norman *et al.* 1995), it is extremely exciting to finally see this discipline being recognized in the game industry. But because UX is still relatively new to this industry, there is a lot of work to do to clearly outline its definition, framework, and practice within game development. Part II of this book represents my personal attempt to do so based on what I identified was resonating the most with the game developers during the years I worked with them at Ubisoft HQ, Ubisoft Montreal, LucasArts, and Epic Games. Before we get to the meat of the subject, let's start with a short history of user experience to better understand its evolution and its first steps in the game industry.

10.1 A Short History of UX

At its core, the user experience discipline considers how the end user interacts with a product and the emotions and behaviors elicited via this interaction by using knowledge from cognitive science and research methodologies. The goal is to ensure that the target audience will experience the product the way its makers intended by shaping the product to fit the human using it. This approach, whereby the human is at the center of the design process (human-centered design), takes its roots in human factors and ergonomics, areas generally considered to have flourished during World War II. At that time, it was noted that people had difficulty operating war machines, especially warplanes, and that some would even die because of fatal errors made while they were interacting with these machines. Psychologists started being hired by the military to alleviate these issues. Back then, machines were mainly designed to facilitate engineering and required long training sessions for the humans operating them to understand how they worked. As highly trained pilots kept crashing airplanes (because of a problem in control configurations, e.g., Fitts and Jones 1947), a mind shift occurred: Maybe it was not the fault of the pilots (who had been meticulously trained) but the fault of the cockpit design that facilitated human errors. Imagine pilots under stress confusing the ejection release and the throttle (as the folklore goes) or the landing gear and flap handles because these controls were not consistently located in the same spot in the cockpit from plane to plane. I'm sure you have experienced something similar as you switched games and had to readjust to a new controller mapping, although the consequences of a mistake were surely less dramatic. Machines started to be designed with humans' capabilities, performance, and limitations in mind. This is how the field relating to human factors and ergonomics was officially born, and it evolved from safety-consciousness concerns for the military to a focus on building human-centric technology for workers and consumers.

Ergonomics is comprised of different fields of research; for example, physical ergonomics is concerned with human anatomy and physical fatigue while operating machines, and cognitive ergonomics is concerned with mental processes such as the ones we saw in Part I of this book (perception, attention, memory, etc.). When computers started to enter people's homes in the 1980s, a new human factors branch emerged: human–computer interaction (HCI). HCI has established and refined laws or principles that can be applied to improve a human's interaction with a computerized interface. The two most well-known laws are Fitts's law and the Hick–Hyman law (see MacKenzie 2013). Fitts's law allows us to mathematically predict the time required for a human to point to a target—either by touching it or pointing at it with a cursor, depending on the distance to the target and the size of the target (Fitts 1954). For example, a small button on a user interface (UI) will take more time to point at than a large button, and two buttons too close to each other will increase the risk of users mistakenly clicking on one button when they wanted to click on the other. Another example is that a button positioned at a corner of the screen will be easier to aim at because the cursor will not be able to get past the button as it reaches the edge of the screen and cannot go any further. This is why application menus on Mac computers (Apple) are always located at the top of the screen instead of being attached to the application window—to allow the target to have "infinite" height because the cursor is stopped by the edge of the screen. Therefore, there is no need to slowdown when the cursor is approaching the target because there are no risks of overshooting. Simply pointing to a target located along an edge is faster. Fitts's law is widely used in UI and interaction design to facilitate the desired actions the designers want users to accomplish. The Hick–Hyman law (or Hick's law) posits that the user's reaction time to make a decision will logarithmically increase with the number of options displayed (i.e., the more options, the longer it will take to make a decision). This law is one of the reasons why designers should avoid complexity in UIs. HCI laws are very important to consider when designing the UI, HUD, and menus for a video game in order to avoid common frustrations that are disconnected from the gameplay itself (unless confusing the player with the interface is part of the game).

HCI is mainly concerned with how to make interfaces more usable and pleasurable to use, but it does not consider the whole experience people have with a product (first hearing about it, seeing it in the store or online, buying it, opening the box or launching the application, using it, telling somebody else about it, contacting customer service, etc.). This is why designer Don Norman introduced the notion of UX in the 1990s—to account for the whole experience humans have with a given product, whether it is an object, a service, a website, an application, or a video game. "Great designers produce pleasurable experiences," says Norman (2013). This is the same approach of user experience that will be considered in this book, although I will more specifically stay focused on what it means for game design. Game UX therefore entails the ease of use (usability) of a game as well as the rest of the player experience—the emotion, motivation, immersion, fun, or flow perceived. What began as a response to a wartime life-or-death situation has now become one of the largest and fastest-growing disciplines in design; user experience can guide the design of virtually every product, system, or service that humans use.

10.2 Debunking UX Misconceptions

Game user experience means using cognitive science knowledge and the scientific method in game development, and there can be some resistance given that it is often a new approach in many game studios. Not so long ago, there were no positions in the industry that had "UX" in the title, and now these UX invaders are spreading around! As is often the case when a new process is introduced, it can generate apprehension and suspicion from veteran professionals, which is quite understandable. As a result, UX professionals (from interaction designers to user researchers) can be confronted with misconceptions about their discipline. When looking back at my own experience advocating for UX or cognitive psychology with development teams, there were five main misconceptions that required some debunking (see Hodent 2015). These are described as follows.

10.2.1 Misconception 1: UX Will Distort the Design Intents and Make the Game Easier

There often is a strong fear among game developers that considering UX will remove all the challenge from a game and dumb it down. Funnily enough, during my training sessions about psychology and UX, members of the audience often ask me how games like *Dark Souls* (FromSoftware) will survive the UX invasion. Somehow, the UX practice is perceived as a steamroller that will smooth out and standardize all games. This misconception has always been the most surprising to me because the whole point of UX is *precisely* to help developers accomplish their vision, certainly not to distort the design intent. Therefore, if your target audience is hardcore gamers and the experience you want for them is suffering (so to speak), then UX practices will absolutely help you accomplish your sadistic goals; rejoice! For example, consider the survival horror game *Resident Evil* (Capcom) and imagine a user researcher who observes the following during a playtest: At some point in the game, players open a closet where a zombie is hidden and now attacks them. Most players being observed are caught off guard, and their first reflex is to try to move backward, away from the zombie, but a table left by a level designer is blocking their retreat (see Figure 10.1). As a result, many players panic as they struggle to move around the table; most of them get hurt by the zombie, and some even die. If UX was about making the game easier, then the user researcher could report to the development team that the table should be removed because it causes player frustration. However, the whole intent of a horror game is, well, to freak people out—so panic is actually a desirable emotion to elicit in that case. Therefore, this observation does not likely constitute a UX issue that needs fixing because it's probably aligned with the design intentions. In fact, this situation would probably be reported to the development team as a positive finding.

Now, what *can* happen is that the development team may have different goals than the publishing or the executive team. Maybe your dream is to design the

Figure 10.1

Resident Evil, Capcom CO., LTD. Released in 1996 on PlayStation. (Courtesy of Capcom Co., Ltd, Osaka, Japan.)

next *Souls* game, but the studio wants a more mainstream game that will appeal to a broad audience and with free-to-play mechanics. In that case, UX recommendations will account for the business goals as well as the design goals, so both must be aligned. When there is no alignment, the UX feedback can be frustrating to the game team because it may echo some business goals that they might not agree with. I can understand this frustration, but it should not be blamed on UX practices; rather, it is a mismatch of priorities or a failed communication within the team and studio as a whole. Good UX practitioners do not have any agenda of their own that they are trying to push, and they are actually not invaders trying to take over. We come in peace and are here to help.

10.2.2 Misconception 2: UX Will Restrict the Creativity of the Team

Many developers consider video games a form of art—which I actually agree with—so they sometimes argue that science should not interfere with their artistic direction. After all, Pablo Picasso never went through a UX process with his art. Games generally are developed with a team of artists (such as art directors, graphic designers, musicians, writers, etc.), and art is crucial to video games—most notably to create an emotional response (as we will see in Chapter 12). However, science and art actually are great partners (e.g., understanding physics is useful for photographers and cinematographers, knowing the mathematical principles of perspective is useful for painters), and video games are a particular form of art. A video game is an *interactive* experience. It necessitates human input to reveal its content. So, if the art direction is conflicting with HCI laws or usability principles, then it will do itself a disservice because it could prevent players from fully experiencing the game (and, thus, its art). As Epic Games' Chief Technology Officer Kim Libreri explains in the following essay, UX can be used as a tool for fine-tuning content. Artists have to create within technical and physical constraints, but they also have to account for human limitations when working on an interactive experience. You can, of course, play with human limitations such as perception, like M. C. Escher or Salvador Dalí did, as long as it is your specific intent. Making enemies hard to detect through their character design might make sense in a horror game, but making a golf ball with a green texture would go against golf usability because the challenge in that game is not about finding the ball. The filmmaker, writer, and actor Orson Welles is credited with once having said: "The enemy of art is the absence of limitations." UX practitioners won't hamper the team's creativity; they will simply reveal more constraints that artists have to take into account (i.e., human mind limitations). Let those additional limitations stimulate your creativity even more!

Kim Libreri, Chief Technology Officer at Epic Games

Ux Is Not the Enemy of Creativity

I have been making what aims to be popular entertainment both in video games and movies for more than two decades and, in my experience, the most important part of audience enjoyment is comprehension. Traditionally, this has been something that was considered instinctual to successful creative leadership, although the reality is that most of the great creative directors are able to project themselves into the audiences' viewpoint while taking feedback from external confidants. When they do this, they are considering the user experience (UX) and how best to express their intent to a consumer.

As an artist, it is too easy to hold on to one's ideas with the justification of creative purity; but if this comes at the audience's or players' expense, you may find yourself catering to an audience of one. UX analysis gives us the tools to have an unbiased, scientific view on how our consumers are reacting to our product, and it has proven to be a reliable and mostly frictionless mechanism for fine-tuning content.

UX testing does not come for free. You need to make sure your content is in the right state of development to not produce random unneeded feedback, and you also have to be very considerate of the questions you ask based on what you actually need feedback on. Although as a project reaches maturity, it becomes more important to understand how users are reacting to the whole surface area of that project.

Nobody wants to deliberately produce a title that misses the mark, especially when millions of dollars are at stake. UX testing is an important tool in avoiding what can often become the echo box of an often insulated creative and executive team. UX feedback can be tough; but, in order to be successful, it is important to remember who we are making a product for.

10.2.3 Misconception 3: UX Is Yet Another Opinion

Making games usually requires coordination from many professionals and, in large studios, the game development team might have to deal with many opinions—from within the game team itself, from the marketing team, the publishing team, the executive team, the audience, and so on. Therefore, UX input can be perceived as yet another opinion the game team has to deal with. Designers might particularly be apprehensive because they are used to everyone already believing they are a designer. As Richard Bartle (2009) pointed out, game developers (whether they are executives, engineers, or artists), journalists, and players all think they are designers. They will tirelessly give their opinion to the game and level designers about certain game mechanics or systems, what they should add or remove, why they believe the balance is off on a particular map, and so on. Just like many people believe they understand psychology because of their experience as human beings, people believe they understand design because of their experience with objects, applications, and video games as a user. This is not to say that non-designers should not give design feedback about the game, but this phenomenon can make some designers defensive. Artists can encounter the same issue because some people believe they understand art because they enjoy stories, comic books, and movies. Engineers are usually less bothered because non-coders can more easily recognize that they don't understand programming. However, engineers are impacted by another kind of issue: Many people don't understand why a modification that seems trivial would be such a big deal to code.

All in all, most game developers usually don't seek any more feedback than what they are already getting (which is often a lot!), and UX practitioners can therefore be seen as yet another newcomer in "opinionland." However, UX practitioners do not give opinions, as I often jokily say to ease developers' worries. They provide an analysis based on their expertise and on data (when available). The UX discipline is about using cognitive science knowledge and the scientific method to identify or anticipate issues that will negatively impact players' experience in a way that was not intended by developers. It's about testing hypotheses through standardized research protocols. It is true that sometimes finding the right problem that needs solving is not always an easy task, and because every game and every experience is different, we do not always know what the right answer is. Iteration will forever be critical to design, even when using a human-centered design approach informed by human factors principles and cognitive psychology. Nonetheless, addressing UX feedback originating from UX tests, expert reviews, or data analyses should not be treated as "just another opinion." If presented correctly, UX feedback is the least biased of all the feedback originating from various channels, while also being the most neutral. As long as UX practitioners know where they stand and have a clear understanding of the design and business goals, they should be the ones providing the most objective feedback.

10.2.4 Misconception 4: UX Is Just Common Sense

When game developers are experienced and competent, it is indeed true that some of the UX feedback will mention issues that they had already anticipated. Trained designers have refined their intuition through experience, and they know about cognitive psychology and HCI principles (whether or not they can formalize their knowledge). Many of the principles known by UX practitioners are actually "universal" design principles (see, e.g., Lidwell *et al.* 2010). However, some conclusions might sometimes appear obvious only *after* they were pointed out. There is a cognitive bias called the *hindsight bias* that makes us believe we knew about something all along because we don't necessarily remember the feeling of uncertainty that we had before all the facts were presented about what happened. Also, many video games ship with what seem to be "common sense" issues. This does not necessarily happen because the developers lacked common sense. It could be because their curse of knowledge prevented them from detecting an obvious problem simply because they knew their game too well and could not anticipate how a new player would perceive it. It could be because they were aware of the issue but got used to it and ultimately forgot it was even there. Or, it could be because they did not have the time to fix this particular issue when faced with all the other priorities. This is why it's always easier to criticize a game after its release, especially when we have no idea what happened during production. However, this also emphasizes the fact that seemingly common sense issues can be overlooked for various reasons.

Most UX recommendations are not common sense, though. As we saw in Part I, the human brain is flawed with perceptual, cognitive, and social biases that affect both developers and players. It's for a good reason that researchers from any field use very standardized protocols to test their hypotheses; it's easy to miss something or misinterpret what is actually going on. Following a good UX process will help you identify most issues your game has and, more importantly, will help you prioritize them depending on how severely they impact players' experience and on the importance of the game feature they affect. For example, an issue that is not impacting players too badly (and they mostly manage to figure it out at some point) but that affects one of your core game pillars will be more highly prioritized than an issue affecting players but that is about an advanced feature that is not essential to the core gameplay. UX methodologies should also help you find where the problems come from, so that you can solve the correct problem. As Don Norman (2013) pointed out, problems usually don't reveal themselves in neat packages; they have to be discovered.

10.2.5 Misconception 5: There Is Not Enough Time or Money to Consider UX

Making games is hard. Very often, developers don't have enough resources— whether it is time, money, or people—to ship the game they want to ship on their deadline. They either have to work overtime, end up cutting a lot of features, and/ or have to sacrifice the game quality. In a 2015 press release, the International

Game Developers Association revealed that 62% of game developers work overtime and that nearly half of these professionals "crunching" are working more than 60 hours per week. On top of this, developing and marketing games is very expensive. This is why adopting a new process and hiring new people can be perceived as adding more complications. However, investing in a UX process is exactly that: an investment. Shipping a game with critical UX issues could end up being extremely damaging to your game, especially given that your audience can choose to spend their time and money on many other games that are now on the market competing with yours. Sometimes even a small usability issue affecting players' shopping flow when they are interacting with the game store interface can have a dramatic impact on your revenue. Most studios utilize thorough quality assurance (QA) testing so that the most critical bugs can be fixed before their games are launched. Similarly, considering the user experience your game offers will help you identify and fix the most critical issues that could impact your players and, in turn, impact the success of your game. Moreover, if you plan for a UX process within your iteration pipeline early in the development cycle, it will help you identify issues as soon as you have paper or interactive prototypes, allowing you to fix these issues in a significantly cheaper and quicker manner than when the features are already implemented in the game engine. As for the features implemented, it will also be cheaper for you to change elements in the game *before* they are fully "arted up" and polished. Of course, not everything can be tested via prototypes, and some game systems can only be tested efficiently in the closed beta stage; but the more issues you can take down early on, the more time you will have to focus on systemic and game balancing issues later in the development cycle. Don't ask yourself if you can afford to consider UX, ask yourself if you can afford not to.

10.3 A Definition of Game UX

The term "user experience" can account for various perspectives. As I mentioned earlier, the term was coined by Don Norman to account for the whole experience a user can have with a product, a website, an application, or a service. Having that philosophy in mind, the game user experience entails the *whole* experience players have with a video game: hearing about it, watching trailers, going to the game website, downloading and/or installing the game, interacting with the game from menus to gameplay, installing updates, contacting customer service, interacting in forums, telling friends about it, and so on. Everything is important to consider to improve the game UX. However, in this book, I will mostly talk about the experience players have when interacting with the game itself.

When considering the video game alone, there is currently no consensus as to how to define game UX. Some developers talk about user experience as accounting for the ease of use of the game only and will label *player* experience as the fun and emotional engagement aspect of the game (e.g., Lazzaro 2008). My perspective about game UX is more general and is aligned with Isbister and Schaffer's (2008) definition describing user experience in a broad sense, namely, what it is like to interact with the software and how engaging this experience is. Some developers might also use the term "user research" to account for UX but, to me, user research entails the tools and methodology we use to measure the game UX and, therefore, is only one (albeit important) gear in the system. There is no best way to define game UX as long as the game developers you work with are aligned regarding what this is all about. My own definition of game UX and the way I communicate about it has been shaped by the numerous interactions and collaborations I have had with game developers at Ubisoft, LucasArts, and Epic Games, and by all the discussions I have had at game industry conferences. This is certainly not to say that my approach regarding game UX is the best one, but it became an efficient and practical framework *for me* in collaborating with my colleagues. And although my framework is informed by scientific knowledge, I have not tested it in the academic sense. It comes from game development practice. Therefore, I'm still refining my perspective and will certainly continue to refine it as long as I work in this industry.

My practical approach to game UX is to consider the whole experience players have with the game itself—from interacting with menus to the emotion and motivation felt during and after gameplay. It includes the totality of what is experienced as players perceive the system image, interact with it, think about it, and admire its visual and audio aesthetics, as well as how they engage cognitively and emotionally with the game, their motivation to keep playing, and how players remember their experience afterward. Having this definition in mind, game UX has two main components to consider: usability and "engage-ability." The *usability* of a game is about its ease of use, how players interact with the game interface, and if this interaction feels satisfying. The *engage-ability* is a fuzzier concept that accounts for how fun, engaging, and emotional a game is. I used to call this component "game flow," but this term can have too many different meanings for game developers. (I now refer to game flow in a more restricted manner, as you will see in Chapter 12.) I will admit that the term "engage-ability" sounds a bit pompous, and you may wonder why I insist on using this convoluted term. I like it for two reasons. The first is that the concept of "engagement" is one that resonates with more people—developers and gamers alike, whereas the terms "fun" or "flow" are usually more ambiguous. When you are *engaged* in playing a game, it means that you care about it, you are motivated to keep playing, your experience is emotional, you are immersed, you feel a sense of presence, and you are likely having fun, whatever "fun" means to you. Why not just calling it "engagement" then, you might ask. That's a great question, and I'm not so sure I have a satisfying answer. But here is my second reason: The suffix "ability" in "engage-ability" entails considering the degree to which a game is able to be engaging in the same way that "usability" entails considering the degree to which a game is able to be used appropriately. Let's hope that these terms will resonate with you too!

In sum, the game user experience entails how players perceive and understand a game, how they interact with it, and the emotions and engagement elicited via this interaction. It considers a game's usability and engage-ability, both of which will be described in the next two chapters. Keep in mind that my attempt to boil down game UX here is intended more specifically for designers, artists, engineers, QA testers, and producers in charge of developing the game, as well as for professionals working in marketing, publishing, or executive teams. I do not consider my audience to be user researchers and UX practitioners exclusively; I believe they should already have deeper knowledge of the subject than what is described here. Therefore, my goal when approaching game UX in this book is mainly to build bridges between professions and perspectives so all developers can work together toward improving the user experience for players. The goal is *not* to exhaustively summarize the research, theories, and frameworks that have been documented so far and that would mainly serve UX practitioners (for an overview of these topics, see Bernhaupt 2010; Hartson and Pyla 2012). Unfortunately, academics or researchers sometimes fail to deliver their message efficiently because their conclusions and recommendations are not understood or are interpreted as "bossy." UX practitioners' main goal is to help everyone on the team create a great experience—not to be considered the "usability police." (I was actually called that way once, and it certainly is not a sentiment you want your colleagues to feel.) Good collaboration starts by making sure we convey our messages appropriately and by making ourselves accessible. Just like I did in Part I with cognitive science, I will, in Part II, simplify and boil down our current UX knowledge and practice in games into what should be the most easily applicable framework for a broad audience of game developers. In order to do that, I will sometimes sacrifice some subtleties and utilize a different vocabulary than the one used in human factors psychology by using a vocabulary more familiar to game developers. The reason why I care so much about advocating for UX and disseminating information about its concepts is because the user experience should be the concern of everyone on the development team (and in the studio) and not just the concern of UX professionals who should only be there to provide guidance and tools for everyone else to use. Therefore, a shared UX language used across the studio is paramount.

Usability

11.1 Usability Heuristics in Software and Video Games

11.2 Seven Usability Pillars for Game UX

According to Isbister and Schaffer (2008), making a game (or software) usable means "paying attention to human limits in memory, perception, and attention; it also means anticipating likely errors that can be made and being ready for them, and working with the expectations and abilities of those who will use the software." Usability is about considering the ability of the system image (i.e., what the user perceives and interacts with) to clearly convey information about what the system means and how it can be used. Given that it is humans who are playing games, game developers must take into account human capabilities and limitations to ensure their game is usable. This does not mean dumbing down the game, as we saw earlier when describing the main misconceptions about user experience (Chapter 10). It is about removing the unnecessary and unwanted frustrations that the system image can induce if it does not account for human perception, cognition, and motivation.

Usability is the first step in offering a great user experience because struggling to understand or accomplish simple tasks in a game can create important enough obstacles that may, in extreme cases, lead players to quit playing the game. At best, a game with bad usability will be experienced as sometimes annoying or might prevent players from discovering or enjoying some features. At worst, your otherwise excellent game may become totally unplayable. If your game is innovative enough, it can *maybe* get away with significant usability issues if players are willing to put in some extra effort to overcome frustrations because it is making a buzz or because all their friends are playing it. Maybe. But that's quite rare; so I wouldn't count on it if I were you. For example, *Minecraft* might have been able to get away with some usability issues because it offered a unique and deep creative experience such as no other game was providing when it was released. However, it is likely that the *Minecraft* successors, which are inherently less groundbreaking, won't have that luxury. In the case of free-to-play games, usability is even more critical because issues could impact initial engagement or retention because players' commitment to play is low when they do not have to invest any money up front. Even small frustrations could prevent them from going further than the first few minutes of your game experience. This could also impact your revenues dramatically if players don't understand why or how to buy an item in the store, for example. As a reminder, I'm talking here about the frustrations that are *not* by design, such as not understanding what an icon in the heads-up display (HUD) means, struggling to equip a weapon, or dying without understanding why. I am, of course, not talking about the challenges provided by gameplay and those that are by design.

11.1 Usability Heuristics in Software and Video Games

UX practitioners often say that a usable interface is one that feels "transparent" to the user. However, this concept can be misunderstood, especially when considering a video game HUD. Game developers sometimes believe that removing the HUD entirely would offer a greater immersion to players, but it could end up being counterproductive because the whole point of having a "heads-up display" is to prevent users from remembering important information or having to search for it. Although you certainly need to avoid a clunky and overwhelming HUD (by making it context-sensitive, for example), removing it entirely might result in creating more friction, more cognitive load, and less immersion for players because they need to open menus to get information they need, which pulls them out of the game world. Of course, if you can give useful information directly within the game world instead of via an HUD, and if that is comfortable for players, all the better! This technique is called "diegetic" interface, and it can turn out to be more immersive and elegant. But keep in mind that it is much harder to get right. How to make a diegetic user interface (UI) consistent with the game world as well as clear and easy to perceive is not obvious. One oft-cited example of an efficient and elegant diegetic UI is the health system in *Dead Space* (Visceral Games). Contrary to most third-person action games, the health bar in *Dead Space* is not displayed in a corner of the HUD or under the hero character. Instead, it is integrated on the character model itself (see Figure 11.1). The game world is pretty dark overall, but the health gauge contrasts because of its brightness. Therefore, it is easy to perceive, and because most action-game players keep their eyes on the center of the screen where the aiming reticle is, giving a quick glance to the health gauge is facilitated by being closer to the reticle than if it were

Figure 11.1

Dead Space (Visceral Games). © 2008 Electronic Arts. (Courtesy of Electronic Arts.)

on the HUD (peripheral vision). Another example of frequently used diegetic interface is the ammunition count displayed on the weapon model. Many first-person shooter games do this, but this generally does not replace the ammunition count on the HUD, which is still needed because it does not move (contrary to the weapon model) and provides additional information needed by players (number of clips, for example).

So, making the UI transparent does not mean removing the HUD. It means giving the useful information at the right time without overwhelming players or confusing them—across the menus, HUD, game world, and pretty much everything in the game. Imagine that you are renting a car model with which you are unfamiliar. The experience you want is driving, so you need the dashboard to be easy to read and the controls (e.g., starting the engine, turning the windshield wipers on, etc.) to be easy to grasp. The car interface feels transparent when you don't struggle to find and read the information you need (speedometer, fuel gauge, etc.) or to control the vehicle. But the interface is still there, supporting you; it just isn't getting in your way. This is what *transparent* means; you do not even think about the interface, which enables you to accomplish your goals. It is when the interface is difficult to use that you realize it is in your way, creating frustration. This is similar to what game usability is about—making sure nothing gets in the way of the experience you want players to feel and removing unnecessary frictions (i.e., points of confusion). Of course, not all usability issues will be detected as such by users; players sometimes simply feel frustrated when interacting with a system without necessarily knowing why, or they might misattribute the cause of their frustration. Players are not designers; they won't necessarily identify the origin of the usability issues they encounter—for example, when they complain in forums. One more accurate way to detect the cause of frictions is to observe and analyze the behavior of players manipulating the game during UX tests such as playtests, where players play the game without guidance as if they were at home. UX tests, usability evaluation conducted by HCI experts, and user research overall will always be critical to improving the user experience of your game (see Chapter 13) because, ultimately, the user experience is relative to the end user. So, you need to verify what *they* experience and analyze what is the possible cause of their frustrations. Iteration is key in the development cycle, so the design-implement-test loop will always be needed. However, designing the interface and interactions with usability guidelines already in mind can help you create a good starting point.

Ensuring good usability is central to the human–computer interaction field. Guidelines were established in the 1990s to evaluate what is important for the ease of use of Web or software interface. These guidelines are called heuristics, or rules of thumb, and they help assess the usability of a product or software. These guidelines will help you save precious time, avoid common pitfalls, anticipate issues, and fix them more efficiently because they can assist you in identifying what is causing friction or in better understanding what user researchers are reporting about the game. Although usability heuristics are different from design standards because their goal is to guide expert usability evaluations, it is useful to keep these rules of thumb in mind. They help you to understand what usability issues are commonly experienced when designing a game.

The heuristics for software and Web design that are most often referenced were put together by HCI expert and usability consultant Jakob Nielsen (1994). Nielsen originally derived a set of ten heuristics, or general principles, for interaction design in collaboration with Rolf Molich in 1990 (Nielsen and Molich 1990). They can be consulted on the Nielsen Norman Group website (https://www.nngroup.com/). The ten usability heuristics are described as follows.

1. **Visibility of system status:** The system should convey information to users regarding what actions can be done (i.e., signifiers). Once users have interacted with the system, they also should get fast and appropriate feedback acknowledging users' intent (when no mistakes occur). For example, when you are in an elevator, the buttons with floor labels indicate where you need to press to get to the desired floor. Once a button is pressed, a good usability practice would be to provide immediate feedback to the user; the button pressed can light up, for example. An absence of feedback can lead to confusion or frustration. In our example, if the light does not work, you might end up mashing the button. Similarly, if you click on the "play" button, you expect a feedback informing you that the game is loading.

2. **Match between the system and the real world:** The system should communicate using familiar language and concepts for the target audience. The system should also use metaphors or analogies to the real world. For example, organizing files in "folders," a real-world concept,

in computer interfaces helps users understand how the system works. For example, in a game, a backpack is a familiar metaphor for player inventory.

3. **User control and freedom:** Users can make mistakes or change their mind—for example, when buying online. Allowing them to undo or change the quantity of an item in the shopping cart or allowing them to delete an item easily are examples enabling user control and freedom. Similarly, let players change their mind and undo when applicable.

4. **Consistency and standards:** It's important to follow platform conventions because familiar words, icons, or actions will help users understand how the system works. For example, the search functionality is traditionally represented by a magnifying glass icon, which constitutes a convention and is likely already understood by users. In games, the O (circle) button on Play Station 4 (PS4) generally is used in Western countries to cancel or go back when navigating menus, for example.

5. **Error prevention:** The system should be designed in a way to prevent user errors from occurring. For example, before allowing the user to complete a potentially harmful action, such as closing a file without saving any changes, the system should ask for confirmation. If players are about to salvage a precious item (maybe to get some crafting ingredients out of it), ask for confirmation in case it was an error.

6. **Recognition rather than recall:** To minimize a user's memory load, it's important to make objects, actions, and options visible. Avoid forcing the user to remember information from one part of the dialogue to the other. For example, when navigating in menus, users should always be able to keep track of their location within the website or the application (which is called a "breadcrumb trail"). Similarly, showing an image of the whole controller and highlighting the button players need to press in a certain context doesn't require a player to recall which button is where, as opposed to when only the button label (symbol) is displayed.

7. **Flexibility and efficiency of use:** Offer users the possibility of tailoring their experience by allowing them to add or remove options and to customize their interface. For example, search engines propose options for expert users to add filters to their search. In games, for example, allowing for a remapping of controls is a good usability and accessibility practice.

8. **Aesthetic and minimalist design:** Remove all irrelevant and distracting information. Every extra unit of information acts like noise that will need to be filtered out by users so they can identify relevant information and focus on it. The Google search engine default page is a great example of minimalist design. The same goes with games; try to remove all unnecessary information on the HUD and in menus, especially on the home screen.

9. **Help users recognize, diagnose, and recover from errors:** Error messages should use plain language to precisely explain the problem and suggest a solution. For example, instead of telling users that the Web page

they are looking for generates a "404 error," the system could instead say something intelligible to anyone, such as "Sorry, the page you are looking for cannot be found" and then tell users what they can do from there. Similarly, do not just play an annoying sound when players try to shoot while out of ammunition. In addition to the sound effect, for example, you can display a text saying, "Out of ammo!"

10. **Help and documentation:** Even though a system should be usable without documentation, it is important to offer users efficient and intelligible help when they need it. Contextual help, frequently symbolized by a question mark in a circle, is an example of additional information provided where it could be needed. Games should not require manuals to play; however, it is a good practice to collect all the tool tips seen in the game so far in a dedicated space that players can consult if they have forgotten about something.

The idea of using heuristics to evaluate games was introduced as early as 1980 (Malone 1980), but it was only in the 2000s that specific video game heuristics truly flourished (e.g., Federoff 2002; Desurvire *et al.* 2004; Schaffer 2007; Laitinen 2008). Here are some examples of game heuristics:

- Controls should be customizable and default to industry standard settings (Federoff 2002).
- Feedback should be given immediately to display user control (Federoff 2002).
- Pace the game to apply pressure on, but not to frustrate, the player (Federoff 2002).
- Provide clear goals; present overarching goal early as well as short-term goals throughout play (Desurvire *et al.* 2004).
- The game should give rewards that immerse the player more deeply in the game by increasing their capabilities (power-up) and expanding their ability to customize (Desurvire *et al.* 2004).
- Players discover the story as part of game play (Desurvire *et al.* 2004).
- Avoid large blocks of text (Schaffer 2007).
- Players should feel in control; they need the time and information to respond to threats and opportunities (Schaffer 2007).
- Don't make it easy for players to get stuck or lost (Schaffer 2007).
- The user interface should be consistent both within the game and between the games (Laitinen 2008).
- The terminology and language used in the game should be easy to understand (Laitinen 2008).
- The user interface should be designed so that it prevents the player from making mistakes that are not part of the gameplay (Laitinen 2008).

If you are a UX practitioner, I certainly encourage you to learn more about game heuristics if you are not already familiar with them. However, these heuristics are not meant to establish a shared language with the development team or to provide easy-to-remember guidelines. They are more specifically meant for user researchers to help them evaluate the game usability. What I'm proposing in the following section is a smaller set of game usability pillars, mixing some heuristics and design guidelines, and using a vocabulary that should be more familiar to game developers.

11.2 Seven Usability Pillars for Game UX

In this section, I will describe a mix of usability heuristics and design principles constituting, in my experience, the main pillars that can help you ensure good usability for your game. They are heavily influenced by the usability training session put together by Ubisoft developers, which described some usability components that inspired my own thinking process. Although these pillars are certainly not exhaustive, I believe they offer a good enough overview of what to keep in mind. Note that some components traditionally associated with usability, such as emotions elicited via interaction with the system, will be instead considered in the "engage-ability" section of this book (Chapter 12). Again, this list of pillars is mostly meant to facilitate a common language and framework within the game studio, so that every developer can be empowered to participate in improving the game UX, should they be interested in doing so.

11.2.1 Signs and Feedback

This pillar is similar to the "visibility of system status" heuristic from Jakob Nielsen (1994). However, none of the game developers I've worked with use this vocabulary. What they often use instead are the terms "cues," "signs," and "feedback." The signs in a video game refer to all the visual, audio, and haptic cues that inform players about what is going on in the game (i.e., informative signs) or that encourage players to execute a specific action (i.e., inviting signs). Signs have specific meanings, and they communicate specific information to players who decode them. In semiotics, a sign has a specific form (i.e., signifier) and a meaning (i.e., the signified), but in game development, we mostly talk about signs (or cues) having a specific *form* to inform about a *function* (see the "form follows function pillar" that follows). Feedback is a specific type of sign providing a perceptible reaction of the system to the player's action.

- **Informative signs**
  Informative signs inform the player of a system state, such as the avatar's level of health as represented by a green bar or red hearts on the HUD (or sometimes directly on the character model in the case of diegetic signs). The HUD is comprised of a multitude of such informative signs telling players about, for example, their stamina level, their ammunition level, their weapon currently equipped, the current score, where they are on the map, what abilities they can use, if some abilities are in cool down, and so on. Informative signs must be easily perceptible, but they

should not be intrusive or distract players' attention for the main action happening in the game. This is why informative signs are mostly on the HUD, in players' peripheral vision. Front-end menus also are comprised of numerous informative signs, mostly in the form of text describing characters, equipment, skills, and so on, which help players understand the game subtleties and make decisions (e.g., which should I buy next, skill A or B?).

- **Inviting signs**
  Inviting signs aim to persuade players to accomplish certain actions. For example, a yellow exclamation mark above a non-player charac-ter (also known as an NPC) may encourage the player to interact with the NPC. Inviting signs in video games are designed to shape players' behaviors and to guide them. In most cases, inviting signs should draw players' attention and therefore should be salient to contrast with the game world. An exception would be when inviting signs are purposely subtle, such as in *A Link to the Past* (Nintendo), where a subtle crack in a wall indicates that the wall can be destroyed. Some informative signs can turn into inviting signs when the state they express requires imme-diate attention. For example, when a player's health is low, the health bar could turn red and flash—therefore inviting the player to regenerate their health (e.g., by taking a health potion or by moving away from com-bat if health replenishes with time).

- **Feedback**
  The feedback is a specific sign informing a player about the reaction of the system to the player's action. The animation of the avatar when the player uses the controller to move the avatar forward is an example of a feedback. Another feedback would be the ammunition number on the HUD, or on the weapon model, which is depleting as the player shoots. All player actions should have immediate and appropriate feedback informing them of the outcome of said actions. For example, in a fight-ing game such as the *Tekken* series (Bandai Namco), when the player hits an enemy, one feedback is a visual effect at the collision. This feedback informs players of the effectiveness of their blow: It's an exciting orange visual effect if the blow hurt the enemy (see Figure 11.2) or a white halo if the blow was parried. It is also important to give players feedback when they attempt to accomplish an invalid action. For example, if they press a button that doesn't do anything, it's a good practice to give a subtle feedback, such as a short sound effect, informing them that the action is invalid so they don't insist on trying to use this button. Another example would be when players try to use an ability that is currently in cool down. In that case, the feedback should be more salient, and it should tell play-ers why they cannot execute this action at that time (e.g., flashing the ability on cool down on the HUD and/or adding a pop-up text under the aiming reticle saying something like "Ability not ready!").

Figure 11.2

TEKKEN™ 7 & ©2017 BANDAI NAMCO Entertainment Inc. (Courtesy of BANDAI NAMCO Entertainment, Inc., Tokyo, Japan.)

All features and possible interactions in a game should have signs and feedback associated with them. It is therefore critical to think about them as soon as the features, mechanics, weapon behaviors (including signs and feedback on the reticle), character behaviors, and so on, are established. By listing all the possible signs and feedback associated with an element early on will help UI designers, artists, and sound designers to start preparing the appropriate assets. It will also help user researchers later on in verifying if all the signs are decoded (understood) appropriately by players. When a game has good signs and feedback, it greatly helps players understand about the game rules through their own perception and interaction within the game world and UI. It can even allow for less tutorial text; if an inviting sign does its job properly (e.g., persuading players to interact with an object), you do not need to add text telling players what to do next. In contrast, when signs and feedback are missing or are not clear enough (see the next pillar, clarity), this can create confusion and frustration. "Signs and feedback" are a central pillar for good game usability.

11.2.2 Clarity

Clarity pertains to the player's ability to understand all the signs and feedback in a game in terms of their perceptibility (e.g., contrast, font used, information hierarchy). If a sign inviting players to interact with an element in the game does not contrast enough with the background, the players will likely not see it. Therefore, good perceptibility is critical to signs and feedback clarity. For example, the fonts you are using should be comfortable to read. It's better to go for a "boring" classic font that is easy to read rather than a creative artsy font that is difficult to read. Of course, if you are able to create an artistic and unique font for the game that turns up being easy to read, go for it! But it's not necessarily easy to verify if it is indeed the case because the font may impact only a subset of your audience that you might fail to consider (e.g., dyslexic players), or the impact may be too subtle to measure (e.g., the font is still legible but takes more time to read as compared to a usable font). Font guidelines exist and are easy to find. For example, it's recommended to use *sans serif* fonts, to keep the number of fonts and different colors for fonts to a minimum (no more than three), to avoid long text using only uppercase letters (all caps text is more suitable for short headings), to ensure good contrast between the text and the background (place the text over a contrasted overlay not directly over the game world), to ensure proper text size, and so on. Text readability is particularly important for interfaces where players need to make important decisions, such as which character class, ability, skill, equipment, and so forth, to choose. Designers can sometimes have a tendency to write too much text to describe an item. Although a good narrative can add some emotions to the experience (see Chapter 12), it is more important to help players in their decisions, especially when the decisions are strategic (as opposed to simply cosmetic). Use bullet points to describe the main particularities and advantages of a class, weapon, or ability. Avoid long sentences that most of your audience won't read anyway. Organize information in such a way that it's easy to compare two items (or more) with each other (see Blizzard's *Diablo III* example in Figure 11.3). Use infographics to make information easier to grasp in one glance. For example, use bars to clearly show what a weapon is good and not so good at doing. In the *Far Cry 4* example shown in Figure 11.4, you can easily grasp that the weapon in focus can cause great damage and has good mobility but that it does not have good accuracy, range, and firing rates.

The Gestalt principles of perception, which we described in Chapter 3, also provide useful guidelines to improve the clarity of the game interface. If you

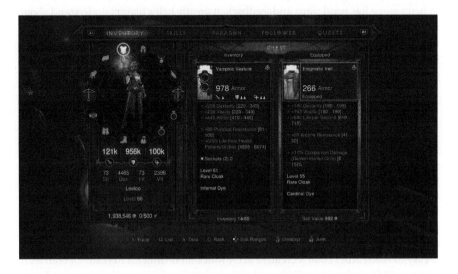

Figure 11.3

Diablo III (Blizzard). Diablo® III. (Courtesy of Blizzard Entertainment, Inc.)

11. Usability

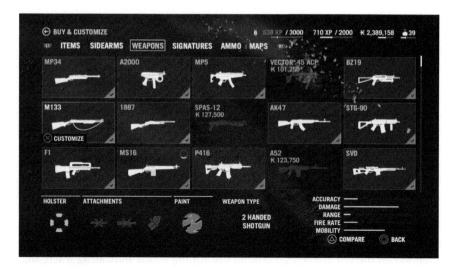

Figure 11.4

Far Cry 4 (Ubisoft). (Courtesy of Ubisoft Entertainment, © 2014. All Rights Reserved.)

remember, these principles have been used to account for how the human mind perceives and organizes the environment. For example, according to the Gestalt law of proximity, elements that are close to one another will be interpreted as belonging to the same group. Applying Gestalt principles can help the designers organize the game interface in a way that will be correctly understood by players. In Chapter 3, we saw, for example, how reorganizing the space between skill icons in the *Far Cry 4* front-end menu could help players correctly perceive and decode information. Make sure that all the iconography you are using in the game is not confusing or ambiguous (i.e., avoid multistability)—unless, of course, perception ambiguity is part of the challenge of the game.

One last core concept to consider regarding sign clarity is signal detection theory, a classic of human factors. The premise of signal detection theory is that all reasoning and decision-making takes place in the presence of some level of uncertainty. It's about detecting the relevant information among the noise, such as finding your keys on a messy table or spotting Wally in Martin Handford's *Where's Wally* game (or *Where's Waldo* if you live in the United States). Let's take the example of enemy detection in a shooter game. If the enemy character design does not contrast well enough with the game world, then it will be harder for players to detect this type of enemy (which you can, of course, plan to do on purpose). You can play with players' perception and thus change the level of uncertainty if it makes sense for the gameplay (see McLaughlin 2016). For example, you can add elements in the game environment that look like enemies (e.g., have the same color or overall shape) to increase "false alarms" and to make a player mistakenly shoot at an inoffensive object. However, when you need players to pay attention to a particular sign in your game, you have to make sure it can be easily detected against the rest of the game environment so they don't miss it. One example is what I call the "red overload." Red is the color of blood and a traditional color convention to signal a warning or a danger; it is often used in games to represent damage taken or a threat. It is also a color that can easily stand out against the rest of the environment if there is enough contrast. However, if too many elements in the game are already red, yet another red sign will not be particularly easy to detect because it will not be salient; it will not stand out from the rest (i.e., the red irrelevant "noise" will be too important for players to rapidly detect a relevant red signal). In the first-person shooter *Unreal Tournament 3* (Epic Games), most of the HUD is red when you are on the Red Team—the score, your health level, your ammunition count, and so on. When you are taking damage, the periphery of the screen turns red as well. All this red "noise" could make it more difficult for players to detect or focus their attention on the red arrow sign around the aiming reticle indicating where the attack is coming from, which is the most relevant information to pay attention to if players want a chance to react fast enough to kill their enemy before the enemy kills them (see Figure 11.5). My claim is quite difficult to verify in a user research lab setup. However, I suspect that the red overload phenomenon could have some distractive effects, especially for novice players. I also suspect that it might take some milliseconds longer for players on the Red Team to detect a Blue enemy, especially if they were on the Blue Team the match before and therefore trained themselves to shoot anything Red moving around. This may have an impact on highly competitive players for whom a few milliseconds more or less in their reaction time and their enemies' could make a difference in the game

Figure 11.5

Unreal Tournament 3 © 2007, Epic Games, Inc. (Courtesy of Epic Games, Inc., Cary, NC.)

outcome. It's somewhat similar to the Stroop effect we talked about in Chapter 5 (i.e., naming the ink color of color words takes additional time when there is a mismatch between the ink color and the color word). You first have to inhibit your trained reflex to shoot at Red elements when you now have to consider Red characters as friendly. This is the reason why I often recommend saving the color red for critical signs only (i.e., to signal an immediate threat, to inform players that they are getting hurt, or that they have low health). Orange is another color that can be used for enemies (i.e., enemy outline or health bar).

Remember that perception is subjective (see Chapter 3). This is why you need to ensure that all the signs and feedback in the game provide good clarity for the gameplay you intend. Remember as well that our attentional resources are very limited (see Chapter 5), so you need to help players focus on the relevant information when this is your intent. You also need to prioritize all information conveyed to avoid overwhelming a player's working memory (see Chapter 4). For example, displaying all the signs and feedback for every element during combat from every character in a multiplayer game can quickly become incomprehensible. You will thus need to define which sound and visual effects should take priority (i.e., usually the ones informing players that they are getting hurt) and which ones should be disregarded when too many things are happening at the same time. Similarly, you need to define which animations, sounds, or dialogs can be cut (e.g., a reload animation is cut if the player starts moving, or a secondary dialog is cut when a grenade surprisingly explodes close to the player) and which cannot. In real life, sound segregation (identifying which sound belongs to which object) is often much harder than visual segmentation (McDermott 2009), so auditory segmentation might be even harder in video games when the sound is coming from a stereo. Although, you might have less trouble if you have a Dolby® Surround 7.1 sound system because, of course, everything sounds better in "Dubly." (I apologize to the readers who haven't seen the movie *This is Spinal Tap* and therefore do not get this joke.) Therefore, sound effect prioritization will be critical to help players make sense of what is happening in the game—so be nice to your sound designers and make sure to keep them informed of your design intentions. (I emphasize this point because I often see sound designers being kept out of the loop and having to catch up later in the process.) In the following section, audio director Tom Bible gives some sound design examples for an enhanced user experience.

Tom Bible, Freelance Audio Director, Sound Designer, and Composer

Sound Design and User Experience

George Lucas once said that, "Audio is 50% of the experience." Audio can have a powerful effect on user experience because it makes up one entire sensory input type. Due to fact that the brain processes audio much faster than other senses, we have a shortcut to subconscious user responses.

Music is known to have a powerful emotional effect on players, and sound design is no less important.

Sound design can contribute to a positive user experience in a number of ways. First, it needs to provide clear user feedback for player actions. It's really important that actions are communicated well through sound so the player instinctively knows whether or not their input led to a successful (or unsuccessful) action. A simple example might be picking up an object in virtual reality (VR). In *Robo Recall* (Epic Games), a sound is played and a white ring expands when the player is able to pick up an object. It's a core action to the experience and often happens out of the player's view. We use an immediate tick sound, followed by a sound to match the animation of the white ring expanding. The player then learns to associate this visually synchronized sound with the sense that an object is ready to be grasped. The simple auditory feedback becomes subconscious after a few minutes of repetition, and the action no longer requires the visual feedback every time.

Second, we need to match a player's expectations of sounds. For example, in VR, we are trying to provide an immersive experience where the player feels like they are in another space. In order to do that, we need to simulate the way sounds work in the real world in order for the audio to "feel" right. Not doing this well can lead to an uncanny valley effect where the player is aware that something isn't right but isn't sure what it is; but simulating acoustic physics can allow the player to enter into an experience with much less cognitive dissonance. We also need to create sounds that follow expectations, depending on players' prior experience. People who have played a lot of video games expect certain sounds to communicate in certain ways. For example, when creating vocalizations for robots that don't speak, we follow human-like speech patterns to try to communicate the character's emotional state or intention. The sounds for R2-D2 do this particularly well, communicating on an emotional level what the character is saying. It's important to note that there are cultural influences; speech patterns from, say, the United States vary a lot from speech patterns from China or Japan. Additionally, we have influences from other media—such as movies—that dictate expectations on how some things should sound, even though those things may not sound like that in real life. Guns are a good example; in films and games, the recordings of real guns have been heavily modified to feel powerful and satisfying—when in real life, they are essentially a "pop" sound.

Possibly the most important element of the user experience for the audio, and the least appreciated, is the mix. Without a good mix, clearly communicated sound design can get completely lost. To create a clear mix is particularly challenging in VR, where we also need the experience to feel natural and follow acoustic physics rules. It's a fine balance to ensure that the different elements of the mix are effectively prioritized (turned up or down) to highlight the most important sounds at any one moment without drawing attention to the fact that the mix is constantly changing. The mix of *Robo Recall* is a good example of this: When sounds in one category play, other sounds are "ducked," or turned down. In order to bring order to the chaos, sounds are put into importance categories, from very low importance up to very high. For example, some sounds that play in the "high importance" category would turn down sounds in the "medium importance" category a little and the sounds in the "low importance" category a lot, but sounds in the "very high importance" category would be unaffected.

Putting this together effectively requires a lot of trial and error, with feedback from players and other audio professionals. Communication can be very subjective, so getting feedback from playtesting on whether players understand what the sounds are communicating is a key piece of the puzzle. This process of iteration is particularly important for interactive audio because players will respond to the audio design as they interpret it and not necessarily as it was intended.

11.2.3 Form Follows Function

Initially associated with modernist architecture, this principle as applied to game design refers to how the form of any given character, icon, or symbol used in the game (form) conveys its meaning (function). In industrial design, the similar concept of "affordance" is used whereby an affordance is seen as "a relationship between the properties of an object and the capabilities of the agent that determine just how the object could possibly be used" (Norman 2013), as we saw in Chapter 3. For example, an object with a handle (i.e., a coffee mug) allows it to be grabbed with one hand and lifted; the handle affords grabbing. Similarly, the visual expression of a game element should intuitively inform the player how to interact with it. For example, an item symbolized by a box with a green cross (form) may inform players that picking up that item will replenish their health (function). Players also may expect that an enemy character carrying a shield (form) is likely harder to defeat (function) than a similar enemy without a shield. I will describe the different types of affordance in Chapter 13. For artists, it means that their assets are constrained by what players need to understand, and that they need to use *form follows function* as an aesthetic guide. The question that needs to be asked is thus, "What aspects of the design are critical to success?" (see Lidwell *et al.* 2010). Success in that case means that players are able to understand what the different elements represent and how to use them (or how to anticipate their behavior) based on their form. You might have good gameplay reasons to not always follow this pillar. However, the more you can support it, the more players will be able to intuitively progress in your game. As mentioned earlier in the section on signs and feedback, signs that can persuade players without ambiguity to execute certain actions because their function is conveyed via their form will spare you (and your audience) some annoying tutorial text that also often requires localization in several languages. In some cases, form follows function can be critical to the gameplay, such as in a multiplayer game where it's important for players to quickly and adequately identify teammates' and enemies' roles based on their form. For example, *Team Fortress 2* (Valve) characters are known to be easily distinguishable through only their silhouette, making it easier for players to coordinate their actions because they know what role (function) the characters nearby have (see Figure 11.6).

To enable form follows function, you need two conditions: The form of the element itself needs to be clearly identified without ambiguity (see the aforementioned section on clarity), and it should accurately convey its function. If an icon that is supposed to represent a radar cone is perceived as representing a pizza slice, it means that the icon needs a little tweaking. However, if a form is correctly perceived but players misinterpret the function it conveys, this means that the metaphor or analogy you are using is not working. For example, imagine that you design an icon representing a magnifying glass (form) to express the ability to zoom in (function). Players may correctly perceive the icon form (i.e., they recognize it looks like a magnifying glass), but it is possible that they might wrongly believe it represents the ability to search something. You can easily test the form and function for your most important icons (or characters, items, etc.) by creating a survey with one icon on each page (displayed in a randomized order) and by asking a representative sample of your audience to first describe what they believe the icon looks like (i.e., to describe its form) and then what functionality they believe the icon conveys (i.e., to describe its function). It will help you assess if some parts of the visual design (or its totality) are not perceived correctly or,

Figure 11.6

Character silhouettes in *Team Fortress 2* © 2007–2017 Valve Corporation. (Courtesy of Valve Corporation, Bellevue, WA.)

11. Usability

when the icon is perceived appropriately, if it conveys the function inaccurately. Admittedly, some functions are very difficult to express via a tiny icon, especially role-playing-game abilities that can be quite specific or complex. It is not the end of the world if players need to learn what some specific icons mean, as long as these icons are not misleading. For example, if an icon is interpreted by most of your audience as expressing a functionality that is far from what it is actually supposed to represent, you should scrap that icon and try a completely different metaphor. It is far more frustrating for players to wrongly believe they understand something only to discover at their expense that what they expected is false than to be confused by the meaning of an icon up-front. When a functionality is not obvious from the form of an element, it places players in a mindset such that they expect having to experiment with this element to understand and learn what it does, which is better than being deceived.

The form follows function pillar is, of course, not only important for your iconography but also for your character, item, and environment designs. All in all, try to convey functionality through form as much as possible because all that is intuitive does not need to be learned, which is good for minimizing cognitive load (see the minimum workload section that follows). When it is not possible to do this, at least make sure you don't deceive players' expectations. Unless, as always, deceiving players is precisely your intent. False affordances, when an element mistakenly affords to something false, can be very frustrating. For example, if an area in the game world looks as if it can be explored (i.e., if it affords exploration), it may be annoying for players to realize that an invisible wall is actually preventing the avatar from going any further. Another example would be an element in the game world that affords climbing (e.g., a ladder on a wall) that is actually not an element players can interact with. Remember that perception is subjective; what you perceive about a design is not necessarily what your audience will perceive, so you will need to test the most important visual designs, as well as the most important audio designs, to verify that they are perceived as intended and that they accurately convey what they are supposed to convey. Remember also that you are under the curse of knowledge; what you find obvious in the game because you know it from the inside out won't necessarily be obvious for new players.

11.2.4 Consistency

The signs, feedback, controls, interface, menu navigation, world rules, and overall conventions in a video game must be consistent. For example, if it is possible to open doors in the game, every door should be able to be opened or, if only some types of doors can be opened, they should have a different visual treatment to avoid confusing players about how the system works. If two elements have a similar form, players will expect them to have the same functionality or to behave comparably. By contrast, if two elements have different forms, players will expect them to have different functionality or to behave differently. Once a certain rule is learned, players will likely be able to apply the same rule to similar items if the system is consistent. For example, once players have learned that their pistol has a limited amount of ammunition and needs to be refilled, they will expect a newly acquired weapon with ammunition, such as a bow with arrows, to behave the same way. They might, however, expect to be able to get the arrow back once an enemy is killed, unless the arrow looks broken or disappears. Now, if you want to introduce a new type of range weapon that has infinite ammunition, you might want to use a completely different type of weapon—one that does not use ammunition, such as a boomerang. Different functionalities should be conveyed via different forms, otherwise players can confuse one sign for another and, therefore, one function for another and make mistakes as a result. For example, if your game has a day/night cycle and uses digits to convey what time it is in the game world, and it also has a countdown that looks very similar to the clock digits but indicates how much time is left to accomplish a mission, it can lead to confusion. Similar functions should have consistently similar forms, but different functions should have dissimilar forms to avoid confusion.

Consistency in controls is also very important, especially because learning the movements your hand or finger needs to do in order to control the game heavily relies on implicit memory (which is sometimes called "muscle memory" because it is tied to action). Sure, in the beginning, players might learn factual information about the controller mapping (such as "Press X to jump" on a PS4 controller), but as they progress in the game and repeatedly execute the same actions, their thumb will automatically make the correct movement to hit the right button without their having to consciously think about how the whole procedure is factually executed. As we saw in Chapter 4, procedural information can become automatic with some practice and therefore is more difficult to forget (just like it can take a very long time to forget how to ride a bicycle once the associated procedure is mastered). This means that you should avoid changing the controller mapping across different yet similar situations in terms of functionality. For example, it's better to use the same button that makes the avatar sprint to also make a horse gallop when the avatar rides one. Similarly, navigating the interface should behave the same way across the game—for example, in the front-end menu as well as when navigating within the avatar's inventory. Consistency can be violated in the game if there is a precise design intention to do so. For example, in *Uncharted 3* (Naughty Dog), when the player is in a sinking ship that is tilting over, the controls are also tilted. For example, you might need to move the thumbstick to the left to go in what seems to be a straight direction according to the camera. Breaking consistency with the camera and controls in this sequence is done on purpose to add an additional (and surprising) challenge.

Consistency among games is also important because it facilitates the onboarding for players who are familiar with certain game conventions. For example, many action games use the same set of buttons to aim, shoot, sprint, jump, crouch, and reload. If your game does not respect the same default controller mapping, it might be more difficult for players to learn or get used to it, which might in turn create unnecessary frustration that could result in some players quitting your game if it requires too much effort to control. Again, if you have a very good design reason to change a convention, go for it; but expect players to need time to get used to it. The game *Skate* (Electronic Arts) is an example of where the controller mapping did not follow the conventions used by previously launched skateboarding games. Instead of requesting that players use face buttons to execute tricks, this game introduced the "Flickit" controls, using only the thumbsticks. This change in convention was likely motivated by a core game pillar, which I imagine was to offer players who were also skateboarders in real life a muscle sensation with their thumbs somewhat similar to what they may experience with their legs on a real board. (Not being a skateboarder myself makes it hard for me to express this.)

If you've been living in the United States all your life and you visit the UK for a few days, it may take you some time and effort to get used to driving on the left side of the road or to remembering to first look right before crossing the road as a pedestrian. Habits die hard, as the story goes, so you should have some precise intent in mind when changing a game convention that might be very familiar to your audience. Otherwise, I would recommend avoiding trying to reinvent the wheel.

11.2.5 Minimum Workload

The player's cognitive load (i.e., attention and memory) and physical load (e.g., number of button-clicks needed to execute an action) must be taken into account and minimized when, as per usual, they are not part of the challenge of the game itself.

- **Minimizing physical load**

  Some games are all about making you sweat (e.g., Ubisoft's *Just Dance*) or rapidly and rhythmically hitting the right buttons (e.g., *Guitar Hero* by Harmonix). However, in other games, the core challenge is not intended to be physical. In that case, reducing the physical load is a good practice for reducing muscle pain or physical fatigue. For example, a game that allows the player to simply hold down a button to sprint (or make a horse gallop), as opposed to repeatedly pressing that button, reduces the physical activity in which they must engage. If your game is fast-paced, you need to make sure that executing frequent actions does not take too many button-clicks (e.g., tossing a grenade, swapping weapons, equipping a new weapon, etc.).

  You can also use Fitts's law to anticipate how much time—and, therefore, physical effort—it will take to go from one interactive area to another. This is a model of human movement that predicts the time it will take to target an area based on its distance from the starting point and the size of the target. If, for example, when navigating menus to equip items in a PC game, you need to first click on a button on the top left of the screen to select an item and you then need to click on a button on the bottom right to confirm your choice, it will require more time and effort (i.e., a wider gesture) to go from the first target to the other. You, therefore, need to pay attention to all the gestures players need to accomplish to execute common actions in the game to reduce physical load.

On a console, it's usually less of a problem (at least in front-end menus) because players have to press different buttons instead of targeting an area with a cursor. One exception would be when the menu navigation is using a virtual cursor, whereby players use the thumbsticks to move a cursor to target certain areas (e.g., Bungie's *Destiny* or *No Man's Sky* by Hello Games). In the case of virtual cursors, it is important to mind the physical load and to use Fitts's law because the movement speed of the cursor is not exactly an analog to players' movement amplitude. Therefore, it can quickly become tiring to drag a painfully slow virtual cursor across the screen if the interactive areas are not thought through in terms of their location. Usually, the virtual cursor speeds up when players push the stick completely toward a direction, and the interactive areas are "sticky" to help players target them (the same principle as the one used in "aim assist").

On a mobile device, physical load is very important to take into account. How your game requires players to hold their phone or tablet (i.e., portrait or landscape orientation) as well as what gestures they need to execute with their thumbs and fingers have to be accounted for. If players are holding a smartphone in a straight position and can play with one thumb, all the interactive areas opposite from the thumb (i.e., buttons located at the top left of the screen, if the player is right-handed) will require more effort and time to reach. You should, therefore, place in these areas (i.e., top of the screen) the buttons players don't need to touch very often (e.g., the settings button is usually placed at the top right of the screen).

Depending on the platform and the type of game, physical load can be more or less of a concern for your game usability. Overall, try to anticipate and minimize physical load whenever possible.

- **Minimizing cognitive load**
  In Part I, we described how limited our memory and attentional resources are. Therefore, you should minimize cognitive load for all the elements in your game that should not require such load as per your design. For example, in the game series *Assassin's Creed* (Ubisoft), the possible actions and associated controls (what button to press to accomplish what action) are constantly shown in the HUD of the game interface, as we mentioned in Chapter 4 (see Figure 4.7). This display reduces the cognitive load with respect to the player needing to remember which buttons to press to accomplish an action. The game developers made the call that remembering the controller mapping is not what was important for the game experience. It was more important for them that players feel that they are free running and climbing everywhere and being badass. You cannot feel as badass if you constantly need to remember what button you need to press depending on the situation. Game design is all about making choices and trade-offs, so you need to define where

you want players to apply cognitive resources and where you will alleviate the load.

Another example would be to force players to execute mental rotations when consulting the radar or minimap on their HUD. If the minimap is not egocentric (i.e., not orientated depending on where the user is standing), it will require a certain amount of cognitive resources for players to mentally rotate the map. Therefore, it's generally a better practice to offer egocentric minimaps. In the case of maps, it's generally less of a problem because opening the map usually pauses the game, and the map UI takes the entire screen. It is, however, a good practice to let players add waypoints on the map that will appear on a player's radar once the map is closed; this reduces a player's memory load because they don't have to remember their itinerary.

In his book, *Don't Make Me Think*, UX professional Steve Krug (2014) clearly explains that anything increasing our cognitive load is actually distracting us from the task we want to accomplish. In the case of games, the cognitive load needed to process information that is not critical to the challenge players want to overcome will likely distract them from that challenge (and/or be felt as frustrating). Taking cognitive load into account is particularly important during the onboarding phase of the game when players learn the main mechanics and rules given that, according to the cognitive load theory that we described in Chapter 5, learning can be hindered if it requires cognitive resources that exceed the working memory limits (Sweller 1994). However, also remember that the deeper the process, the better the retention. Therefore, you do want players to attribute more working memory resources to the mechanics or features you want them to learn while alleviating cognitive load for irrelevant elements. Lastly, to be engaged in an activity to the point of experiencing flow, players will also need to concentrate on a challenging task without being distracted. So, remember that the minimum workload pillar applies only to all the tasks that are not directly relevant to the core experience in order to allow players to allocate more cognitive resources to the core experience. (See the game flow section in Chapter 12.)

11.2.6 Error Prevention and Error Recovery

Players make mistakes in video games; they die. This is part of many game experiences, and it often wouldn't feel as satisfying to overcome a challenge if it was too easy (see the game flow pillar in Chapter 13). However, that does not mean you cannot be generous with your players and prevent some mistakes from occurring when that agrees with your intentions. You can also help players recover from errors, especially when errors can cause frustration that does not bring much to the game experience. Keep in mind that, because of cognitive dissonance, if players do not absolutely clearly understand what they are doing wrong, they will likely not blame it on themselves. Like the fox in Aesop's fable (see Chapter 6), they will instead probably blame it on your game as a way to handle the discomfort of their failure; they will call the game stupid and move on with their lives (unless they are truly motivated to keep feeling the pain of failure to progress in your game).

- **Error prevention**

  We have numerous cognitive limitations; therefore, we cannot pay attention to all that we are doing all the time, and we cannot remember all information we encounter. As a result, players will likely make mistakes. It is your job as a designer to anticipate all errors users can make so you can design to prevent such errors. To take a simple example, if you have two buttons very close to each other but with opposite functions, such as "confirm" and "cancel," Fitts's law predicts that the likelihood of a player clicking the wrong button is greater than if both buttons are more spaced out from each other. So move away from the players' easy reach those buttons that could lead them to wrongly executing a costly action (such as cancelling the download of their game when it was almost complete). Also, add confirmation messages when the action is particularly dramatic or irreversible. For example, in *World of Warcraft* (Blizzard), it was particularly difficult to accidentally delete a character: You had to type in the word "DELETE" and confirm your intent. Overall, any action that leads to destroying or deleting something should usually require confirmation (or allow for recovery).

  Errors are not only frustrating in menus. Within a game world, you can also think of ways to be generous and prevent errors from occurring. For example, in *Mario Galaxy* (Nintendo), the collision zone of enemies is smaller than their actual three-dimensional model. It allows players to get closer to enemies without being penalized, which is a thoughtful detail given that it is not always easy to estimate how close Mario is from other objects and characters in the game. In games with platforming mechanics, allowing for air control or letting players safely reach a platform even if only one pixel of the character model actually collides with the platform are examples allowing error prevention. In games with crafting mechanics, for example, you can prevent errors from occurring if you help players identify which weapons they have equipped and therefore which ammunition they should craft. By understanding how the brain works (Part I), you can anticipate some errors players will likely commit and decide (or not) to prevent them from happening. Observing players naturally discovering and interacting with your game in playtest sessions will also allow you to identify what the common errors are that players are committing. Remember that you need to account for human capabilities *and* limitations in your design. If players often commit the same mistakes, it is likely because your design favors such errors occurring. Remember that even highly trained pilots can make fatal mistakes when an airplane cockpit is poorly designed. It won't help you to grumble and raise your clenched fist at players behind the one-way mirror. If the playtest participants were chosen to accurately represent your target audience, their errors will likely also be experienced by the audience at large once the game is launched. So, if your goal is to offer a great experience to your audience, you need to empathize with them and find out why your design is encouraging them to make those mistakes.

One last thing—never ever let players quit your game without saving it. These days, most games autosave a player's progression (which is another great example of error prevention), but sometimes a game needs manual saving. If that is the case for your game, do not allow players to unwillingly quit your game without saving their progression, especially because this is no longer standard procedure (unless your system only has one save slot, which players might not want to overwrite if, e.g., they want to retry from their last saved point). The cost for players to catch up to where they were in the game might be too intense and too frustrating. Similarly, if your game has checkpoints, make sure to inform players appropriately of what will happen if they leave the game before reaching the next checkpoint (e.g., tell them how far away they are from their latest checkpoint). Lastly, in multiplayer games, clearly inform players of what will happen if they abandon a match in progress. Many games penalize players who abandon matches, but not all players understand why quitting is not nice for other players and what will be the consequence for them if they do quit. Additionally, on consoles, players may quit the game by turning off the console, which means that they may not see any messages telling them that there are consequences for quitting (e.g., a ban or warning). Consider showing these warnings when players relaunch the game, for example.

- **Error recovery**
  You have probably experienced some relief several times in your life after committing a mistake when the system allowed you to recover from it. "Undo" is such a lovely feature! It's not always easy to offer an "undo" functionality in games, unless it is one of the core mechanics of your game (e.g., Number One's *Braid*). However, allowing players to retry from a checkpoint close to where they committed an error (and died) has a similar effect. You can also think of adding an "undo" button in some particular cases. For example, *League of Legends* (Riot) allows players to undo their last shop purchase or sale. One other example would be to allow players to reset all the points they have spent in a skill tree, so they can recover from a bad decision they later regretted.

11.2.7 Flexibility

The flexibility pillar refers to the customizations and adjustments the player can choose in the game settings. The more customizable the game is—for example, in terms of control mapping, font size, and colors—the more accessible it will be for all players, including for players with disabilities. Remember that perception is subjective; what you find to be the most comfortable in terms of UI (e.g., font size) is not necessarily what some, or maybe most, of your players would prefer (e.g., if they have impaired vision or simply if they need to read the subtitles). Approximately 8% of the male population has some sort of color blindness, so you should account for these people as well.

In terms of controls, some people are right-handed, others are left-handed, and others might have a temporary disability (e.g., wrist sprain) or a permanent disability (e.g., rheumatoid arthritis). The more setting options you can offer, the better the accessibility and overall usability. If you do offer such flexibility, make sure that players are aware that customization is possible in your game because most people don't dig in menus before hitting the "play" button. For example, Naughty Dog's *Uncharted 4* does a great job at presenting accessibility and customization options when players first launch the game. In addition, offering numerous option settings should not prevent you from carefully choosing what the default settings should be. Most people go through the path of least resistance and, therefore, won't change any option settings. Only power users will play around with the settings. So, think about your mainstream audience when choosing the default settings (use industry standards and conventions). It is easy to forget that many people do not experience the world the same way we do. Designing for flexibility and accessibility is not only a generous thing to do for your audience, it is also a good business practice because you will increase the size of your potential audience. Making your game accessible does not necessarily require more time to implement if you think about it up front. UX designer Ian Hamilton explains in the following section why accessibility matters and why it should not be hard to achieve. I also encourage you to consult the website http://gameaccessibilityguidelines.com/, which offers clear guidance for inclusive game design.

Flexibility also means letting players decide the difficulty level they want to play. Some players want to be greatly challenged, while others simply want to casually cruise along. You might also want to consider allowing some players to access parts of your game that are usually only unlocked after some amount of gameplay. This is particularly important for party games that sometimes do not allow players to access any minigame until they go through the "story mode" that unlocks one minigame after the other through an artificial and unnecessary story (the main interest of party games is to play with random friends at random times, just like with a board game). It can be particularly frustrating for someone who just bought your party game to have fun with some friends coming over in the evening. There is no reason why you should prevent players from experiencing all the different aspects of your game, especially when players have to pay up front. If you care about the replay value of your game or its retention, there are other less frustrating mechanisms you can apply (see Chapter 12 about the motivation pillar).

One last phenomenon you should be aware of is the "Pareto principle," otherwise known as the "80/20 rule," which basically states that 20% of the variables in a system are responsible for 80% of the results. For example, 20% of a product's features are responsible for 80% of the product usage. Therefore, most people will only use about 20% of the features in a game. So, keep the default UI simple for most players; only display the widgets they absolutely need to progress in the game (at the moment they need them), and let power users add options and add-ons to their UI (e.g., *World of Warcraft* offers a great example of such flexibility in the UI widgets).

Ian Hamilton, Accessibility Specialist and UX Designer

Accessibility is a hugely important field for our industry for many reasons. One is the size of the market—according to government data, around 18% of the population has some kind of disability. Not everyone encounters barriers in gaming, but there are also conditions that do that aren't covered by that government data, such as color blindness: 8% of males; difficulty reading: 14% of U.S. adults. Developers can't afford to miss out on that business. Another reason why accessibility matters is the human benefit. Games provide access to recreation, to culture, to socializing—things that so many of us take for granted. But if your opportunities to access those things are in some way limited, games can become a powerful contributor to a person's quality of life.

For these and other reasons, it has been a beautiful thing to see the field advancing, and the pace of change ever-quickening. The industry is not yet where it needs to be; but it is on the right path.

This isn't difficult. Consider it from the early stages, identify what barriers to enjoyment or participation there might be in your game that relate to motor, hearing, speech, vision, and cognitive ability. There will always be some barriers that are a necessary part of what makes the game fun; this is fine. Focus on the others, figure out what you can do to avoid or remove the unnecessary barriers.

Most barriers can be addressed either through communicating information in more than one way, such as a symbol as well as a color, or text as well as speech, or by just offering a bit of flexibility, such as difficulty levels or remappable controls. If considered early enough, there's a huge amount that can be done very easily, and the impact is often wide-reaching. Avoid small, fiddly interface elements and you've made the game more enjoyable for people with all kinds of different permanent physical motor and vision impairment—also for people playing on a bumpy bus or in direct sunlight. Provide good subtitles and you've made it playable for someone playing on mute without headphones because the baby is asleep. One-handed controls work for people with one arm, people with a broken arm, people who are holding onto a subway handrail, a bag, or a beer. Using an icon as well as a color on a map is just extra reinforcement for all players.

Accessibility is relevant to all disciplines but, of them all, it is user experience (UX) that has both the greatest responsibility and the greatest power to make a difference. It is the only discipline where standing up for the needs of all of your players is literally written into the job title—the U does not stand for "subsection of users who don't currently have any kind of impairment." And the tools are already there in the UX arsenal: expert review, data analysis, user research. Familiarize yourself with best practices for use in expert reviews. The knowledge is already out there through free resources such as http://gameaccessibilityguidelines.com.

Games are a powerful force for good in our world, and UX is a discipline uniquely placed to both facilitate and communicate that good. We just have to make it happen.

12

Engage-Ability

12.1 Three Engage-Ability   12.3 Emotion
     Pillars for Game UX   12.4 Game Flow
12.2 Motivation

Good video games are typically described as being "fun," so game designers are usually striving to reach that outcome. For game designer and educator Tracy Fullerton, designing a game is about creating an "elusive combination of challenge, competition, and interaction that players just call 'fun'" (Fullerton 2014). Therefore, one of the goals of iterative design is to verify if players are having fun (Salen and Zimmerman 2004). The problem is that what makes a game "fun" can be difficult to assess. As game designer Jesse Schell points out, "Fun is desirable in nearly every game, although sometimes fun defies analysis" (Schell 2008). For example, game designer Raph Koster describes fun as "another word for learning" that makes our brains feel good and evade boredom (Koster 2004), but researcher Roberto Dillon considers that, "Fun is a very personal activity that can be completely different from individual to individual" (Dillon 2010). As game designer Scott Rogers put it, "The problem with fun is, like humor, it is completely subjective" (Rogers 2014).

12.1 Three Engage-Ability Pillars for Game UX

Although there is not yet a widely established theory and predictive measurement for fun, several models and frameworks have been proposed, describing, for example, player enjoyment, presence, immersion, or game flow. These frameworks, originating from either academia or game development practice, are not necessarily easy to unify. One of the models that provided me with good practical help when working with developers is the *game flow* model from Sweetser and Wyeth (2005). They identified that player enjoyment, the most important goal for video games, had similarities with the concept of *flow* (Csikszentmihalyi 1990), which outlines what makes experiences enjoyable and people happy. We already approached this concept in Chapter 6, and I will describe it in greater detail here, in the "Game Flow" pillar section. Briefly, game flow proposes a model of enjoyment in game evaluation, combining user experience heuristics that align with the concept of flow. For game designer Jenova Chen (behind the games *Flow*, *Flower*, and *Journey* developed by Thatgamecompany), a well-designed game is one that transports and keeps players in their own flow zone, whereby challenges are not too easy or too hard (Chen 2007).

Just like my approach with usability, the idea is not to make an exhaustive list of theories and frameworks for fun, enjoyment, and immersion. Instead I propose some broad pillars that helped me speak the same language as the development teams. These pillars, informed by cognitive science, can assist us in comprehending what may be the most important factors for player engagement and retention, while staying true to the game experience developers want to offer.

The usability pillars described earlier provide a framework for removing unnecessary barriers, which could create frustration and disrupt players' suspension of disbelief. Whereas usability pillars focus on the ease of use of a video game, engage-ability pillars focus on the level of engagement and immersion a game provides. It is admittedly easier to measure game usability because we can apply established human factors principles, observe if players make mistakes, and check what they understand about the game and whether they know what they have to do. User experience (UX) practices can thus quite accurately predict what will be the quality of a game in terms of its ease of use. On the other hand, assessing player engagement is more complicated because we cannot easily *objectively* measure how much fun (immersion, or flow) players are experiencing and, more importantly, how this measurement can help predict the level of success of a game. Sure, you can always ask players to tell you how much fun they are having, but self-assessment is highly biased, and fun scales so far are not a particularly good predictive tool for the later success and enjoyment of a game. Although I will talk about user research methodologies later, in Chapter 14, it's always important to keep in mind how to measure success. One of the most-used key performance indicators for the success of a game, and especially for free-to-play games, is the player retention rate. Analytics and data science will be touched on in Chapter 15, but the main idea is that the retention rate measures how long you can keep players *engaged* in playing your game. This is why the concept of "engagement" is central to crafting a successful (and fun) game.

This concept certainly needs refinement, and the following "engage-ability pillars" are merely an attempt to identify the broad factors influencing player engagement that allow some level of objective measurement. It's a starting point aiming to provide some broad guidelines to identify what are the engagement strengths and weaknesses of a game and, hopefully, to help developers fix issues early and make sense of analytics data once the game is in the beta stage. Because there cannot be any behavior or any engagement without motivation, *motivation* is the core pillar of engage-ability, supported by the *emotion* and *game flow* pillars.

12.2 Motivation

I tried my best to provide an accurate yet broad overview of our current understanding of human motivation in Chapter 6. We know that motivation is the motor to satisfy our drives, needs, and desires. Although there is currently no consensus or unified theory of motivation, we understand that there are different types of motivations (mainly implicit, intrinsic, and extrinsic) related to different needs (biological needs, learned needs, cognitive needs, and individual needs). These motivations interact with one another to influence our perception, cognition, and behavior in ways that we do not yet clearly understand. Depending on your personality and on the internal and external context (i.e., biology and environment), you will be motivated to do different things at different times. Therefore, researchers cannot easily predict someone's behavior, especially outside of the science lab where all variables cannot be controlled and carefully manipulated. As far as video games are concerned, game designers can manipulate the environment, but they cannot control players' biology or personal needs; although they can account for the latter. What developers are able to do, though, is design the environment (the game) in such a way to stimulate players' intrinsic motivation and/or they can use extrinsic motivation in the shape of feedback, reward, and punishment. This is the reason why the game industry has mainly approached motivation in games through the distinction between extrinsic motivation (i.e., engaging in an activity to obtain a reward external to the task itself) and intrinsic motivation (i.e., engaging in an activity for its own sake). It is important to understand that this distinction is in the mind of the player. A specific gameplay event (e.g., obtaining a new skill point as the player is leveling up) can be perceived as being both an intrinsic reward (feedback on an increase of competence) and extrinsic reward (skill point to spend). Besides, video games being per definition an autotelic activity, we could argue that all rewards in a game are inherently intrinsic, because they are usually related to the activity itself (the rewards are used within the game). Some exceptions would be with "serious" games because they are usually not played for the pleasure of the activity itself but to gain real-life benefits (e.g., lose weight), and games with a strong player-driven economy, with valued in-game currency. I'm not entirely convinced that approaching motivation in games through an intrinsic/extrinsic dichotomy is the most accurate perspective, but it is a comprehensible segmentation often used by developers, so I will use it here for lack of a better angle. However, keep in mind that the following segmentation might be somewhat unstable because we have yet to truly understand how different motivation types interact and influence our behaviors.

12.2.1 Intrinsic Motivation: Competence, Autonomy, Relatedness

Intrinsic motivation occurs when one pursues an activity for the sake of the activity itself, not as a means to getting something else (see Chapter 6). One perspective often used as an intrinsic motivation framework in game development is self-determination theory (SDT). Based on this perspective, a game should aim to satisfy basic psychological needs for competence, autonomy, and relatedness to be engaging (see Przybylski *et al.* 2010). Competence refers to the feeling of being skillful and of progressing toward clear goals. Autonomy needs relate to the sense that one has been offered meaningful choices and venues for self-expression. Relatedness refers primarily to the need to feel affiliated with others. Some games rely more heavily on facilitating players' sense of competence. For example, *Super Mario Bros.* (Nintendo) progresses in difficulty, requiring players to become more skillful and thereby increasing their navigation competence and reflexes. Other games stress the autonomy component through the experimentation they allow for (i.e., Mojang's *Minecraft* allows player to experiment with the world in a creative way). Lastly, relatedness is often addressed through multiplayer features allowing players to interact with each other in real time, via cooperative or competitive goals, or asynchronously. The need to feel affiliated with others might also be satisfied with non-playable characters that contribute meaningfully and emotionally to the game (or even, maybe, inanimate but endearing objects such as the Weighted Companion Cube in Valve's *Portal 2*, but that's a little bit of a stretch).

- **Competence**
  One of the most important ways to satisfy players' need for competence is to make them feel skillful, in control, and to feel a sense of progression and mastery. It is therefore critical to clearly express to your audience what the short-term goals are—but also the mid-term and long-term goals (or gameplay depth) of the game—so players can put forth more effort and engagement when playing it, knowing that it can be a long-term investment. For example, in the *Pokémon* series (Nintendo), short-, mid-, and long-term goals are very clear: Players (designated as *Pokémon* trainers) need to win the next match and catch more Pokémon (short-term goals), beat the "Gym Leaders" and level up their Pokémon (mid-term goals), "catch 'em all" and beat the "Elite Four," the best trainers in their region (long-term goals). Reaching a goal constitutes a clear intrinsic reward, but goals are also usually associated with what could be perceived as extrinsic rewards. (I find it difficult to draw a clear line between intrinsic and extrinsic rewards within an autotelic activity, though.) Defeating a powerful enemy usually results in gaining experience points, in-game currency, or items. For any features and elements in your game, you need to ask yourself how you can clearly express meaningful goals to

your audience, with the two important notions here being "clearly" and "meaningful."

Goals have to be *meaningful* for one main reason: We pay more attention and allocate more cognitive resources to the things we care about when we clearly understand "why" we should care. As we saw in Chapter 5, allocating attentional resources to working memory is key to deep information processing and learning. Game designers don't need UX practitioners to remind them that setting goals is essential in games. After all, it's an important part of their craft. What can happen, however, is that the goals set might not be as meaningful as they should be for players at the moment they encounter them. Consider, for example, a skill tree, which is one of the most straightforward expressions of goal setting in a game. For game designers, it might be meaningful to emphasize a skill early on that allows players to carry around a bigger inventory (e.g., in the form of a bigger backpack) because they can anticipate that it will soon be a very useful functionality to have in the game. However, many players, especially because they are just discovering your game, might become more easily excited about progressing toward skills having more dramatic impact, such as a powerful weapon with spectacular visual effects or an ability that allows the character to double jump or fly. Such skills make it easier for players to project their growth of competence in the game. Of course, once players start experiencing some inventory limitations, it will then be meaningful to them to seek out a bigger pouch. So, when designing a skill tree and setting goals overall, make sure to express how meaningful to players' competence acquiring a certain item (skill, resource, weapon, etc.) will be. Being able to consider *what* will be meaningful to the players *when* is where all the challenge resides—in placing yourself in the players' shoes. Players do not have the same level of knowledge you have about your own game, so don't expect them to consider certain goals intrinsically engaging when they are not truly meaningful at the moment players encounter them. For example, proposing to start a mission offering valuable resources as a reward won't be as compelling for players if they have not yet experienced how scarce those resources are or if they cannot craft anything they find valuable with that resource. Don't think about how valuable certain elements in your game are inherently, think about what *perception* players will have of their value (remember that perception is subjective). If you find ways to set goals at the right time that will be perceived as meaningful by your players, then you'll have a much greater chance of engaging them more intensely and for a longer time period.

The other important notion is that those meaningful goals, as well as players' progression toward them (e.g., progression bar), need to be clearly expressed in the game—through the user interface (UI) at the very least. Many motivational issues arise, not because goals are missing or because they aren't meaningful and valuable to players, but simply because their expression lacks clarity. Ensuring good usability for all the goals you are setting for your players is paramount. For example, if in your skill tree you offer an ability allowing players to execute a super-badass action in the game, make sure that the icon representing this skill looks just as badass and that its form expresses its function as much as possible. You can also add a short video clip to show the ability in action because it will help players project their growth in competence and make them dream about when they will be able to earn and execute that ability. Another way to make certain goals compelling outside of front-end menus is by teasing players in the game world. In multiplayer games, for example, when another player has earned a certain desirable item or ability, making it clearly perceptible and clearly awesome will draw other players' attention to it. When you play *World of Warcraft* and you are starting to feel the pain of walking around, seeing higher-level players showing off their hard-earned mounts is both meaningful and clear. Even if it weren't clear from the UI that at a certain level the ability to ride a mount could be acquired, seeing it in action most likely stimulates players' curiosity to figure out how to get one. It also allows players having earned a mount the ability to show off, therefore satisfying their need to express their superior competence (until, of course, they encounter a player on a flying mount). In solo games, goal clarity can be expressed via teasing, which also stimulates curiosity, another intrinsically motivating factor in humans. Nintendo is particularly good at teasing players. For example, in *The Legend of Zelda: A Link to the Past*, players can place bombs next to certain locations to open secret passages. At some point in the game, players may encounter a specific type of cracked wall that cannot be destroyed with common bombs (i.e., tease). Later in the game, as players encounter a new type of bomb, they can clearly recognize why this super bomb is meaningful and what to do with it (i.e., use it against the big cracked wall). Similarly, in *The Legend of Zelda: Phantom Hourglass* (Nintendo DS), players encounter poles, sometimes next to inaccessible areas, before they are given a grappling hook. As a result, once players obtain the grappling hook, they already know why this new tool is meaningful and how it will increase their competence: They can now grapple the poles to reach the previously inaccessible areas. Showing locks (i.e., obstacles) before giving the relevant keys (i.e., a super bomb or a grappling hook in our examples) can be a very clear and compelling way to set goals for players, while supporting a sense of growth and stimulating curiosity. Another way to do so would be to have areas in your game that players cannot enter because they do not have the required level or areas that players can enter but where they are immediately slaughtered by enemies much stronger than them. Showing players early on that these zones exist and that they require a growth in competence to enter is a clear (and sometimes meaningful) goal. All in all, make sure that your players understand the goals you are setting for them; verify if they can perceive which skill or item would be meaningful to acquire, how it would empower them, and if they can tell what is going to happen once they accomplish a certain mission or reach a certain level. Can they identify some of their immediate, mid-term, and long-term goals? Are they looking forward to acquiring a certain level, skill, or item, and do they perceive how it will increase their competence? If not, either these goals are missing (i.e., game design issue), they are present but not identified via the front-end menu or via the game world (i.e., usability issue: clarity), they are identified but not clearly understood (i.e., usability issue: form follows function), or they are not meaningful enough from your players' perspective in terms of growth in competence (i.e., engageability issue). Remember to provide clear feedback regarding their progression and especially which goals are close to completion because this might encourage players to play just a little more to accomplish a goal. Providing clear information regarding the progress made and what is left to accomplish is a critical element to competence. Offering a moment-to-moment game feel, such as the avatar having a cool animation as players execute a newly earned ability, is another way to enhance the feeling of competence, but we will discuss game feel later.

Goals are associated with the intrinsic reward of reaching them, but they also are often associated with what could be perceived as extrinsic rewards. For example, defeating a powerful enemy is intrinsically rewarding because it provides feedback on a player's competence. However, it's usually also associated with a reward in the shape of in-game currency, experience points, or items. With rewards being additionally relevant and meaningful within the game world itself, I find it difficult to clearly draw a line between intrinsic and extrinsic motivation in games. I will, however, describe the different types of rewards in greater detail, and their potential relative impact on intrinsic motivation, when addressing extrinsic motivation. All in all, the key element is to make players feel a sense of purpose for their goals in the game and to give them clear feedback on the progress made so they also can feel a sense of achievement. One last question to keep in mind is whether or not players understand *how* to be competent in the game. Players who die or fail objectives because they are not using the appropriate ability against the right threat, because they don't detect that they are in danger, or because they don't clearly understand the rules of the game won't feel any mastery. And they will likely churn or have heightened aggressive feelings (see Przybylski *et al.* 2014). Usability and learning curve are very important to competence. If you neglect the usability of your game or if you treat tutorials as a chore that you will address at the last minute, you will very likely fail to correctly onboard your players so they can feel a sense of control and mastery. The user researchers testing *Paragon* (Epic Games), a multiplayer online battle arena (MOBA) game (played five vs. five), identified early on in the development cycle that many players (including adept players)

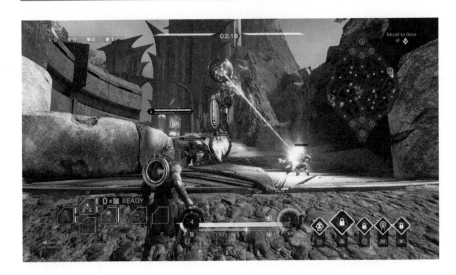

Figure 12.1

Paragon © 2016, Epic Games, Inc. (Courtesy of Epic Games, Inc., Cary, NC.)

were dying due to towers (powerful obstacles) over and over again. They seemingly did not fully understand when it was safe to get close to an enemy tower (see Figure 12.1) without being targeted—and quickly killed—by it and what could trigger such tower "aggro" (i.e., if you hurt an enemy hero while within an enemy tower area, it triggers the tower to shoot at you). Understanding the rules of tower aggro was revealed to be one of the most substantial factors for quitting the game, as we were able to realize once the game was live, after the data analysts could mine the data. Players who were killed by towers the most often were also among the most likely to churn. Craft your onboarding carefully so players can understand *how* to become competent after you've teased them about *why* they should care because this will have an impact on retention.

- **Autonomy**
  Satisfying players' needs in autonomy mostly entails allowing them to make meaningful choices and to have a sense of volition but also to make the game systems clear so they feel in control and can experience a sense of purpose. One of the most powerful meaningful choices players can make is to express their creativity. *Minecraft* represents the quintessence of autonomy in games because this procedurally generated game offering deep systemic design allows players to experiment and create in nearly infinite ways. Other means to support players' autonomy would be to allow them to customize elements in the game—the appearance of their avatar, the name of characters, the name of their base, the choice of a banner, and so on. The more customization options you can offer, the better. There is a cognitive bias called the "IKEA effect," named after the

Swedish furniture retailer, which increases the perceived value people have of a product when they participated in its conception (Norton *et al.* 2012). Therefore, when players participate in creating their base or their avatar, they might likely attribute more value to these elements. Of course, those customizations have to be meaningful to the players; if you make them spend time tweaking the appearance of a character that they won't often see (e.g., because the game has a first-person camera view), it might not be felt as being a valuable endeavor. Unless you can add features allowing players to see their avatar at certain times, such as by transitioning to a third-person camera view when players perform emotes, or by offering replay features during which players can see how awesome their avatar looked as they were executing some impressive combat moves in the match.

Role-playing games (such as *Skyrim*) and simulation games typically offer personal agency because the choices players make in these games either allow them to specialize in certain abilities (i.e., setting their own goals), impact the game story, or to shape an environment differently (e.g., Sid Meier's *Civilization* or Will Wright's *SimCity*). Again, the choices have to be meaningful, their purpose should be understood during decision-making, and their impact overall must be perceivable. For example, depending on the actions you choose to take in games like *Black & White* (Lionhead Studios) or *Infamous* (Sucker Punch), the impact on the game world can be perceived through the environment art, the artificial intelligence (AI), the visual and sound effects, and so on. If the impact of player choices cannot be clearly perceived (which can, e.g., happen when the choice is associated with a probability algorithm, such as equipping a certain item that offers a 5% chance to get a critical hit), it can result in a lack of meaning, and players might not feel agency. Meaningful choice can be experienced when players have several ways to overcome a challenge or solve a problem, such as in Konami's *Metal Gear Solid V: The Phantom Pain* in which you can choose to play in a stealthy manner or … not so stealthily. It can also be experienced when the game story meaningfully changes according to player choices, such as in *Mass Effect* series.

Whether players are offered a large or small number of options, it is critical that they understand the purpose and/or perceive the impact of their choice—why they are choosing to do the things they do and how it is impacting their personal agency. If the purpose is not clear, or if its impact is not perceptible enough, it will likely influence players' level of engagement toward the game, especially if autonomy features are core to the gameplay. So offering autonomy does not mean letting them figure things out on their own with no guidance in the name of complete freedom because players won't feel autonomous, nor they will feel competent, if they are confused or overwhelmed. Autonomy has to be guided so that players can fully experience control over their meaningful decisions.

- **Relatedness**

Satisfying players' need in relatedness means offering meaningful social interactions in the game. Humans are very social creatures that could not have survived without connecting with each other. Games offering various channels to communicate information or emotion among players (i.e., chat system or emotes), to compete against each other, or to play cooperatively increase their likelihood of being engaging. As always, the social features will likely be felt as more engaging if they are meaningful. For example, playing cooperatively might be more compelling when each player has a specific role to play and can perceptively contribute to the success of the team. It can mean being able to group up for a short time to overcome a specific challenge or organizing into guilds or clans for a long-term relationship. Note that allowing for long-term relationships encourages players to care more for the social interaction and be more collaborative. For example, it is well-established in game theory that players in the prisoner's dilemma game collaborate more when they know that they will be playing a certain number of rounds with the same partner (Selten and Stoecker 1986). Imagine a game in which you and your teammate are arrested for a crime you have committed together. However, the police do not have enough evidence to keep either of you in jail for long. Because you and your partner are both interrogated in separate rooms, you are offered a choice: to either rat (defect) on your partner or to remain silent (collaborate). If both of you collaborate, you both serve one year in jail. If both of you defect, you each serve three years. But if one of you collaborates while the other defects, the betrayer is immediately freed while the other has to serve ten years in jail. When players are only playing one round with a random partner under these conditions, the average decision is to defect—it seems to be hard to trust a stranger we will never play with again! However, when players know they will play several rounds with the same partner, they show a greater tendency to collaborate, especially during the first rounds (collaboration declines as the end of the session gets nearer). The moral of the story is that players are more likely to troll or take advantage of a random teammate they will never interact with again, when there is no need to maintain a trust relationship (see Ariely 2016b). Consequences matter. So, by offering longer-term social relationships—such as via guilds or simply making it easy (and meaningful) to friend strangers—it's helping to create a more favorable environment for collaboration. Of course, ideally, you want your players to bring their "real" friends over and to be able to facilitate friends of friends being able to identify and easily play with each other. It's easier to trust and be willing to help someone you know or someone who is within your social circle. Humans have a tendency to favor their "ingroup," the people who are close to them, who are part of their social group. This is called the ingroup bias. So make sure that you implement features that make it easy for your players to invite friends to join the game (e.g., by allowing them to automatically import social media friends). Make it easy for players to quickly jump in a mission or match where their friends are already playing. Consider informing them via the front-end menu about what mission their friends have recently completed or what goodies they have earned because behavior can be influenced by peer effect. Offer ways for players to show off their status to the group. For example, obtaining a specific badge after completing an epic quest is a way to confirm a player's competence in a social context. It can feel particularly rewarding for the player who earned the badge, and it can also tease the others to obtain it (peer pressure works). Lastly, make it easy for players to be nice to one another. For example, allow for gifting or add features to let players give tips to each other, such as tagging an item so that teammates can see it appear on their minimap so they can go check it out. There are many ways to design for collaboration.

Competition is another way to experience relatedness. This type of social relationship poses more problems than cooperation, though, mainly because it can be very frustrating to be the loser, especially if the game feels unfair or if humiliation is possible (e.g., "tea-bagging"). On the other end, it can be satisfying to be the best player; it clearly expresses one's competence. However, there can be only one (best player), and all others might feel demoralized not to be at the top of the scoreboard. And those players who are at the top of the scoreboard have to live through the pain of losing status as soon as someone else takes their rank. Although celebrating the best player or the best team generally is a good practice, game designers need to also find ways to portray losing in a more positive light and/or turn it into a chance to learn and progress. Just as we mentioned in Chapter 7 about emotion (because none of these UX pillars are independent), we can use cognitive reappraisal to regulate negative emotions that can be tied to losing. For example, you can emphasize what the player was the best at compared to the others or, even better, how she or he improved on personal metrics. *Overwatch* is particularly good at this, pointing out at the end of the match when players beat their "career average," and it can be about many different metrics, such as number of kills (eliminations), time stayed on the objective area, healing done, weapon accuracy, and so on (see Figure 12.2). If your player versus player game has cooperative features (team features), I encourage you to not only focus on the number of kills but to celebrate actions that helped the team in different ways, especially regarding the match objectives, and not just celebrate who was the best "killer" of the game. Consider valuing the different roles when applicable, making them matter, and gratifying players across many different metrics. By doing so, you will likely increase the chance to motivate a larger audience, not just the best shooter and most competitive players. Support roles matter as well. Lastly, make sure that players understand why they have lost and what they can do to improve. Humans can have a strong reaction to unfairness, so if the game is not well balanced—or

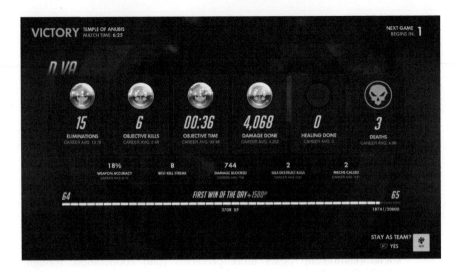

Figure 12.2

Overwatch (Blizzard). Overwatch®. (Courtesy of Blizzard Entertainment, Inc.)

simply perceived as unbalanced whether that's true or not—or if the reason why they failed is unclear, it could create some significant frustration. Allowing for a death camera (whereby the player who died sees a replay of what happened) can help, but it must be truly informative. Reliving the pain of failure without clearly being able to identify what caused it and how to avoid it next time can actually be more harmful than helpful. At the very least, make sure the death cam can be easily skipped.

Both cooperative and competitive games can suffer from multiplayer toxicity—when a very small percentage of players are insulting or harassing others, thereby ruining their fun. Toxicity is a serious problem that you must address—not only for your audience's well-being but also for your revenue because there are good reasons to believe toxicity has a negative economical impact. Being insulted as they play might deter some players. After all, harassment usually is not what most people sign up for. The best way to address the problem is to design the game to prevent toxicity early on. For example, allowing friendly fire will likely encourage trolls to take advantage of it. Allowing for collisions between players might encourage some players to block others in corners. If only the player who gives the final blow to an enemy or when gathering resources gets the loot, it will encourage trolls to steal loot by just giving the final blow. Letting players have a line of sight on the opposite team's spawn point will allow for spawn killing. These types of behavior, when occurring with strangers, can be at worst perceived as harassment and at best felt as unfair. Both feelings are not particularly motivating—except perhaps in pursuing retaliation—but escalation of violence is another topic. Give players the means to block other players they do not want to encounter again and to flag players who displayed an inappropriate behavior. Define inappropriate behaviors in your game and make players read and accept the code of conduct. Do not tolerate violation of this code of conduct. Explain to the violators why their behavior is not allowed and give them a chance to redeem themselves, but do not let toxic behavior go without consequences (remember the lessons from behavioral learning principles in Chapter 8). Give feedback to the victims of toxic behavior that their voice has been heard and action has been taken toward the player they have signaled (once the toxic behavior is verified). Find ways to celebrate civil players—for example, by allowing other players to express their sympathy toward them. And so on. The environment can shape behavior, and toxic behavior is no different. As user researcher Ben Lewis-Evans explains in the essay that follows, the game can (and should) be designed to reduce toxicity, but it will be easier to do this if you think about it early on. Unless, of course, it is part of the design intent to allow for trolling. But keep in mind that it will most likely reduce the breadth of your audience because being trolled can demotivate many players.

Ben Lewis-Evans, User Experience Researcher at Epic Games

Reducing Antisocial Behavior in Games via the Three Es

Players don't typically play a game to be harassed or to have their game spoiled by someone going AFK (away from keyboard), team killing, feeding, cheating, or many of the other negative behaviors other players can perform. Antisocial behavior will also hurt your profitability, with both Riot Games and Valve Corporation reporting that experiencing antisocial behavior is a strong predictor of players churning out of a game. Both of these factors make reducing antisocial behavior in games a key user experience issue.

Thankfully, reducing antisocial behavior has been a focus of scientific study in psychology for more than a century. For example, in road safety, the area I studied before moving to games, we examine preventing antisocial behavior (e.g., drinking and driving) via the "Three Es"—education, enforcement, and engineering. These same three approaches can be used in games:

- *Education* is, simply put, to tell people what not to do, OR, more effectively, to tell people what to do. Strangely, despite the fact that we know that people don't often do what they are told, people have faith in education, and it is often the first thing they try. It also helps that education is cheap to accomplish and puts the weight of the responsibility for change on the people being "educated." Unfortunately, education is the least-effective thing you can do to tackle toxic behavior.

It has its place, for example, with loading screen messages, codes of conduct, and providing examples of good sportspersonship but don't expect it to be the solution.

- *Enforcement* is backing up the rules you have educated people on with penalties. It can also include encouragement, where you give people rewards for doing the things you want (which is more effective than penalties but is more difficult to implement well!). Enforcement is more effective than education and has a preventive effect via the perception of enforcement—specifically, the certainty and speed at which an unwanted behavior will be punished. The severity of the punishment is the least important factor. What matters is people get caught, and get caught fast, and that they believe this is the case so they won't perform the behavior in the first place. This is a problem for traditional police enforcement because they can't be everywhere and the legal system moves slowly. However, in games, we control the environment and the data, so we can detect and punish or reward behaviors quickly. This environmental control also leads us to…

- *Engineering*, which is designing to reduce or eliminate the issue. For example, in road safety, you can tell people not to drink and drive (education), which won't work very well; you can add random stops to breath test people, with fines for being over a certain limit (enforcement), which will have more impact, and you can put a sensor in cars that simply stops the car if it detects alcohol on the driver's breath (engineering). Similarly, the relatively simple engineering of putting in a median barrier and dividing a road can cut fatalities by more than 50%! The antisocial behavior we see in games is not just "kids" or "what gamers do." Instead, it is (unintentionally) enabled by game design. For example, does a game need general or voice chat? If not, don't add it because it is just another channel for harassment. If so, does it need to be on by default or can a player opt in? Making it an opt in will connect those that want to talk while reducing the antisocial tendencies of just throwing a bunch of people together. Another example would be to not have a "draft" in a MOBA (multiplayer online battle arena) and instead reduce within-team competition at the start of a match by letting players choose their preferred hero and position. Engineering isn't often the easiest path, and it requires that the social outcomes of design decisions be considered at every stage and level of development (much like other user experience factors). But engineering is generally the most effective option. When we create the systems, we can design to solve the issues the systems enable.

- **Meaning**
As you may have noticed, one concept has been recurrent throughout the description of the needs of competence, autonomy, and relatedness—the

concept of "meaning." Meaning is about "having a sense of purpose, value, and impact," as Dan Ariely (2016a) put it. This is why it is important to reveal the reasons behind anything the player needs to do or has to learn. I do not mean the functional reason (i.e., green potions can regenerate health), but the meaningful reason (i.e., you have been hurt; therefore, you need to find a way to heal, which can be done by using a health potion). Before introducing a system, a mechanic, or an item, think about how you could place the player in a situation where learning this mechanic or earning this item will be meaningful. It will help players understand their value. Lastly, make sure to associate clear signs and feedback with these elements, so they are perceived the way you intend. We will talk again about the importance of meaning when tackling the learning curve within the game flow pillar and again when talking about how to put together the onboarding plan for a game in Chapter 13. But this is a key concept you need to keep in mind at all times.

12.2.2 Extrinsic Motivation, Learned Needs, and Rewards

Just as we saw in Chapter 6, extrinsic motivation is about learned needs shaped by the environment. We learn about our environment by experiencing it and identifying what behavior leads to a pleasant outcome versus a negative outcome. Our motivation is influenced by the reward value of a given behavior and by our probability of obtaining this reward. If when you click on a cookie—in Julien Thiennot's game *Cookie Clicker*—you gain another cookie, and if you experience this feedback as a positive reinforcer (reward), you will likely click again. Many free-to-play games use extrinsic rewards to encourage players to log in every day—for example, if you log into the game, you get a reward in the shape of a daily chest. Even if some players did not really want to play your game on a given day, they might, for example, want to receive some in-game currency (or other goodies) that they will be able to use later on to unlock some very good-looking skin they were interested in acquiring for their main hero. And, who knows, as they log in and collect their daily reward, they might also see a new quest offering some other interesting rewards, or maybe they will be poked by a friend who was about to start a match and therefore invites them to join. Proposing players to accomplish an action in order to obtain something that they find valuable is a way to keep them engaged with the game. The concept of the daily chest and overall push-up notifications is probably as close as we can get to pure extrinsic rewards in games. As I mentioned earlier, because playing a game is an autotelic activity by definition, the rewards earned in the game only have a purpose within the game itself, in most cases. Daily chests are a little bit different in that they lure players into launching the game only to acquire a reward, even if they did not necessarily feel the intrinsic need to play the game at that moment. If you remember the "overjustification effect" mentioned in Chapter 6, you may wonder if giving extrinsic rewards to players for engaging with your game might undermine their initial intrinsic motivation to play. For this undermining effect to happen, the rewards need to be perceived as external to the activity and, more importantly, they need to stop occurring.

The research studying the impact of extrinsic rewards on intrinsic motivation generally highlights a drop in player motivation to pursue an activity for people who were initially intrinsically motivated—after an extrinsic reward was introduced (e.g., money) and then removed—when compared to people who were not introduced to the extrinsic reward. For example, think back to the study in which the schoolchildren who were rewarded for drawing (which they usually do for its intrinsic value) were less likely to draw spontaneously later on compared to children who were not extrinsically rewarded (Lepper *et al.* 1973). Therefore, for the rewards that are felt as external to the play activity (i.e., daily chests), you want to make sure that you do not remove the reward at some point in time because that could undermine players' intrinsic motivation to play your game. This is why it is generally risky to punish players who did not log in your game to collect their daily chest. For example, imagine a game requiring you to log in every single day so that your reward increases the more consecutive days you log in. One day, you will forget or won't be able to log in and it will break your streak, moving you down the reward ladder. It is likely that, the next time you do log in, you will feel that some reward was taken away from you, and it could impact your intrinsic motivation to play the game. Therefore, if you want to use this feature, avoid punishing players for not logging in. Once you introduce an extrinsic reward, it seems unwise to remove it or to reduce its value. Keep in mind, though, that here I'm talking about truly extrinsic rewards, and many game rewards won't necessarily be perceived as extrinsic to the activity.

Another important concept to keep in mind regarding extrinsic motivation is the type of incentive used. Rewards that feel "controlling" are mainly those that could deter intrinsic motivation. Some self-determination theorists are moving away from a strict extrinsic/intrinsic motivation dichotomy to focus instead on the distinction between autonomous and controlled motivation (see Gerhart and Fang 2015). Within this perspective, an incentive will have a different impact on intrinsic motivation if it is task-contingent (i.e., rewarding engagement, completion, or performance) versus noncontingent (i.e., not tied to any particular behavior). Noncontingent rewards are considered to be less controlling because they are not related to what people are doing. An example in the workplace would be to receive an unexpected bonus not related to your performance at work. An example in games would be to receive a reward randomly that is not related to any behavior whatsoever (e.g., receiving an e-mail from the game publisher simply offering some in-game currency you do not have to earn). In games, however, rewards are mostly a specific sort of feedback for players' actions; therefore, they are task-contingent incentives. There are three types of task-contingent incentives. They can be engagement-contingent (you get a reward for engaging with a task), completion-contingent (you get the reward as you complete the task), or performance-contingent (you get a reward if you do the task well, or the value of the reward depends on how well you accomplished the task). Performance-contingent rewards are the most likely to be perceived as controlling because they are given when players match a certain standard of excellence. However, they also provide a powerful expression of a sense of mastery and progression, which is not the case with the other task-contingent rewards.

Overall, extrinsic motivation is no longer seen as being bad for intrinsic motivation, and in some cases, it can actually enhance performance and creativity. For that to happen, extrinsic rewards have to be instrumentally important and valuable for players' goals. This is why, again, making sure that rewards are meaningful from the perspective of your players is paramount. If you offer gems as a reward for a quest, for example, players need to understand their value and what they will be able to do with them. This is a very important notion to keep in mind in order to make your game more engaging: Receiving a key reward should not be perceived as an ending point but as the *starting point for the next goal*. Moreover, rewards are a common practice in video games so they are expected, and they also inform about players' performance in the game. Rewards should, therefore, be treated as a certain type of feedback, with all the usability concerns associated with it. The value of performance-contingent rewards should increase with the difficulty (or duration) of the task. Harder missions should offer better rewards. Those rewards do not always have to be tangible and instrumentally important for accomplishing other goals. When they are given for small achievements, they can also be less tangible (such as verbal praises) as long as the praise gives information on a player's skills. For example, a verbal praise merely expressing "well done!" is not as informative as something like "double kill!" The latter clearly provides specific feedback on what the player has accomplished. The reward could also take the shape of the game world reacting to what the player is doing. For example, if the player has saved a village from a terrible evil, the non-player characters could react by being happy again, thanking the player, partying on the streets, and so on. Because rewards are a specific type of feedback that can inform players about their mastery, absence of reward will likely be felt as a punishment. So, if the player saves the world but the game world does not react, this can be somewhat disappointing. For example, if you allocate time and effort in collecting the 100 flags scattered around the *Assassin's Creed* world, although you are intrinsically rewarded for the exploration you did and for a sense of completion, the reward for such an effortful endeavor can be felt as underwhelming (i.e., players only get an achievement unlocked). Even if no great reward was advertised for collecting the 100 flags, players might still have expected a more meaningful reward than a mere achievement. So, remember to reward players' time and effort accordingly.

12.2.3 Individual Needs and Implicit Motives

Humans are more similar than they are dissimilar; however, individual differences and preferences do exist. These differences clearly impact our perception, as we saw in Chapter 3, and they also impact what we find intrinsically motivating. For example, depending on how strong your power, achievement, and affiliation drives are, you won't be motivated in the same degree to dominate others, improve your skills, or be connected to others. As a designer, if you have strong power motives, you might design a game that is highly competitive, therefore targeting players with strong power drives while alienating others. If it is your intent to target a very specific population with specific motives, it's up to you, of course. But, otherwise, I would recommend offering systems and mechanics that can appeal to a wider population.

Beyond implicit drives, humans also have different personality types. As mentioned in Chapter 6, personality models overall are not particularly reliable, especially for predicting behavior. The model of the Big Five personality traits currently seems the most robust. Five factors have been defined as broad traits that encapsulate most of the personality differences observed: openness to experience (O), conscientiousness (C), extraversion (E), agreeableness (A), and neuroticism (N), or OCEAN. This model does not accurately predict behavior, though. However, it can be used in games to help designers think about various personality traits and how to satisfy individual needs in their game, especially those that might be different from the developers'. Very recently, Nick Yee suggested that the five-factor model might align with gaming motivations (Yee 2016). In a blog post, Yee presented the three high-level clusters for gaming motivations, based on data collected from more than 140,000 gamers who replied to a survey: action-social, mastery-achievement, and immersion-creativity. "Action" entails the need for destruction and excitement and "social" the need for competition and community. "Mastery" entails the need for challenge and strategy and "achievement" the need for completion and power. "Immersion" entails the need for fantasy and story and "creativity" the need for design and discovery. According to Yee, the action-social cluster correlates with extraversion; the mastery-achievement cluster correlates with conscientiousness; and the immersion-creativity cluster maps to openness. However, neuroticism and agreeableness were not found to map any gaming motivation clusters. Other types of gaming motivations have been theorized. For example, Bartle (1996) suggested a taxonomy of player types: achievers (motivated by mastery and accomplishment), explorers (motivated by discovery and exploration), socializers (motivated by social interactions), and killers (motivated by competition and destruction).

As far as I know, there currently is no personality model that can reliably predict how different types of players will behave in a specific game. What you can do, though, is account for all personality types and implicit motives. For example, offer different types of activities, missions, ways to solve a task, and rewards to satisfy a variety of needs and engage a broader audience. If your audience is children, know that they are not behaving like little adults. This is not the subject of this book, so I won't get into any details about child development but make sure to learn about the specificities of your younger audience, which depend on their age.

Our understanding of human motivation is increasing, and we are now starting to have a better grasp of what motivational ingredients to use in games. As experimental psychologist Andrew Przybylski points out in the following essay, we now need to explore these ingredients in greater detail, collaboratively.

Dr. Andrew K. Przybylski

*Oxford Internet Institute, Department of
Experimental Psychology, University of Oxford*

It is a very exciting time to be a scientist or user experience specialist studying and applying motivation to video games and virtual worlds. In the last decade, we have "landed on the island," so to speak. We know that psychological and motivational theories can help anticipate player behaviors (e.g., churn) and emotions (for good and ill), and we have some hints as to why this might be. The outstanding challenges before us for the coming decade—"exploring the island"—will require us to figure out exactly how to apply these principles to specific game mechanics and play experiences. The only way we'll be able to do this is by building open, robust, and multidisciplinary collaborations among game designers, user experience researchers, and social data scientists. I'm cautiously optimistic such collaborations will inform both effective game design and expand what we know about human play.

12.3 Emotion

As Don Norman (2005) expressed, "The emotional side of design may be more critical to a product's success than its practical elements" (p. 5). Accordingly, how it feels to play the game, what surprises are offered, and the overall emotions evoked, are critical parts of UX in games. The emotional side of video games is frequently addressed through visual aesthetics or through music and narrative. However, an important aspect of emotional game design is often overlooked: the "game feel." According to game designer Steve Swink (2009), the game feel includes, "Feelings of mastery and clumsiness, and the tactile sensation of interacting with virtual objects" (p. 10). Designing the game feel entails paying attention to the controls, the camera (how the players see into the game world), and the characters. For example, if the camera of the game has a very narrow field of view and is angled in such a way that it is difficult to see the horizon, the player may feel claustrophobic, which would be inappropriate for a relaxed exploration game (albeit appropriate for a tension-ridden horror survival game).

12.3.1 Game Feel

A game that feels good to interact with has controls that feel responsive and enjoyable to manipulate. Game feel is about giving the player a sense of presence in the game world. It is also about how the avatar, controlled by the player, evolves on the screen as well as about the other characters. It's about the ambience, the cohesion, and the art direction. According to game developer Steve Swink (2009), a definition of game feel is "Real-time control of virtual objects in a simulated space, with interactions emphasized by polish" (p. 32). Swink describes great-feeling games as conveying five types of experiences for the player: aesthetic sensation of control, pleasure of learning a skill, extension of the senses, extension of identity, and interaction with a unique physical reality with the game. I encourage you to read Steve Swink's book, if you wish to dig deeper into the subject. Most of these elements will be briefly and superficially tackled here (I'm not a game designer and I'm even less of a gameplay programmer), except for pleasure of learning, which will be instead covered in the game flow section. UX pillars are not independent; this is why different people, game developers or academics, may classify differently some of the concepts I discuss here.

- **The 3Cs**

  The 3Cs stand for Control, Camera, and Character, and are critical to many game developers. At Ubisoft, where I was first exposed to the 3Cs, they are considered one of the most important elements to define in a game. Let's first discuss controls. One of the first things that come to mind is the controller or keyboard mapping, which should feel natural. There's a reason why shooting is usually set on the right trigger on controllers, and that is to simulate pressing on a real trigger. Players aren't octopuses so controls should also be comfortable to operate. Another important consideration is that players should have the sensation of being in control (which is also an important element for intrinsic motivation). This is why there should be immediate feedback to player's input. If the response is not instantaneous, the controls may feel sloppy. Character animation, therefore, has an important impact. If the time between the moment when the player pushes the thumbstick in one direction and the moment when the avatar actually moves is too long, it could be felt as awkward. Swink (2009) uses the example of the original *Prince of Persia*, explaining that it takes 900 milliseconds for the prince to go from a standing position to a full speed run because the animation takes too long (although it looks cool). The aesthetic feel of control is closely related to character animation because it has an impact on input responsiveness. If players are being attacked while reloading, for example, and the reload animation is not interrupted or does not complete fast enough as players try to escape, they won't feel as much in control and can become frustrated as a result. Another example for platformer games would be to consider how much inertia a character has, how collision works (is there a friction between the character and the ground, for example), and if air control is allowed. For shooter games, it would be important to consider the acceleration in between targets and the stickiness of targets when aiming. Remember to consider the Weber–Fechner law, whereby the greater the physical intensity, the more difference between two magnitudes we need to detect a difference (Chapter 3), which also applies to the physical intensity applied to analog controls and the expected response. These are only a few examples but, overall, the relationship input-output should be predictable and the feedback to an input should be perceptible, clear, and immediate. I strongly recommend you create various gym levels (i.e., testing rooms) to assess players' reactions and expectations via task-analysis UX testing (see Chapter 14). Controls allow for player agency; this is why they must be carefully considered. If players don't experience real-time control, then they will likely feel *controlled* by the game, which will negatively impact their sense of autonomy.

The camera is another critical element because it defines players' perspectives on the game world. What view should the game have? Top-down, isometric, behind-the-shoulder-third-person, first-person? Is the camera still or scrolling? How fast should it scroll, and how should it follow the character? Does the player directly control it? What is the field of view? And so on. All these parameters will modify the game feel and therefore should be carefully chosen to transcend the game design intent and allow for greater player control, while reducing usability frictions and motion sickness. One of the elements to consider is taking the camera control away from players at certain times, while the rest of the time they mostly freely control the camera. Because you cannot easily control how to encourage players to position themselves in such a way that the camera angle will give some indication of what is next, it is tempting in action-adventure games to temporarily take away camera control from players to show them a specific element in the world. Doing so could make players feel controlled, though, so make sure at the very least that they can easily anticipate when control will be taken away from them (although finding a way not to do so would be even more elegant). Virtual reality (VR) is a special challenge here because taking camera control away from players is likely to make them sick. How to treat the camera as the character stands close to a wall when in third- or first-person view is another example of an important parameter to consider for the game feel. In that case, you might want to force a certain camera view to avoid awkward or unsettling angles that could distract players away from the action and, again, hamper the sensation of control. Getting the camera stuck in geometry won't make players feel particularly skillful. You can ask level designers to avoid narrow corridors or corners if camera collision behavior concerns you. Be mindful also of how much the camera is moving to avoid motion sickness (and simulation sickness in VR). Camera shake can be a nice effect to simulate the physicality of an explosion blast, but it can also be disturbing and, again, make players sick (especially in VR). Another option would be to shake the UI instead. The camera represents your players' view of the game world, so it will have a considerable impact on game feel.

Lastly, what all the characters (and interactive items) look like, sound like, and animate will have an impact on players' understanding of the game rules and on their expectations. Carefully determining the character form in such a way that players can anticipate their function, but also their behavior, is one of the key elements. A large enemy entirely protected by plate armor except for their back that carries a big sword and makes heavy and loud footsteps will be anticipated as being slow, resistant, able to inflict a large amount of damage, and to have a weak point in the back. A player's avatar should be even more carefully designed because it represents an extension of the player within the game world, and it will be seen a great deal of the time (unless the game is in first-person view). How a character animates is particularly important: how it moves, its weight, its inertia, and so on should match the proprioception feedback from thumbs moving the controller sticks to feel believable. A simple change in animation can sometimes make a big difference in perception. For example, in a third-person camera game, if players complain that when their avatar is moving backward it feels too slow, you can change players' perceptions without changing the actual velocity of the character by changing the animation so that the character seems to be moving faster. Beyond characters, objects in the game will have a different feel depending on their texture, shape, and interactive properties. For example, players will expect pointy objects to be either dangerous or useful for combat. The same applies for the UI, and more particularly for icon shapes. A triangular icon will probably be associated with combat, while a round icon might be more likely associated with health. Carefully craft and polish your main characters and items so they can appear alive, with a unique physical reality, and relatable. They should express human-like emotions. Suspension of disbelief is an exciting goal to achieve in terms of game feel, and character design has an important role in it.

- **Presence**
Presence is experienced when players have the illusion that nothing is between them and the virtual world, when they perceive that they are simply in the game with no mediation. Questionnaires have been developed to measure presence (e.g., Lombard *et al.* 2009), which has been found to be positively linked to enjoyment (e.g., Horvath and Lombard 2009; Takatalo *et al.* 2010; Shafer *et al.* 2011). Moreover, research indicates that games satisfying motivational needs allow for a better presence (see Przybylski *et al.* 2010). This can be broken down into three components: physical, emotional, and narrative presence, which have connections with game feel. Physical presence happens when players feel that they are actually in the world. This notion is very similar to Swink's notion of "extension of the senses," which he says can be reached when the screen, the speakers, and the controller become an extension of a player's sense of the game world. When the camera and the controls are well-defined and intuitive, players "substitute their visual sense for one in the game world" (Swink 2009) and the avatar they control feels like an extension of their body in the virtual world. Emotional presence is

the feeling that what is happening in the virtual world happens to the player and that it has real emotional weight. This notion can be somewhat associated with Swink's concept of "extension of identity" whereby once a player's perception extends into the game world, so does his/her identity. Narrative presence happens when players are invested in the story and find the characters believable and relatable—for example, when player's choices and actions have real consequences on the events unfolding (see Isbister 2016). Carefully designing control, camera, and character (known as the 3Cs) addresses many of the components for presence because control and camera are central to physical presence, character design can have an impact on narrative presence, and all the 3Cs combined influence emotional presence. Physical reality and game flow (as described later in this chapter) are also important components to enhance presence.

Art direction, audio design, music, and narrative all contribute to presence through the emotions they can convey. Remember that emotion (both the physiological arousal and, potentially, the associated feeling) influences our mind and guides our behavior but that perception and cognition can also induce emotion (see Chapter 7). According to Donald Norman (2005), any design has three levels of processing that interlace emotion and cognition: visceral, behavioral, and reflective. The visceral level triggers automatic emotional responses, such as the fight-or-flight response facilitated by the limbic system, or a conditioned behavior, such as players raising their awareness when hearing the *Metal Gear Solid* alert sound effect. It helps us determine what seems good, bad, safe, or dangerous. The behavioral level has to do with the pleasure and ease of use, already largely covered with the usability pillars and the game feel component. Finally, the reflective level is about the intellectualization of a product, such as the message and values it conveys, the self-image reflected by using it, the memories it triggers, and so on. For example, a piece of clothing can look and feel good on the skin (visceral level), and it can be easy to put on thanks to a zipper (behavioral level), but you end up not buying it because you know that the manufacturer is involved in child labor or was one of the manufacturers implicated in the Rana Plaza tragedy when a sweatshop factory in Bangladesh collapsed, killing more than a thousand workers (mostly women). Game narrative design, in particular, can trigger interesting emotions that movies or books cannot, such as guilt. Let's take the example of the IndieCade award-winning tabletop board game, *Train*, by Brenda Brathwaite Romero, as explained by Katherine Isbister (2016). In this game, players have to move boxcars full of passengers from one place to the other, overcoming obstacles and challenges along the way. At the end of the game, players realize that the train destination is Auschwitz, which may trigger strong emotions in them—notably guilt because they feel complicit. This could be interpreted as an example of the reflective dimension (i.e., reference to the horror of the Holocaust) that influenced the visceral level (i.e., feeling of repulsiveness informing moral judgment, if we analyze the visceral reaction using Damasio's somatic markers theory seen in Chapter 7). No wonder players allegedly did not want to play this game twice! Although narrative can have an important role in a game, you must be careful that it does not hamper gameplay and player control. For example, having to sit through a 20-minute cutscene at the beginning of a game is both very expensive to produce and often detrimental to engage-ability. Use cutscenes parsimoniously and favor a narrative design embedded in gameplay, letting players be in control.

Music is also a powerful conveyor of emotions. As Norman (2005) pointed out, music is part of our evolutionary heritage, is universal across the entire human species, and can trigger visceral responses. Research suggests that music can, in fact, modulate activity in brain structures commonly associated with the limbic system that are known to be involved in emotion, such as the amygdala, the hypothalamus, and the hippocampus (Koelsch 2014). Rhythm follows the natural beats of the body; a fast tempo (beats per minute) is suitable for action, while a slow tempo is more suitable for relaxing. Music has the power to move people, literally. It has also the power to evoke various emotions. Music with a fast tempo and large pitch variation might express joy, whereas melodies played in minor keys are often perceived to be sad. (I've heard that D minor is the saddest of all keys—I apologize, this is another *Spinal Tap* joke.) Nonlinear music with dissonance can evoke fear. And so on. Lastly, music can have rewarding effects; the human brain is attracted to certain stimulus repetition, and there are inherent tendencies toward repetition in music (Sacks 2007). Therefore, music can be inherently pleasurable and is a powerful tool you can use to evoke specific emotions in players. However, reactions to music are also subjective, and some players might find one type of music annoying while others would find it stimulating, for example.

All these elements (and others, such as the 3Cs, physical reality, and game flow) have an impact on physical, emotional, and narrative presence. They influence how much players will consider themselves as being "inside" the game world, how much pleasure they will have interacting with the interface, how much they will care about what's going on, what emotions they will feel as they progress in the game, and so on.

- **Physical reality and living virtual worlds**
  Whether your game is an immense and realistic open world or made of cartoony UI only, it has a physical reality that needs to be believable. Humans have a strong intuitive understanding of the physical world. Even young infants have specific expectations about physical events; they expect that a solid object cannot pass through another solid object or that if an object is bigger than a container, it cannot fit into the container

(see Baillargeon 2010). Physical events in the world don't necessarily have to exactly mimic reality, but they have to be credible. Again, here comes the importance of signs and feedback and form follows function. The events happening in the world, what players can do within the world, and feedback from players' actions should be clear, and their physicality should make sense. For example, the sound of bullets missing the enemy and instead hitting a metallic surface should not be the same as the sound effect when players hit an enemy. When a brick or a tile is being hit by, say, a player's finger, the shock should have physicality via cracks and then destruction associated with particle effects, for example. In a racing game, cars can look increasingly damaged as they hit other cars. In a platform game, the character can spread his arms when running around. (Mario has such fun animation.) In menus, as players hover over buttons, there could be a feedback associated with it: Buttons could lift and a sound effect could be played (e.g., in Ubisoft's *Just Dance 2* on Nintendo Wii, as players focus on buttons, a different musical note can be heard each time a button is the focus, which makes navigating menus playful and melodious). In *Fortnite* (Epic Games), players can hit a piñata in the shape of a llama (which is the metaphor the art team found for opening a card pack in the game store) and, before hitting the llama, its eyes follow the cursor movements (see Figure 12.3). In open worlds, different creatures could inhabit the world depending on the day/night cycle and the weather. AI agents should react accordingly to what is happening in the world, to each other, and to what the player is doing. To take an

Figure 12.3

Fortnite Beta © 2017, Epic Games, Inc. (Courtesy of Epic Games, Inc., Cary, NC.)

example from a mobile strategy game, when players upgrade a building in Supercell's *Clash of Clans*, a builder character rushes to the building and seems to be working on it while hammering sound effects can be heard. And so on. All of these are only limited examples of how to turn an interface into a toy and how to give life to the virtual space, which will make interacting with it more playful, observing it more interesting, and, therefore, will enhance game feel overall.

12.3.2 Discovery, Novelty, and Surprises

Once players are familiar with a game, a lot of their actions become automatic after being repeated over and over. Just like when you learn to skate or to drive a car, you do not need to think hard about what to do once you have practiced enough for the behavior to become automatic. Moreover, if you are used to skating or driving on the same familiar terrain, you will not pay attention to the road as much after a while. To raise your awareness, novelty needs to be introduced. This actually is how child development researchers study preverbal children—by introducing novelty or by creating a surprising event to see how they react. For example, to determine if infants can discriminate between a triangle and a circle, researchers test their "reaction to novelty" by measuring fixation times (how long the infant stares at an object). Let's say that an image of a triangle is repeatedly shown to an infant. At the beginning, the baby may fixate on the image for a certain time, but her attention response will progressively wane as a result of repeated presentations of the same image. When the infant stops being interested by the image, it's called "habituation." The stimulus (i.e., triangle), now familiar, is no longer deemed interesting, and fewer attentional resources are allocated to it. But then the researcher changes the image for one of a circle. If the infant does not react to the novelty, it could mean that no difference was perceived. But if the fixation time on the new item increases, if "dishabituation" is observed, this suggests that the infant perceives the difference and is reacting with interest to the new stimulus. Similarly, infants have a tendency to look longer at "surprising" events, such as an object disappearing or violating some physical rules (such as a solid object passing through another solid object instead of colliding with it). Our brain reacts to novelty and surprises because we need to quickly learn and adjust to any new element from our environment; we are conditioned to react to novelty and surprise, so to speak. However, if too many things are new at a given time, this can be felt as overwhelming because there are too many stimuli that demand our attention, and this can be exhausting (see Chapter 5 about attention).

A somewhat similar reaction happens with games. Once players are comfortable with the game world, controls, and rules, introducing novelty or surprise will break automatic behaviors and stimulate players' attention and curiosity. The novelty can be expected, such as acquiring the mind-controlling abilities in *Middle-earth: Shadow of Mordor* (Monolith), which offers a quite satisfying novelty in combat when those filthy Uruks start fighting for you. The novelty could be in the shape of an exotic gameplay mission whereby a mechanic is removed to create the novelty. For example, in the *Uncharted* series, the navigation mechanic is removed by placing players inside a vehicle moving autonomously so they only need to aim and shoot. When the novelty is completely unexpected, it's a surprise. In *Fortnite*, for example, players are used to opening chests as they find them in the world. At some point in the game, though, some chests are zombies in disguise that attack players as they innocently try to open those chests. Although it is essential for game feel and usability to ensure that the game world and input outcomes are predictable and consistent, it is also important to introduce some novelty and surprise every once in a while to raise players' awareness and refresh their interest. Be careful about what you keep as a surprise, though; revealing a whole new area of the game could be satisfying for players still engaged, but you might have lost other players on the way there if they failed to identify long-term goals. This is completely anecdotal, so take it with a grain of salt because it has to do with my own biased and naïve perception of the game, but when I played *Shadow of Mordor*, I nearly churned before discovering a whole new area in which you can gain access to the most powerful and satisfying abilities (such as the ones when you mind-control enemies). I was frustrated while painfully progressing in the first area (the only one I thought existed until then) because I didn't feel any sense of mastery and the disgusting Uruks kept taunting me when they were defeating me (making cognitive reappraisal difficult...). I couldn't project my progression, and I didn't clearly identify a longer-term goal (i.e., discovering a whole new area). It's only because a friend of mine told me to keep going because it becomes exquisitely satisfying when the second area is discovered (thanks Jonathan!) that I persisted. And he was right; I greatly enjoyed my experience after reaching the second area, but I needed external encouragement to keep playing. So yes, offer novelty and surprises, but not at the expense of clear short-, mid-, and long-term goals and players' sense of progression. And remember that perception is subjective; not all players will be able to project their progression through careful examination of skill trees. To solve the *Shadow of Mordor* UX issue that I experienced, a "fog of war" could be used to tease players that a new area would be accessible at some point. It would show that something is there without revealing exactly what it was. Teasing curiosity and enabling discovery is important because discovery brings pleasure, and pleasure is what evolution has found to motivate humans in choosing an efficient behavior (Cabanac 1992; Anselme 2010).

12.4 Game Flow

Flow is a state of enjoyment when we are totally engaged and immersed in an activity that feels intrinsically motivating—for example, when you put a lot of effort into learning to play a musical piece that you deeply care about on the piano (see Chapter 6 about motivation). For psychologist Mihaly Csikszentmihalyi, flow is the secret to happiness because people seem to be happiest when they experience this sense of optimal and meaningful experience (Csikszentmihalyi 1990). As he puts it, "The meaning of life is meaning: Whatever it is, wherever it comes from, a unified purpose is what gives meaning to life," and this is what the state of flow is all about. This is the reason why the concept of flow is so important for engage-ability because meaning is a key concept in motivation. According to Csikszentmihalyi, there are eight components involved in the experience of flow:

- A challenging activity that requires skills (which we know we have a chance of completing).
- The merging of action and awareness (the person's attention is completely absorbed by the activity).
- Clear goals (when the goal is challenging to accomplish and is meaningful).
- Direct feedback (feedback is immediate and related to the goal).
- Concentration on the task at hand (we forget the unpleasant aspects of life and information that is irrelevant to the task).
- The sense of control (developing sufficient skills to master the task).
- The loss of self-consciousness (no room for self-scrutiny).
- The transformation of time (losing track of time).

These components are greatly relevant to video games. In fact, Sweetser and Wyeth (2005) have adapted the components of flow into "GameFlow" heuristics, offering an interesting model for evaluating player enjoyment in games. The GameFlow model consists of eight core elements: concentration, challenge, player skills, control, clear goals, feedback, immersion, and social. We have already tackled most of them through the UX lens. For example, the concentration component entails grabbing a player's attention and maintaining it. Therefore, it is mostly tied to signs and feedback and minimum workload related to what is not relevant to the core experience. The player skills component is related to motivation (e.g., competence and rewards) but also to the learning curve, which we describe later in this section. Control is mostly related to the 3Cs and to autonomy (within the motivation pillar). Clear goals are mostly related to competence (within the motivation pillar). Feedback is obviously part of the signs and feedback usability pillar. Immersion is partly related to game feel but also to the game flow components described here. Lastly, social interaction is mainly connected to relatedness (within the motivation pillar) and social presence (within the game feel pillar). The one GameFlow component that we haven't discussed yet is challenge. Beyond this evaluation model, the concept of flow was also concretely and compellingly implemented by game designer Jenova Chen in games such as *Flow* or *Journey* (Thatgamecompany).

As you can see, a large number of game UX concepts overlap among different frameworks and theories, which explains why unifying these frameworks is particularly challenging. This also explains why it is probably impossible to strictly and independently categorize UX pillars and components. Consequently, in this section, we will more specifically tackle the game flow components related to the difficulty curve (level of challenge, pacing, and pressure felt by players) and learning curve (a particular type of challenge that needs to be considered separately given its importance). As always, these components are not independent of each other.

12.4.1 Difficulty Curve: Challenge and Pacing

Defining challenge is central to game design, and the level of challenge *perceived* is at the core of the traditional definition of flow in games. As the game progresses, the player should ideally be in the "flow zone," wherein the challenge is never too easy or too hard (Chen 2007). A game that is too easy or too simple (relative to what your audience experiences—not what developers experience as they play and evaluate their game under the curse of knowledge) can lead to loss of attention and become boring. On the other hand, a game that is overly challenging—to a point where players don't feel that they can overcome the challenge—will raise anxiety and become too frustrating (see Figure 12.4). The level of challenge needed will differ depending on a player's expertise; players with different level of expertise have different flow zones, with the most expert and hardcore players usually needing a more challenging experience than the most novice or casual ones. One way to accommodate the different flow zones is to offer variable levels of difficulty that players can choose from (e.g., relaxed, normal, hard, nightmare, sadistic, up to eleven, etc.). Another way to address it is to use a dynamic difficulty adjustment system based on a player's skill and performance, but it's also much more complicated to implement and to fine-tune. Jenova Chen instead proposes focusing on a way for players to control their own

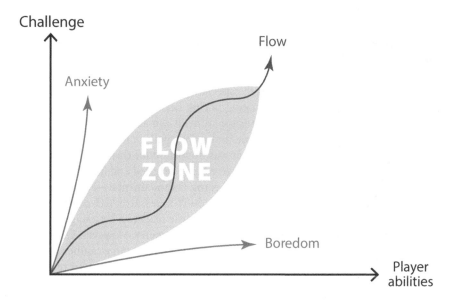

Figure 12.4

Game flow.

flow experience by offering a wide spectrum of activities and difficulties so that each player can choose to navigate in the game however they want and to set their own level of challenge.

In any case, for players to experience game flow, a good balance of the relationship between challenge and a player's ability must be found, and it shouldn't be linear. First of all, the beginning of the experience (i.e., onboarding) should be easy and rewarding because players are discovering the game and have a lot of things to process. We will talk about onboarding and the learning curve in more detail in a moment, but it's something to keep in mind. The other important thing to keep in mind is that, if the level of challenge of the game linearly increases with player's mastery (ability), then it might be difficult for players to have a sense of growth and progression, which is critical to motivation. This is the reason why a sinusoidal curve is represented inside the flow zone in Figure 12.4. Ideally, you want to offer moments of deep challenge alternated with moments that are less challenging, so players can lower their awareness, relax for a moment, and simply feel awesome as they are easily dominating enemies or the situation for a little while. This is what game designers call the "challenge saw tooth," and it's paramount to expressing a player's mastery. There are various ways to design a challenge saw tooth, and creative director Darren Sugg gives examples in the following essay. A simple way would be to let players encounter enemies of a much lower-level every once in a while, and it's even better if players can clearly recognize that these enemies were previously challenging to defeat. *Shadow of Mordor* offers a great example of that, especially because players can keep track of the Uruk captains who previously defeated them. Another example would be in *World of Warcraft*, where players sometimes need to (or choose to) go back to lower-level areas populated with less-challenging enemies. Setting the right level of challenge at the right time is key, but it's also, well, challenging. Game developers have a tendency to overestimate the right level of challenge needed, mainly because as they are playing the game themselves over and over, they usually feel less challenged as compared to a first-time player (i.e., curse of knowledge), especially QA testers who know the game inside out. A game that is seen as being boring because it's too easy can make some players churn, but a game that is too difficult can also make players churn, especially if they die early in the game and if their failure feels unfair. This can happen when players did not learn what was important for them to succeed, or if they did not fully understand why they were being defeated and how to overcome obstacles. This is why polishing the onboarding is fundamental—and even more so in free-to-play games with which players don't necessarily feel committed to engage. Balancing difficulty is tricky until the game reaches a beta stage and can be experienced by a large audience tracked with telemetry. However, UX testing your game via playtests, whereby a small sample of your target audience plays through your game as if they were at home, with no guidance from user researchers, will give you precious hints regarding the level of difficulty experienced by players. Playtesting your game will be incredibly informative for you, even at the early stages of development and more specifically when you design the onboarding (because you *are* designing this critical part of the game early on, right?).

Pacing—determining the tempo of a game—is also an important component of challenge. It's impacted by the perceived pressure relative to the level of stress and cognitive load imposed on the player, including time constraints, harsh punishment for failures and missteps, or the need for sustained attention for long periods of time. A challenging enemy will be perceived as even more difficult to beat if it appears right after a sequence during which players had to deal with many things happening simultaneously for a long period of time. Player fatigue, therefore, has to be accounted for when balancing difficulty. It can be important to offer breathing spaces to players—for example, by playing a cutscene *after* some intense action if your game has cinematics (instead of before the action, if you need to be parsimonious with cutscenes given their production cost) or by varying activities that do not require the same level of attention. For example, combat generally implies more pressure and cognitive load because moments of inattention could easily result in a player getting hurt or killed, whereas navigation challenges can usually be experienced at the player's own pace, unless there is a time pressure (e.g., the avatar is chased by a gigantic boulder and therefore cannot stop and think). Be careful not to create a situation where difficulty increases dramatically with players' missteps, which could be considered unfair and stressful. Rogers (2014) uses the example of blood splatter that fills the screen the more a player gets hurt, with the screen growing dark when health is critical: This can be perceived as a punishment for players already in trouble because it brings an additional disadvantage of not being able to clearly see around them. It's very satisfying to be able escape death *in extremis*, so try to encourage this outcome instead. Another more efficient tool to control pacing is to use AI to adjust the game pressure depending on a player's assumed stress level. This is what *Left 4 Dead* (Valve) is doing. As explained by Rogers, the game uses an "AI director" that measures the supposed stress level of players using variables such as health level, skill mastery, and location. Depending on these variables, the AI director will adjust the number of zombies that spawn, the ammo and health generated, and so on. The most relevant pacing can be (depending on the player's performance *and* on the level of stress needed to offer the right level of challenge) the better the perceived game flow.

Darren Sugg, Creative Director at Epic Games

The Power of the Saw Tooth, or "Why You Need Variance in Challenge"

First off, the idea of saw tooth difficulty isn't an original one. It is a staple of modern game development. So, as we look at the reasons people play games, it's often for their personal sense of fun and the thrill of "winning." In this case, we define winning as the thrill of meeting the challenge the crafty (or cruel) game designers have put before players. Did you ever stop and think about how game designers create and regulate the amount of difficulty they throw at players? Here are a few guidelines that might help in creating a challenging experience.

1. Agree on your audience. This is essential to how you can craft your experience. Some game difficulty curves rise quickly, demanding players adapt and overcome challenges like an octopus on ten espressos, while other games choose an easier curve relying on things like adaptive difficulty or user selection of difficulty in order to maintain challenge. The difficulty controls you should design are frequently determined by the audience for the game.

2. Once you've settled on how much difficulty you'd like to have in your game, you should endeavor to create a fixed level of challenge that progresses over time along your agreed-upon challenge curve.

3. Continue to give the player more power and ability to overcome the challenge curve at various points in time (thus forming the saw tooth). A good example: One room before your boss creature, the player unlocks a new ability and is able to kick the butt of mundane enemies with very little skill only to be challenged by a boss who requires the player to have developed true mastery of their newfound power in order to succeed.

4. Allow players to feel masterful and awesome at the height of their power and continue to introduce new enemies that balance out their newly found skill/power.

5. When players are about to get bored with being so awesome using their new skill or incredibly powerful weapon (which would make them exit their flow state), it's time to introduce a new enemy who can counter or survive their newly boosted power. This then requires the player to pursue a new skill or to gather a new weapon to recapture their previous "badassery."

Let's examine this principle as applied to our fictional game called *Crypts & Creeps*. When players first begin their adventure in *Crypts & Creeps*, they are a single adventurer with a rusty sword, with one type of attack called "quick stab." As players progress through the first level, they are faced with slow creatures that enable players to time their attacks in order to gain a sense of mastery. However, as players progress, they begin to encounter creatures that are more numerous and a bit faster, and "quick stab" just isn't enough. Before the game introduces hordes of them, players unlock a timing-based attack called "energetic slash" that, when unleashed at the right time, can slay these fast imps in one wide slash—another opportunity for mastery. Just as this attack "should" be mastered, the game introduces a boss that requires the use of both attack types to win. If the player learns these attacks (and the difficulty curve to learn should be determined by the type of audience the game is trying to serve), they will then beat the vile creep to much heroic fanfare.

In order to take *Crypts & Creeps* to the next level of polish, the game should also include some bets on what the player would do in real life after their exhausting boss fight. They'll probably need a break afterward. Some users even end a session after a tough level. When the user takes on the next level, a good potential flow would be to have them faced with the same enemies as last time for the first minute or two, so they can once again get into their flow AND feel powerful before being introduced to the next challenge.

So when you are at a loss as to how to create the right flow for your game's challenge, always remember the basics of the saw tooth structure as it can shortcut some of your iteration.

12.4.2 Learning Curve and Onboarding

One key for an engaging game is for it to be "easy to learn and difficult to master" (attributed to Atari founder Nolan Bushnell). A video game is a learning experience: The first minutes or hours of play are about learning how to play (i.e., onboarding), and the rest of the experience is about learning how to master the game and often about learning new mechanics along the way. Part I of this book gives an overview of how the brain processes information, how it learns, and Chapter 8 describes some learning principles. All this "gamer's brain" knowledge can be directly applicable to game design, level design, UI design, interaction design, sound design, and, well, pretty much everything in your game that players will perceive, feel, think about, and interact with. To offer a good learning curve, the first important thing will be to refine all the signs and feedback, provide good form follows function (i.e., affordances), and ensure that no critical usability issues are impairing players' understanding of the game. All the things that can be explained in the game through clear cues of what to do and clear and immediate feedback of what's going on and what is the outcome of player's actions will only facilitate the learning process while making it less patronizing than tutorial texts. Then, you need to craft the onboarding in such a way to ensure that all the key game mechanics, systems, and goals are efficiently taught. Generally, the best way to onboard players is to have them learn by doing, in context, with meaning. This means that, for the core features and the most difficult to grasp elements in your game, you will need to place the player in a meaningful situation justifying the need to learn something through guided experimentation with the environment, which is what I call a tutorial. A contextual tutorial is one that is well-integrated in a mission, allowing the player to experiment with a new mechanic in a situation at the moment it is taught. A meaningful tutorial is one that makes sense within the experience (relative to a player's current goal and interest) and piques the player's curiosity. Players must understand *why* it is meaningful for them to learn about a feature.

Let's use three examples to illustrate what I mean:

Example 1: No context and no meaning. Tutorials that are blocks of text pausing the game, that you read first before being able to execute the actions described, are tutorials without context. Players cannot learn as they do. In that condition, any sort of meaning is difficult to convey because the tutorial will be probably be interpreted by a player as receiving an annoying list of instructions.

Example 2: Context but no meaning. At the beginning of a platform game, a tutorial text is displayed onscreen, without pausing the game, instructing "Press X to jump." However, there is no meaningful reason at that moment for the player to jump because there is nothing to jump on to. This time, the tutorial is in context (players can jump as they are taught) but their motivation to practice the mechanic will be low.

Example 3: Context and meaning. Let's reuse the previous example, but this time, players can see some loot on an upper platform. Some tutorial text explaining about how to jump only pops up after a few seconds *if* players haven't figured it out on their own. This time, the instruction is much more meaningful because the mechanic is taught as a means to an end, which should enhance player's motivation to learn about this mechanic.

The examples I'm using here are very simple, but the same principle applies to teaching more complex mechanics and systems. The more complex a mechanic, the more you need to provide a deeply meaningful and contextual learning experience. Learning that "sticks" requires active learning. Remember that the deeper the process, the better the retention. Therefore, key mechanics need to be taught through situations requiring players to allocate their cognitive resources to learning the mechanics, while removing all other distractions to avoid cognitive overload. This is why you need to define your onboarding plan (see Chapter 13) and consider tutorials not as patronizing instructions to follow but as learning experiences that are part of the level design itself. Consider learning the game as an integral part of the game user experience—because it is.

Some designers consider tutorials controlling and would rather avoid them in the hope of letting players be autonomous and have the satisfaction of learning the game on their own. This perspective is a misconception for two main reasons. First, tutorials don't necessarily have to feel patronizing and controlling. If they are designed carefully (i.e., contextual and meaning learning by doing) and well-integrated to the level design, players should feel in control instead of being bossed around. Second, players actually will *not* feel in control, competent, or autonomous if they do not understand what they have to do and, more importantly, *why*. If some players get lost, you increase the chance of seeing them churn. And even if some hardcore players complain about tutorials and tell you that they don't need them, UX tests usually reveal that they misunderstand or completely omit important elements of a game when it lacks proper tutorials, and they can view a game negatively because of this. That is why it is not particularly useful to ask players if they found the game easy to understand—beyond the mere assessment of their perception—because most will reply that it was clear enough. However, asking them objective questions about the purpose of an item or the goal of a mission will be much more informative. We will discuss some user research tips in Chapter 14. All in all, it is up to you to design compelling tutorials, but this is difficult, requires a lot of test-retest loops, and therefore needs to be considered very early on. When tutorials and the overall onboarding is overlooked, games generally end up with screens of tutorial texts that won't be efficient for teaching players or that will be considered annoying, or both.

When you design your onboarding, you will have to pay close attention to how teaching mechanics or systems is distributed over time. Remember that distributed learning is much more efficient than massed learning. So, be careful about how many elements you are trying to teach at the same time and pace this out depending on the complexity of the learning (which is not easy to define, but give it your best guess depending on how familiar the feature should be to your audience and, hopefully, based on early UX tests). Mind players' cognitive load during the onboarding because this is not the time to challenge them if they are not yet familiar with the game mechanics. The other element you need to consider is to *not* punish players as they are learning new mechanics. By punishment, I mean a frustrating failure or an unfair death. For example, the first time that players learn to jump over a precipice, don't make them die and go through the pain of a reload if they miss their jump and fall down the precipice. Instead, consider ensuring that the fall won't be fatal and provide a ladder so that the player can climb up and try again. Players should definitely receive clear feedback that the action attempted was not effective. By all means, hurt the avatar—because players' actions should have consequences. But do not punish them too harshly when they are learning. Dying as a player learns will likely feel unfair, and unfairness is a strong negative feeling you will usually want to avoid. Players should feel encouraged to try again and be excited at the idea of progressing. They should not feel incompetent and clueless. Of course, once players start to master a mechanic, feel free to challenge them accordingly. Dying can then be fine if players understand why they died and how to overcome their failure, and it will only make future success more meaningful and satisfying.

To sum up, designing for game flow implies accounting for the level of challenge (difficulty curve), the amount of pressure (pacing), and it requires distributed learning by doing (learning curve), preferentially through level design. One last thing to keep in mind is to avoid "flow breakers." These are frictions in the game that are intense enough to break a player's suspension of disbelief. Flow breakers can take the shape of unfair or misunderstood deaths and failures, taking player's control away through a screen freeze (usually to insert a non-contextual and nonmeaningful tutorial text) or a camera pan, a cutscene that is too long, making players lose hard-won possessions (loss aversion is a strong phenomenon), too harsh of a punishment, a seemingly insurmountable obstacle, and so on.

Overall, this UX framework can guide you in considering the usability and the engage-ability a game offers to a target audience. The UX pillars described constitute, in my experience, the main ingredients influencing the enjoyment and success of a game. Whereas usability pillars are about removing unnecessary friction points, engage-ability pillars are about enhancing player engagement, through motivation, emotion, and game flow (see an example of how to use engage-ability pillars for the UX of casino games in the following essay by Anouk Ben-Tchavtchavadze). You will find an overall summary and a UX pillar checklist in Chapter 17.

Anouk Ben-Tchavtchavadze, Lead User Experience (UX) Designer at King

UX of Social Casino Games

You may say that social casino games are not your cup of tea, but looking at what makes a successful slot machine can help to show how the casino industry has used psychological principles to improve their games' UX and, consequently, to have great retention and engagement. When working on social casino games, you quickly understand how important motivation, emotion, and game flow are to the success of your games.

MOTIVATION: VOLATILE REWARDS, BONUS ROUNDS, AND PLAYER TYPES

Rewards are front and center in slot-machine design; players know and understand intuitively which symbols they are rooting for. Bonus rounds feature different types of mini games offering varied game play, a sense of excitement, and player agency. Players continue to play often not just for the rewards but for the bonus rounds themselves. When rewards are given or bonus rounds triggered, a long fanfare and show ensues, making everyone that witnesses the spectacle feel like a winner.

When speaking of design and math models, there are generally two types of slot machines: high volatility or low volatility. Machine payouts can be large but infrequent or frequent and small. Each type caters to a different audience and style of play. Understanding the different type of players and what motivates them has led to optimizing reward schedules and types in this manner and has become an industry standard and best practice.

EMOTION: THE IMPORTANCE OF WINNING AND AUTHENTICITY

There are common assumptions in gaming about losing. For example, you may believe that players on a losing streak expect to get lucky soon. However, we have seen in social casino games that engaged players are most likely to stop playing if they are on a losing streak. We have also seen that, after a big win, engaged players are more likely to up their bet amounts and to continue playing. When loss aversion kicks in, this will make your players stop playing, but it can be countered by their winning as long as the game does not feel rigged—even if it is in the player's favor.

When looking at new player retention rates, we also see that players are less likely to retain if they lose their first few games. The importance of mastery and success in the first few games are crucial. When we look at weekly retention rates, we see that players that win 25% to 75% of the time retain and engage more. Either losing too much or winning too much can reduce retention and engagement.

GAME FLOW: CONTROL, CLARITY, AND CONCENTRATION

Studies show that players who engage with slots machines frequently do so to "turn their brains off" and relax—mostly to forget about the stress in their lives. Slot games are not complicated games; when done well, they have the right balance of user control, variation, and ease of use that keeps players attentive and focused on the simple task at hand. Providing strong feedback and clear rewards keeps players interested. Feedback comes in the form of rich animated visuals, sound, and haptic effects for full immersion, allowing players to relax and easily lose track of time.

13

Design Thinking

13.1 Iterative Cycle   13.3 Onboarding Plan

13.2 Affordances

Design thinking refers to the strategies applied to solve design problems by placing the user at the center of the process, while recognizing that this user has human capabilities and limitations. And it starts by understanding what the real issues are. It's a mindset allowing for human-centered design. "Human-centered design (HCD) is the process of ensuring that people's needs are met, that the resulting product is understandable and usable, that it accomplishes the desired tasks, and the experience of use is positive and enjoyable," says Don Norman (2013). Of course, when it comes to games, the product also has to be fun, or *engage-able*. In the game industry, HCD is sometimes called the player-centric approach (Fullerton 2014) and can be described as considering the user experience during the development process. This approach entails an iterative cycle that will be repeated until the design is satisfying. It entails (but is not limited to) prototyping ideas, testing them with a representative sample of your audience, and iterating.

According to Norman (2013), the iterative loop consists of observation—idea generation—prototyping—testing, and it necessitates embracing failure. You need to fail early and frequently so that your iterative process can be fruitful and you truly nail the design you want to offer to your audience. However, many developers (including executives) do not understand this notion. "Why don't good designers get it right the first time? Ain't that their job?" I have heard many non-designers saying such things, and it's mostly followed by "Even I would have done a better job on the first pass, it's just about applying common sense. I've got ideas." First, it is true that expert designers can create a good starting point (by applying design principles, usability pillars, and HCI principles); however, designing a great experience is inherently impossible to get right the first time because user experience is not inside the design, it's *relative to the user* (see Hartson and Pyla 2012). I am not a designer myself but a great part of my job is about trying to help designers figure out what user experience is evoked by their design. I can assure you that it's always easier to criticize design choices after the facts (i.e., hindsight bias). Only those who do nothing don't make mistakes, as we often say in French. Second, everybody can generate ideas. I have no doubt that anyone in the game industry, including players, can have brilliant ideas; there is no question about it. But simply having an idea is not enough. It's not even 15% of the work. Executing the idea is what truly matters. According to entrepreneur Guy Kawasaki, "Ideas are easy, implementation is hard." A great idea implemented poorly can end up being worse than an average idea carefully nurtured and matured. In the end, it's not what the "people with ideas" had in mind that matters the most; it's how the end user will experience the product. This is why the "common sense" argument is a fallacy (see Chapter 10 describing UX misconceptions). As Don Norman pointed out, design thinking is not about finding solutions, it's about finding what the real issues are relative to what experience is desired for users. It's about solving *the right* problem. It's about considering a wide range of potential solutions and choosing the one that makes the most sense for your project. Often, the solution chosen isn't perfect, but it should be the most suitable for your design intent. Supercell developers explained in an interview for *VentureBeat* that they killed 14 games before they were able to successfully launch their fourth game, *Clash Royale* (see Takahashi 2016). Design thinking is about making the right trade-offs all throughout the development cycle and sometimes even across the studio.

In the next section, John Ballantyne, game technology lead at Oculus Story Studio, gives us an interesting example of a UX design challenge in virtual reality. I will include some more examples below of how a UX process can impact design here, but I won't get into the weeds of game design, interaction design, or user interface (UI) design, especially because I am not a designer myself. This section is therefore more about the design process, as seen through the broad UX lens.

John Ballantyne, Game Technology Lead at Oculus Story Studio

User Experience (UX) Design Challenges in Virtual Reality

Virtual reality (VR) poses many interesting challenges to content development. Not least among them is that, in VR, the user brings more of themselves into the experience than in any other medium. This has caused UX design considerations to jump to the forefront of our process at Story Studio.

As a small example, in games, we have taken for granted that the player avatar is always the same size (e.g., Master Chief is seven feet tall). However, in VR, people of different sizes will remain different sizes in most positionally tracked VR experiences. This happens because an experience will often feel "wrong" if a user is positioned such that their real-world feet are either above or below the virtual floor. Users will feel they are either buried in the world geometry or floating above it. In order to get a user's feet in the correct location, we need to effectively adjust the camera height in-game to be reflective of their real-world height.

It turns out that experience design changes in some interesting ways when the avatar is no longer the same size. We have discovered small edge cases such as very tall people being taller than trigger volumes and breaking scripting. But we have found bigger experience–design challenges such as players potentially not feeling "heroic" because they are short in real life and thus also short in the game world. Can you still feel like a super powerful Master Chief if you are shorter than all the NPCs (non-player characters) in the experience?

We have found that we have to test our experiences over a very diverse set of users as we prototype our mechanics and set designs. Beyond typical user segments that we would test for game development, we must also now test over a wide variety of physical player attributes as well. This leads to new and challenging UX questions. How can we cater to people who can't, or don't want to, walk? How can we set a consistent narrative feeling for people of widely varied heights? How can we create a believable player avatar that caters to both men and women?

Answering these questions poses significant challenges to our development process. Thankfully, UX design practices provide us with a path forward. Like all science, the processes don't provide immediate answers, but they do provide a great framework for the pursuit of answers.

13.1 Iterative Cycle

Many things happen before entering the iterative cycle, which I won't discuss in great detail here. For example, a general game idea might have been proposed that the studio wants to explore (or is commissioned to develop), or a small group of developers might have been playing around with some prototypes, or a game jam has generated a broader idea for a game. Then, during the concept phase, game pillars, gameplay loops, and overall features are outlined, and hopefully, a target audience is chosen and defined (i.e., user) as well as design and business intents (i.e., experience). Once these pieces are in place, the iterative cycle will come on full speed during the preproduction phase because this is when most of the prototyping happens, and it should continue as long as the game is not done. Therefore, if you are working on a live game, the iterative cycle never really ends.

As Hartson and Pyla (2012) said, "Most interaction designs are born bad and the design teams spent the rest of their lifecycles in an iterative struggle for redemption."

The iterative cycle for a given feature consists of designing, prototyping or implementing, testing, analyzing, and then defining the design changes needed in order to refine the feature and go through the cycle again. This "enlightened trial and error" cycle (Kelley 2001) is a critical process in design. Ideally, you should start with paper prototypes (or the equivalent) in the first iterative loops, then move on to interactive prototypes, and only then should you start implementing the feature to test again. Prototyping before implementing is beneficial, mainly because it's much more costly to change a design once implemented in the game engine than to tweak a cheap prototype. Also, it's a very natural human reaction to become attached to a feature. Therefore, if the feature is already implemented or already has polished art, it will be much harder for everyone to stay open to tear it all down if it turns out to not be working as intended. However, one of the main problems in product development is that, "The day a product development process starts, it is behind schedule and above budget," as Don Norman (2013) humorously pointed out. And this seems to be particularly true in the game industry, which is plagued with overtime (nicknamed crunch time). Because of that, fairly often a feature can be implemented without being truly designed—let alone prototyped and tested. "There's no time!" Tight deadlines and/or a weak production process can lead developers to cram features in as fast as they can so they can ship the game on schedule and hope it won't collapse. Unfortunately, at least in my experience, it does collapse when implementation is too rushed. The game or the update/patch may have been shipped on time, and some revenue may have been made, but it often turns out that either more players than expected churned or that less players than expected bought the monetization items that were critical to the financial health of the game. And when the new features are finally tested (too late) in a UX lab, critical UX issues that could have been avoided, or at least improved, are often easily identified. Once a feature is committed, it is extremely difficult to change the system because then it is harder to concede that drastic changes might be needed. And if these changes are implemented, they will likely impact all of the production in ripple effects. Therefore, even if paper prototyping and continued iteration before implementation may appear to be a waste of time at first glance, keep in mind that this process will likely save precious time and money down the road. Consider iterative cycles as an investment for the future. As Frederic Markus, president of Feerik Games, explains in the essay later in this chapter, prototyping "just works," especially when including user research in the loop.

The testing part of the iterative cycle is what concerns UX practitioners the most. This evaluation must be guided by the predefined UX goals (i.e., how is the player supposed to understand and interact with the feature) and executed using UX pillars and metrics. Carefully analyzing the results of a test is of the utmost importance. Cognitive biases and hastily jumping to conclusions are a threat to every developer (even the UX people, but they should at least be aware of these biases). Some examples of user research methods and tips are described in Chapter 14. Keep in mind that experimental protocols are heavily standardized in academic research for very good reasons. A game studio may not have the luxury of following a strict standardized testing protocol, but the scientific method should at least be understood and applied as much as possible. Remember that design thinking is mostly about solving the *right* problems.

At some point in the development stages of your game (hopefully at the end of preproduction but usually during production), the iterative cycle won't only impact isolated features but entire systems or even the game as a whole. It will then be important to cut elements of your game that are not truly enhancing the experience you want to offer. We have a natural tendency to add more features even if the core experience is not yet nailed or if all the critical elements for a system to work properly aren't defined and implemented. Dan Ariely (2008) explained that humans couldn't stand the idea of closing doors on options. However, it's not the number of features that will matter the most, it's how compelling the experience is. The difference between the BlackBerry and the iPhone is often used as an illustration for this notion. BlackBerry was once the leader of the smartphone market and proposed many more features and functions than Apple's iPhone when it first came out. Yet the iPhone quickly became the new leader in this market. Purity is often described as being the ultimate goal for product design. The problem is that the depth of the experience is also important, especially in games. Therefore, you will need to identify the features that truly offer meaningful options and enhance gameplay depth, while determining which other features should be let go. Depth is good, but it usually comes with more complexity and, worse, more confusion. Confusion could create frustration and make players feel that they are losing control and autonomy, which could then lead them to churn. (Of course, we could also argue that a game lacking depth will become boring and also lead to player churn.) If you believe that a feature cannot be cut because the depth it provides is important to the gameplay experience, then it is essential to ensure that its representation in a game is not confusing (try to remove as much noise as possible in the interface to improve usability) or that it's introduced later once players have grasped how the core systems work. You may also want to put complicated features in a less prominent position in the UI, such that only the more experienced or determined players will be likely to find them.

Game design is a balancing act. There are no predetermined solutions. It will all depend on your production constraints (time, resources, budget, etc.) and your priorities. Try to keep in mind who is your user (because sometimes features are added more to please the developers than the audience) and what is the core experience you want to offer. This will help you adopt a player-centric approach as you define what trade-offs you should make (because you cannot have it all), what should be cut, and in what priority the important features will need to be implemented for the game UX.

Frederic Markus, President of Feerik Games

User Experience and Prototyping

I have enjoyed working on video game prototypes for many years; slowly but surely, the feeling grew that there was something bigger than gameplay and story involved in making a great game. It turns out that everything about a title—from the package, the installation on your console, to your computer, the first menu, the game, the ending... everything from sounds to color tones, every input—all these elements are, I found out (maybe a bit late) user experience—THE user experience as a whole.

The discovery that this was a field involving research in human behavior, the working of the brain, and so many other subjects was a breakthrough—the missing link among all industries involving users as their reason to exist—and it changed everything for me. It meant that we could learn user experience from other industries, that we could get what we experienced and observed by ourselves confirmed or disproved, and that we could implement processes.

Now this part about processes—the fact that this is completely in opposition to the belief that video games are all and only creative work—is what made me very curious. And it made sense.

The idea is to integrate users, as early as possible, in testing the quality of the experience, in getting feedback, in being open-minded about what we would get, and in reacting to it accordingly. The next step, of course, is to iterate, then test it again, and see what we have improved or not.

This loop is an iteration loop, and all I have learned in game prototyping is about iterating as often as possible. So actually including users from the very start of the design process, as unremarkable as it seems now, just works.

And the most amazing result of this integration? Because so many fields are involved in UX and so many things have been learned from it, we are now UX builders, with gameplay and story important satellites. The discovery is that a game gravitates around UX and not the other way around.

13.2 Affordances

As explained in Chapter 3 and in Chapter 11, perceiving an object affordance allows people to determine how an object could be used (Norman 2013). For example, a mug handle affords grasping. Affordance is an important concept in game design and UX in general because what is intuitive doesn't need to be learned (or remembered, consequently), thus requiring less attentional resources to process and understand. The more perceived affordances you have in the game, the less you need to explain how things work. This will improve both usability and game flow. Therefore, you need to polish the perceivable part of an affordance (i.e., signifier) so that it is perceived and understood accordingly. Hartson (2003) has defined four kinds of affordances:

- **Physical affordances**
  Physical affordances designate features that facilitate physically doing something. For example, some beer caps do not need a bottle opener; you can twist them open with your bare hands. That's a physical affordance. In video games, this could mean facilitating the physical action of pointing at a button with the cursor or the finger—for example, by making the button large enough. On mobile UI design, it could mean placing the most useful commands close to where the thumb rests to make interactive areas comfortable to reach. And so on. Fitts's law (see Chapter 10) is one important HCI principle that can be used to enhance physical affordance.
- **Cognitive affordances**
  Cognitive affordances help users to learn, understand, know about something, and decide what can be done with it. Button labels, icon shapes, and metaphors used to convey functionality, and so on—all are cognitive affordances. Form follows function is about cognitive affordances.
- **Sensory affordances**
  Sensory affordances are features that help the user sense something. It's about helping users to see, hear, and feel things. For example, using a font size large enough to be legible is a sensory affordance. Signifiers (or signs and feedback, as we call them in games) should be noticeable, discernable, legible, and audible. The clarity usability pillar is about sensory affordance.
- **Functional affordances**
  Functional affordances are design features that help users accomplish a certain task—for example, being able to sort items in an inventory. Item-comparison features, filtering, and pinning are functional affordances.

I have already stressed this several times, but polishing your affordances is a critical aspect in design. Affordances help players understand and use an interface. Ensure the usability of your signs and feedback and allow for form follows function. Avoid false cognitive affordances (see Chapter 11) that could confuse your players and frustrate them. For example, if an area of a map is not accessible to players, it should not look as if it were (that would be a false affordance). Work with user researchers (if you can) to test the affordances in your game early on. Are buttons easy to click on, are signs and feedback perceived and clear, do players understand the functionality of items only by looking at their shape, can they anticipate the behavior of an enemy by looking at its character design, can they understand what their immediate next goal is just by looking at the environment and without the use of walls of text, would certain tasks be made easier if players had different functionality available?

Thinking about features and systems through the lens of affordances can help you define how to convey their functionality as intuitively as possible in the game. Also, during the testing phase of the iterative cycle, keeping the different types of affordances in mind can help you ask your testers the most useful questions (e.g., showing a screenshot of the heads-up display and asking them what each element is) and find the most critical problems faster.

13.3 Onboarding Plan

Engaging your audience within the first minutes of play is a delicate endeavor and has become a critical aspect of development in the era of free-to-play games. If your game fails to captivate your audience's attention quickly, there won't even be any retention challenges to care about. When looking at the average cumulative playtime for free-to-play games that are considered successful (e.g., on SteamSpy. com), it is not rare to see that about 20% of the audience is already gone after only one hour of play, so that the first hour is critical to the first-time user experience (FTUE), during which most of the onboarding takes place.

Don't get me wrong, though, even a great onboarding experience does not guarantee success. As we saw in Chapter 12, engaging players for the long term is tremendously important, too. Also keep in mind that you may still onboard players even after hours of play whenever you have new features, systems, or events to introduce or teach. However, we will focus more specifically on the early onboarding here. As we saw in Chapter 12, one of the important aspects of the game flow pillar is the learning curve. You need to find an efficient way to teach your audience about how to play your game. You need to excite your players' curiosity. You need to make them feel competent and autonomous and allow them to project both their short-term and long-term growth in the game, all while minding their cognitive load to avoid confusing and overwhelming them. And everything needs to happen as fast as possible because you do not have a lot of time to reach your audience if they haven't paid for the game up-front. On a mobile device, this window can be very short, on the scale of minutes. This is why designing the onboarding and the tutorials can be particularly tricky if you want to do it right—that is, make the onboarding meaningful (engaging) and efficient (learning occurs). One way that I have found helpful in reaching this goal is to put together an onboarding plan. It works as follows: Designers create a list of every element the player has to learn in the game, categorized by overarching systems, and then define the most important elements to learn for the core experience because these will need to be handled with care. You'll end up with a massive list, but you can make the process easier by only focusing on what you believe are the most critical mechanics and systems for players to learn during the first hours of play. Use a spreadsheet; list all the elements in one column, one element per line. The other columns should have the following information:

- **Category** (overarching system)
- **Priority level** (to define the most important features in your game)
- **When** (when, approximately, should the teaching of the element take place; use integers to roughly define what should happen when. For example, tag "1" everything that should be taught during the first mission or the first 15 minutes, "2" what elements are taught in the second

mission, etc. Several elements may have the same number; this will be refined in the tutorial order column)

- **Tutorial order** (the order in which the teaching takes place; each element should have a unique number in this column so you can sort the table according to this order, for example 1.1, 1.2, 1.3, 2.1, 2.2, etc.)
- **Difficulty** (how difficult to learn do you anticipate the feature to be—e.g., difficult, moderate, simple)
- **Why** (define why it would be meaningful for players to learn this feature, how it will make them more competent, how it can help them achieve their goals. Doing so will help you create meaningful situations to teach the feature; e.g., "If I do not learn how to craft a weapon, I will be killed by the monsters")
- **How** (tutorial method you will use—through UI only, through learning by doing, through dynamic tutorial text, etc.)
- **Narrative wrapper** (once your list is ordered chronologically using the tutorial order filter, this will help you write the story that will support the onboarding plan)
- **UX feedback** (if you have UX specialists on your team, they can mention early UX test results or what they anticipate the difficulties for players could be)

You can see an example of an onboarding plan in Figure 13.1 using a few features from *Fortnite* as an illustration. Start by listing the features and assigning them both a system category and an importance number (e.g., 0 = critical feature, 1 = important, 2 = nice to have, 3 = if players never figure that out it's okay). Then define how difficult it will be for players to learn the feature. Knowing your audience and their prior knowledge will be important in figuring this one out. Having the help of a user researcher will be valuable, too. Overall, a mechanic that is common to many games and works the same as yours should be easy to grasp (e.g., shooting mechanic). By contrast, a mechanic that is specific to your game or is less standardized might be medium to difficult to learn and master (e.g., cover mechanic). Setting up an onboarding plan may seem daunting, but it will help you have a better understanding of what sort of cognitive load you will put your players under and if you can identify that too many features are taught at the same time (which will be easy using the spreadsheet sorting features); it will help you to spread it out. Remember that distributed learning is more efficient than massed learning, so this process will allow you to distribute the teaching more efficiently over time, depending on the difficulty of each feature (the more difficult the feature, the more cognitive load required, and the fewer other features you can teach at the same time). As a rule of thumb, try to avoid having two difficult features to teach one after the other. Once you think that you have attributed the right tutorial order for each feature, filter the tutorial column in ascending order; it will reveal your onboarding plan.

You do not necessarily have to complete every column for every single element, but I strongly recommend you at least fill out the "why" column for all the features that are not easy to learn. (By using "simple," "medium," and "hard" labels, you can

WHEN	Tutorial order	Category	WHAT	Difficulty	WHY (meaning)	HOW	Narrative wrapper
0	0	Metagame	Player controls a roster of heroes. Player is the Commander.	Moderate	I'm the Commander of many heroes. I can send them to missions and I get to control them during missions.	Learning by doing	Player is introduced to the concept of Commander: world needs saving from zombies and a stranded hero needs leadership during a mission. Player becomes Commander of this first hero.
1	1.1	Navigation	Basic movement controls.	Simple	I need to move around to explore.	Contextual tutorial text	Now the player controls the hero.
1	1.2	Shooting	Basic shooting controls.	Simple	I need to aim and shoot to destroy zombies efficiently.	Contextual tutorial text	Enemies are coming but player can shoot them from a safe place.
1	1.3	Harvesting	Materials for building and crafting can be found in the word.	Simple	I need to explore and harvest elements in the world to gather material to craft cool weapons and build cool forts.	Contextual tutorial text	Player's gun broke as last enemy was killed so harvesting is needed to craft some new.
1	1.4	Crafting	Basic crafting.	Moderate	I need to craft guns when none can be found in the world.	Learning by doing	Player can now craft a new gun.
1	1.5	Building	Placing a staircase piece.	Easy	A staircase allows me to reach unaccessible higher grounds.	Learning by doing	Player is in an underground cave and sees a chest above. Only stairs can get player there.
2	2.1	Metagame	Home base power is the most important element for player progression.	Difficult	I become more powerful the higher my home base power gets.	Learning by doing	As first mission is completed, player is introduced to home base power.
2	2.2	Building	Editing a door.	Moderate	Editing doors in walls allow me to get to the other side without having to destroy the wall.	Learning by doing	In the next mission, a strong wall takes too long to destroy but player can edit a door.
2	2.3	Building	Building entire forts to protect an objective.	Difficult	Forts needs to be strong enough so zombies cannot reach the thing I'm protecting. Traps can help me. I need doors to move around inside the fort.	Learning by doing	Player needs to prepare for a zombie invasion and is explained how to build an efficient fort.

Figure 13.1

Onboarding plan example.

13. Design Thinking

easily order the features by difficulty using the alphabetical filter.) Every feature that is not easy to learn should be taught more carefully and might also need repetition later on. These are the features your audience should learn by doing, in a meaningful context. Filling these cells out will help you define why these features should be meaningful to learn, using the player's perspective, and will allow you to think about a way to implement these learning experiences within the design early on.

This onboarding plan will also help you allocate the right amount of resources for each feature you have to teach. Usually, all the "simple" features can be taught via tutorial text or even dynamic tutorial text that is only displayed if players do not naturally execute the correct action (e.g., only display the tutorial tip explaining how to move if players haven't done so on their own within the first few seconds). After you start user testing your game, you might need to rearrange your plan because some features that you thought would be easy to teach may turn out to be more challenging for players to learn. You can also use this onboarding table to define which tutorial tips can be displayed on the loading screens and when. Because you will likely need to give reminders to players and repeat some tutorials, you can use loading screens to provide reminders or to give low-importance tips. Just be careful not to teach too much via text on a single screen. Don't explain more than three simple things and, if you are using loading screens to teach about mission rules, focus on the *why* (main goals) rather than the *how* (to reach these goals) or the *what* (items in game you need to interact with).

Using loading screens to teach about features is usually not very effective. However, it is a good way to occupy players because waiting can be painful. And it is also a matter of perception. For example, waiting times will seem shorter if:

- There is a progression bar that has animation on it.
- This progress bar accelerates (rather than decelerates and stops).
- If players have something to do while waiting (instead of looking at an empty screen).

So, while you should use loading screens to convey tutorial or gameplay tips, you shouldn't rely on them too heavily; keep in mind that players might not read the text if there's too much information or, if they do read it, they are not likely to remember much of it. Remember human limitations in perception, attention, and memory.

In summary, this onboarding methodology will allow you to make faster decisions and build hypotheses about the game and its experience that you will be able to test with playtest and analytics. It will also allow you to build the narrative wrapper that will bring all the pieces together to support the onboarding plan and the player's learning journey. If you start by defining the narrative (which is tempting because we all love stories), you will take the risk of needing to adjust your onboarding to the narrative, which could hurt the user experience (by hurting the learning curve). Just like any other discipline, narrative design should be at the service of gameplay, at the service of the user experience by taking into account player's motivation and game flow, and therefore should transcend the onboarding plan.

14

Game User Research

14.1 The Scientific Method
14.2 User Research
    Methodologies and
    Tools

14.3 Final User Research
    Tips

The main role of user research is to evaluate a game (or an app, a website, a tool interface, etc.) in terms of its ease of use and its propensity to engage players. User researchers will ruthlessly track down as many usability and "engage-ability" issues as possible and offer fix suggestions for the development team to consider. They can help developers challenge their curse of knowledge, take a step back, and see their game from a new perspective (the one of their target audience, who will be discovering the game). Their main mission is to identify the barriers getting in the way of a compelling user experience, while keeping in mind design intentions and business goals.

User research relies on two main tools to accomplish this mission: knowledge (i.e., cognitive science knowledge, human–computer interaction [HCI] and human factors principles, heuristics) and methodology (i.e., the scientific method). We have extensively covered the former all throughout this book, so let me introduce you to the scientific method should you not be familiar with it already.

14.1 The Scientific Method

The scientific method allows for a systematic way of thinking in order to find the solution to a problem or to answer a question. It's a hypothetico-deductive model whereby measurable evidence is gathered and analyzed using a standardized protocol in order to confirm or disprove a hypothesis without, hopefully, introducing any biases. The scientific method is an iterative process, which is not too far from a design-thinking iterative process. It usually starts with general theories, and then there is a conceptualization phase whereby scientists review the current literature about a specific subject, make some broad observations, and define questions to explore. The next steps are as follows: hypotheses—experimental protocol design—test—results and analysis—confirm, reject, or refine hypotheses—circle back to general theories (so that the same research-ers or other researchers can iterate on the findings). When researchers outline a hypothesis, they also postulate a "null hypothesis" stating that the variable tested does not have an impact. For example, applied to games, an experimental hypothesis could be: "Players who learned the rules of the game by doing die less often during the first hour of play than if they had simply read tutorial texts." A null hypothesis would be: "Players who learned the rules of the game by doing *do not* die less often during the first hour of play than if they had simply read tutorial texts." After the experiment is conducted and results are analyzed, if sig-nificance tests posit a likelihood of, typically, 95% or more that the results found cannot fit the null hypothesis, then it is rejected in favor of the experimental hypothesis. Experimental protocols must ensure that the difference measured between two groups (e.g., a learning-by-doing group and a learning-by-reading group) can truly be attributed to the variable developers are interested in (learn-ing by doing impact). For example, if it was determined that players who learned the mechanics and rules of the game in a learning-by-doing environment died less often than those who read tutorial text about the same content, and that this difference was statistically significant, it could be, for example, because reading took less time on average than learning by doing. Therefore, the effect measured could be caused by the difference in processing time instead of the type of learn-ing per se. And that's why research has rigorous standardized protocols in order to make sure the correct conclusions are drawn.

In academia, the experiment(s) can be described in a paper, reviewed by sci-entific peers, and then published in a journal, if the methodology was deemed solid, so that the whole scientific community can incorporate the findings within their own theoretical framework and subsequent experiments. At least, that's how it should be. The problem is that, when the null hypothesis cannot be rejected, researchers often don't bother to submit papers about their study, or when they do they are likely not accepted for publication. This is likely biasing some scientists to try too hard to confirm their experimental hypotheses (from introducing unconscious biases to intentional fraud), and it deprives the whole community of interesting results. Not finding an effect (i.e., not being able to reject the null hypothesis) *is* an interesting result as well. In his fascinating book, *In Search of Memory* (2006), Nobel Price recipient and neuropsychiatrist Eric Kandel recounts these words from neurophysiologist John Eccles, who won the Nobel Prize in 1963 for his work on the synapse: "I learned (…) to rejoice in the refutation of a cherished hypothesis, because that, too, is a scientific achievement and because much has been learned by refutation."

There is currently a "replication" crisis in many scientific disciplines (see Przybylski 2016), although there has been a lot of focus on the area of social psychology more specifically. Indeed, some results found in an original study aren't always replicated as the same experimental protocol is repeated by different researchers (or sometimes by the original researchers themselves). Being able to reproduce the outcome of an experiment is very important because it means that the methodology was solid, the biases reduced to a minimum, and the effect measured was not random. An inability to replicate is therefore concerning and probably contributes to public confusion, especially because these studies, before being found nonreplicable, are sometimes broadcast by the media through clickbait headlines removing all the caution and subtleties researchers usually have with their results. Sloppy experiments, conducted with loose protocols and small sample sizes, are probably hurting science's reputation. Moreover, some fraudulent practices, usually led by industries trying to convince people that their products are not dangerous so they will keep consuming them, are further generating doubt in people's minds. For example, it is a well-known fact that the tobacco industry corrupted scientists and experts to create controversy about established scientific findings linking smoking with cancer (see Saloojee and Dagli 2000). Also, think about the impact that *one* study had on the misled belief that vaccines increase the risk of autism. Only one study was enough to create doubt and feed on parents' fear of harming their children—even though it was later *completely discredited* because of a serious lack of rigor and despite the fact that *numerous studies* have found *no evidence* to support this hypothesis.

This increase in distrust of science is a real problem because it allows fake news (or "alternative facts") to thrive and for public opinion to be more easily manipulated, which could, by extension, perhaps complicate the life of a user researcher. Science is a commitment to find the truth; it should not be a competition to determine who is going to be right, nor should it be used as a tool to sway people's minds. It is therefore of the utmost importance that user researchers stay neutral. They are not here to push anyone's agenda. They should not give their "opinion." Instead, they should provide their analysis of a situation, using their scientific knowledge and data when available. A user researcher's job is to provide objective evidence to help developers make decisions while trying not to fall in love with the game, which could induce some biases. Although I believe it's important for user researchers on a project to be embedded in the game development team because trust needs to be established and they must collaborate closely, it also is important that they try to keep some emotional distance from the game itself or let other researchers conduct UX tests to avoid biasing the results. That being said, user research can be a very powerful tool to help developers identify very early on what *the right problems* to solve are, to define their severity order, and to find solutions.

14.2 User Research Methodologies and Tools

Although game user research uses the scientific method, game studios are not academic labs. They have games to ship, usually on tight deadlines. Game user research is therefore a balancing act between fast turnaround and scientific rigor, which is what user researcher Ian Livingston calls "good enough" research (Livingston 2016). Let's say, for example, that you design a test to measure the impact of one condition versus another, such as the time spent (in minutes) to complete a mission with a certain controller mapping (Condition A) versus a different mapping (Condition B). After you have measured the performance for each condition and calculated the standard deviation within each group (i.e., dispersion of the data values), you can look at the results with different confidence intervals (i.e., how much uncertainty lies in your data). In the fake data presented in Figure 14.1, for example, at a 95% confidence interval (which is usually the minimum required in research findings), the performance between the two conditions is not significantly different. However, by looking at the data with an 80% confidence interval, the conditions could be considered to be generating different player performances. Although an 80% confidence interval would certainly not be accepted in a research paper, it could be good enough to decide which controller mapping should be the default, and it's certainly better than making this decision without collecting any data. That being said, we usually don't even have the luxury of recruiting sufficient participants to have a large enough sample size to allow for such statistics when conducting user research; this is why we cannot easily compare different conditions in a UX lab. However, when sending surveys to a large sample or when collecting telemetry data during closed beta while modifying a few variables (i.e., A/B testing, whereby performance or the conversion rate observed with condition A is compared with condition B), defining an acceptable level of uncertainty will be important (see Chapter 15).

User research cannot be as rigorous as academic research, mostly because we usually cannot have large enough sample sizes to conduct quick tests each time

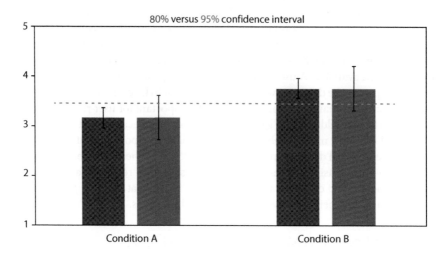

Figure 14.1

Confidence intervals. (Modified from Ian Livingston's Game UX Summit 2016 Presentation.)

the development team needs insights to make a decision. This is a limitation we must accept given the heavy constraints of game development (especially the time constraint), but this is why test protocols should carefully remove as many potential biases as possible. For example, recruited participants should match the audience profile to which the game is targeted; game developers should not interact with the test participants to avoid increasing their hype (gamers are usually pretty excited to test a game in development at the studio's offices); participants should not be able to watch what other participants are doing (to avoid peer pressure and to prevent them from understanding something by observing others playing, etc.); and participants should always be told that it's the game itself that is being tested not their ability to understand the game. A good practice is to make participants realize that all the difficulties they will encounter and all confusion they will want to report, even mild, will help improve the game for all players, including those who aren't as skilled as they are. (Otherwise, some participants may have a tendency to not report some confusion they might have because they do not want to appear incompetent at playing games.) Make sure to tell participants that the researchers and moderators interacting with them do not work directly on the game; therefore, their feelings cannot be hurt no matter how harsh the feedback. Participants have a tendency, in my experience, to be soft and tolerant, because they are mostly happy to play a game in development while being compensated. Remind them to give cold, blunt feedback, and to explain concisely *why* they loved or hated something. Whatever they do, UX test observers must stay as neutral as possible and must not react to what's happening—no laughter, no sighs, no cheering when participants finally overcome a hurdle, nothing. Participants should forget that they are being watched, if possible, and they should never feel that they are being judged in any way because, otherwise, it could influence their performance (e.g., see the "Pygmalion effect" or "Rosenthal effect," whereby teachers' expectation can influence students' performance; Rosenthal and Jacobson 1992). UX test observers should also be very careful not to infer any player intention from the behavior they observe. For example, if they observe some players spending a long time on the screen where they need to, say, name their base, observers should code the behavior as "stayed a long time on naming-base screen" and not immediately draw hasty conclusions, such as "players struggle with the naming-base interface." Maybe players were only thinking about what name they wanted to pick and were not struggling with the interface per se. It's only *after* analyzing data from observation notes, player performance in the game, and test survey answers that player intent and struggles can be inferred. But if the observation is already tainted with bias, it will pollute the rest of the analysis. So, be careful to stay neutral when you write down player behavior. Also be careful that game developers behind the one-way mirror don't draw hasty conclusions themselves. If it's highly beneficial that developers watch the test, they must understand that their own knowledge and expectations will bias the way they interpret what players are doing (and not doing). They should therefore wait until receiving the UX report before drawing conclusions about what players understand and intend to do in the game. The whole point of the scientific method is to avoid such biases; so make sure everyone understands why it is important.

Lastly, be sure participants sign a nondisclosure agreement (NDA), and remind them that they cannot talk to anyone about what they experience during the test. I have never experienced any leak originating from UX tests, but the risk is real and a leak would definitely hurt the trust between the user research team and the rest of the studio. It's usually a good practice to have participants empty their pockets and place all their recording devices (such as smartphones, USB keys, etc.) in a locker for which they keep the key.

Now, I'm going to give a quick description of the main user research methods and tools that can be used in the game industry (see also Lewis-Evans 2012). Most of them require recruiting participants that are representative of your core audience; therefore, you must have a good idea of who your core audience is. The recruitment part is particularly time-consuming because you need to find players in the correct age range you are targeting (certain legal constraints apply if you wish to recruit minors, so be extra mindful of that) who play games that are similar to yours at the frequency wanted (casually playing or intensely playing), and they need to be available at the time and date you wish to plan the test. So, make sure to plan to recruit ahead of time. It usually takes at least a week to find a good sample of players.

14.2.1 UX Tests

UX tests are the main methods utilized in game user research. They imply recruiting external participants (players representative of your target audience) who will interact with parts of your game (or website, application, etc.). Therefore, you will need to work closely with the development team and particularly with QA to ensure that you have a build that is good enough (i.e., not crashing all the time) and that does not contain bugs that would impact the elements you are interested in. For example, if you are testing a specific feature, a bug affecting that feature is a problem. Other non-severe bugs are fine, as long as you know how to work around them. For example, if choosing a particular hero or using a particular ability can break the game, you can instruct your participants not to use them. Depending on what development stage the game is at and what you are testing for, different types of UX tests can be used.

- Task analysis is when you want to see if players are able to complete a specific task in the game, such as building a deck of cards, for example. These tests are usually short, and specific metrics are measured—such as the time it takes to complete the task or the number of errors made by participants. It's useful to conduct these types of test using gym levels (testing rooms) to observe how fast players aim, if they overshoot or stop before the target, and so on. You can create all sorts of gym levels to test all sorts of things that would be important for game feel. You can also use specific tasks such as a card-sorting task when you are prototyping a feature. To use the example of a card deck builder, before anything is implemented, you can give players paper cards and ask them how they would create a deck for a specific hero. By looking at how players are organizing the cards in what categories, it can help you build a system that would be fitting their intuitive thought process. This task is often used on the Web to help design the information architecture of a site (e.g., what pages should go in what categories). Task analyses are conducted one on one (one participant at a time, observed by one researcher). It is usually recommended to test at least 15 participants, but that can be too time-consuming if you are in a rush to prototype and then implement a feature, so define how rigorous you can be.

- A usability test (or playtest) is when participants are playing parts of the game (not its entirety) and the focus is essentially about usability but also engage-ability issues. If some elements are not yet implemented in the game, you can give players paper information. For example, you can give the tutorial information on sheets of paper. These tests are usually conducted with several participants at the same time (usually around six, but it can be more if you are testing a multiplayer game needing a five vs. five configuration). Even though we know that multitasking is a myth, one moderator can observe two players at a time. Recordings are also taken of the game and can be reviewed later if time allows.

- Think aloud (or cognitive walk-through) is a specific way of conducting task analyses or usability tests whereby you ask participants to talk through what they are doing and their thought process. This is very useful for understanding what the first reaction of a player is in front of an interface and can give very good insights about what players expect. If you use this method, make sure to encourage participants to talk as they think and tell them that there is no wrong way of doing the task. It's the software that is being tested, not them. Encourage them to ask questions because it will reveal what they find confusing, but mention that you won't be able to answer most of them because you want to see if they can find the answers on their own. If they do ask questions, you can reply: "Well, what do you think?" Lastly, if they stop talking in the middle of a sentence, avoid completing the sentence yourself (that would be biasing their thought process) but simply repeat the last words. For example, if they say "I'm not sure how…" and then stop talking, simply say "You're not sure how?" It usually does the trick. This method has an important limitation that you must take into account: By asking people to talk through their thought process, you make them focus on a task much more than if they were left to their own devices. It means that they are more likely to figure out how a feature or system works. So keep in mind that it's more the time it takes them to figure out the task than the success or failure that is important to note. These tests must be conducted one on one, usually with about six participants.

- A playthrough test is when players will play through a large chunk of the game or its entirety. Although researchers will still be on the lookout for usability issues, the main purpose of these tests is to look for engage-ability issues, such as where the game is too easy, too difficult, where players stop being excited by specific goals, and so on. These tests usually require a larger sample size (if possible) because you want to cover player variability. However, these tests usually also require participants to come to the UX lab over several days (sometimes even a week), so it can be tricky to find enough participants who are available across multiple days. Also, given that closed beta (or alpha) are becoming more common and allow for a much larger sample, if you can get around eight players for a playthrough test, it would still be better than not doing any. Those tests are very good complements to analytics findings because they will offer good context (*why* players do the things they do) as to what the telemetry data is revealing (*what* most players are doing; see Chapter 15).

Depending on the studio, these tests can have different names. Moreover, some game developers sometimes label "playtest" the activity whereby they are themselves testing the game to discuss its features. I would agree with game designer Tracy Fullerton that these should not be called playtests but "internal design reviews" (Fullerton 2014). All the UX tests mentioned earlier require external participants who do not know anything about your game most of the time (unless your test requires players who already know about certain features). In any case, a test requires good preparation. Researchers conducting the tests (or researcher assistants, such as moderators or test analysts) must play through the build themselves (which is why it's important to have the build in advance) and prepare an observation sheet so that those observing the test can more quickly write down the issues they identify. It's also important to avoid writing down everything while observing the test and to instead focus on specific objectives. Some systems might not be completely finished, other features might have bugs, so it is more efficient to focus on what is ready for testing. (It's quite impossible to observe everything anyway.) Moreover, it's particularly irritating for game developers to receive some feedback about a feature or system that they know is not yet fully functional (unless they expressly asked for such preliminary feedback). And by "functional" I do not mean aesthetically attractive or polished; I mean that the feature can be used, even if it looks ugly or has placeholder elements. So, work with the development team to define the objectives of the test (more about test questions in a moment).

It's important for the development team members to be able to observe a test as it is happening—preferably behind a one-way mirror because it allows them to look over the players' shoulders without being seen. This will help developers to put themselves into players' shoes and to adopt a player-centered approach. Also, if developers observe the test together in a room (as opposed to individually via a live stream directly to their desktop computer), it will likely spark conversations about why players are not doing what was expected and what should be done to fix an issue. It's my favorite part of UX tests—being behind the one-way mirror, listening to what developers have to say, what they truly intended, and why they believe players are behaving unexpectedly. In my experience, it's a critical part of the user research process to build trust with the development team and make them participate in the study. It will also allow user researchers to ask questions about the intentions behind specific features or systems. As an example, Figure 14.2 shows how Epic Games' UX lab is organized. You can see the testing room, where the participants would be playing while the test observers behind them would be observing gameplay via the overhead screens. And you can see the "secret room" (or the "speakeasy room" as we like to call it) where the UX researcher in charge of the test and development team members would watch what's going on and discuss everything. (This room is entirely soundproofed, so developers can express their frustration loudly—watching a UX test can be painful at times, when you realize that what you thought would work is actually not working.)

Several tools can be used during UX tests. The most important of all are observation and the notes taken by the observers of the test. These notes will be compiled at the end of the day and compared with those of other observers when applicable, so that the researcher in charge of the study can have a good idea of what players were able to do easily, what they had difficulty with, and what they misunderstood or missed completely. Another useful tool is to record the sessions, so you can replay a section and extract clips to include in the UX report. You can use the free and open source Open Broadcaster Software (OBS), which allows you to record and stream from multiple sources, such as the gameplay and a webcam pointing at players' faces. (However, I do not recommend relying on players' facial expressions because they can be very misleading, unless you have a powerful tool that can identify micro-expressions.) Eye tracking is another great tool to use, especially to enhance observation. Some cheap eye-tracking cameras can now be embedded directly in OBS; they allow test observers to see, as an overlay, where players are looking on the overhead screens. Note that eye tracking

Figure 14.2

Epic Games' UX lab. (Courtesy of Bill Green, © 2014, Epic Games, Inc.)

allows you to see a player's gaze but not necessarily what they are paying attention to. Some eye-tracking software can allow you to create heat maps in order to see what, on average, people are looking at. Eye-tracking heat maps can be useful especially for still elements (e.g., heads-up display [HUD]) or for invariably short experiences (e.g., trailers); otherwise, the cost (in time, mostly) often is not justified for the benefits gained when compared to efficient observation. Another useful tool would be to add a controller or keyboard overlay via OBS, such as Nohboard, which allows test observers to see what keys players are pressing from the overhead screen. Lastly, you can add the local time on the OBS video, using Snaz, allowing you to monitor more precisely how much time is needed for players to complete a task. Most of these tools (except for the eye-tracking cameras, the overhead screens, and the material needed for participants to play the game) are free. You can see an example of what a UX test recording looks like in Figure 14.3, from Epic Games' UX lab. (That's me playing *Fortnite* to show you what it looks like—without compromising participants' privacy.) If you have a fancy lab, you can think of adding biometrics, such as galvanic skin response (GSR), which measures sweat activity from players' fingers to identify when they are getting emotionally aroused—although it doesn't tell you about the valence of the emotion (negative or positive). At the moment, however, biometrics such as galvanic skin response and others aren't really practical to use. They are costly, and the data analysis takes a lot of time. They could be interesting to use for short sessions or to test trailers. Otherwise, well-prepared and rigorous observation remains your best tool to date in game user research. One last "tool" you should use is to have participants answer surveys from time to time. If prepared

Figure 14.3

Example of a UX Test Capture at Epic Games, used with permission.

well, a survey can be more efficient than an interview because it's less biased. (Answering a survey doesn't require dealing with human interaction, which can induce all sorts of biases.) I'm describing surveys in greater details below, but use them regularly during a UX test session and especially with screenshots of what participants have just experienced, asking them to describe the elements on the screen and what they do. Surveys will tell you what players have understood and misunderstood in the game.

After a UX test is done and the data analyzed, the user researcher in charge will produce a UX report listing all the UX issues encountered, usually categorizing them by type (UI, tutorial, metagame, etc.) and severity (critical, medium, low). The severity depends on how much of a blocker the issue was for players and how much frustration resulted from it but also what feature was affected. If a UX issue affects a core pillar of the game, or monetization features, the severity might be heightened even if players finally find a workaround. Some features cannot allow any level of friction, or you might lose players with little patience and a large library of other free-to-play games to try. Reports should have a short headline describing the issue, another part describing the issue in greater detail—preferably by adding screenshots or clips taken from the recording of the session. Lastly, it should *suggest* some possible fixes, depending on developers' objectives. Make sure that these suggestions do not sound bossy. They are meant to clarify the issue and offer options—not to make the developers feel that you want to design the game for them. Don't forget to add what was good in the report, too! If the test had the main objective of testing the understanding of the HUD, do not only mention what players had issues with, also mention what parts of the HUD were efficient. Lastly, if what was a UX issue in a previous build is no longer an issue, mention it, too. It's important to celebrate UX victories, even the small ones.

14.2.2 Surveys

You can use surveys during UX tests or send them out to your closed beta participants, for example. Surveys can be a very powerful tool, if used with caution. Like neuroscientist Joseph LeDoux (1996) said, "Introspection is often a blurry window into the workings of the mind. And if there is one thing about emotions that we know well from introspection, it is that we are often in the dark about why we feel the way we do." If you need to explore what players felt about your game, try to be as precise as you can be in your questions. For example, if you ask them if they found the game difficult, fun, or confusing, make sure to ask them to explain why as well. Ask them to mention their top three favorite things and top three least favorite things about the game and why. Also, when trying to find out how players would define the game, we ask them how they would describe it to a friend. This will help respondents focus on more tangible elements rather than vague emotions that are not always easy to describe. Try, as much as possible, to ask them objective questions, especially regarding usability. For example, instead of asking if they found the tutorial mission clear, ask them what they remember having learned during this mission. You can ask them if they found the HUD clear at first, to measure their perception, but then show them a screenshot of the HUD, with a letter associated with each element, and ask them to describe what they believe each element does.

When designing a survey, only ask one question at a time. For example, if you ask "Was this ability clear to use and powerful?" you won't know if respondents' answers are about the ease of use or the feeling of power the ability gave them. Also, make sure to avoid leading questions. For example, instead of asking "Did you find [name ability] powerful?" ask "How would you describe [ability]?" with an open-ended answer. If your survey needs to be sent to hundreds of respondents (or more!), it would be better to avoid open-ended questions as much as possible (that would later need text analysis) and propose a seven-point "Likert scale" question (or five points if you don't need granularity or have a smaller sample). For example, you can ask respondents to indicate how much they agree with certain claims, such as "abilities made me feel powerful in the game," with the following possible responses: strongly disagree, disagree, somewhat disagree, neither disagree nor agree, somewhat agree, agree, strongly agree. These types of questions will be very useful to measure how engaging your game is and to see what needs tweaking. Think about the core pillars of your game and the core experience you want to offer and go through the engage-ability pillars to build your Likert scale questions. Ask about how much they felt compelled to pursue specific goals, if they found that teammates were helpful, if they were feeling helpful toward others, if they felt they were progressing in the game, if they felt a sense of mastery, if they found that interacting with the interface was pleasant, if they found the game too difficult/too easy, if they felt in control, if they believed they had meaningful choices, and so on. This will help you identify the strengths and weaknesses of your game in terms of engage-ability, so you can decide if you should try to focus on the weak areas of your game or double down on its strengths. You can make your own questionnaire or use existing ones, such as the player experience inventory (see Abeele *et al.* 2016), the game engagement questionnaire (which can be requested online at http://www.gamexplab. nl/), the immersive experience questionnaire (which you can find online at the UCL Interaction Centre website, see also Jennett *et al.* 2008), or the player experience of need satisfaction questionnaire (which is copyrighted, see Przybylski *et al.* 2010). One study suggested that the three last questionnaires mentioned here showed considerable convergence (Denisova *et al.* 2016). Whatever type of survey you choose, make sure to use simple wording and to try to keep it short. Add a progression bar on your questionnaire because, as you know, people like to see their progress toward an end goal.

14.2.3 Heuristic Evaluations

A heuristic evaluation is conducted by a UX expert (or, preferentially, by several) to evaluate the usability and engage-ability of a game. Heuristics, or rules of thumb, are used as guidelines. The usability and engage-ability pillars described in Chapters 11 and 12 are examples of heuristics, although experts would use a much more exhaustive list. This method can be useful when you need to evaluate a game in a very rough stage or when you cannot conduct UX tests. Note, however, that UX tests will still be needed to determine most of the UX issues because nothing can replace observing your target audience as they try to figure out your game. After a heuristic evaluation is conducted, the researcher in charge writes a report to send out to the game team.

14.2.4 Rapid Internal Tests

Rapid internal tests can be done using employees that do not know anything about a specific feature of the game in order to quickly test iterations on this feature. For example, you test a feature with a colleague, you tweak the design according to your observations and your colleague's feedback, then you retest again with another colleague, and so on. Researchers Medlock *et al.* (2002) from Microsoft Games Studios have been developing such a method, which they called rapid iterative testing and evaluation (or RITE). It's very similar to a task analysis test, but it focuses on a very narrow aspect of the game—one feature for example—iteration after iteration for a quick turnaround. It could be done with external participants (always better!), although I would recommend using this method with internal employees simply because recruiting external participants takes time and might be overkill for narrow tests like these. Using internal participants induces heavy biases, given that game developers have a very different view of games than gamers and that they probably know the person who has designed the feature tested. However, internal participants can provide some good feedback until UX tests can be conducted.

14.2.5 Personas

The persona method allows defining a fictional player who will represent the core audience for the game. The process involves the marketing team bringing their market segmentation and the development team bringing their core pillars and the experience they want to offer in order to make a first assessment of who the audience might be. Then, some interviews with users within the target audience will help define what their goals, desires, and expectations are for the type of game in development. In the end, a fictional character will be created, with a name, a photo, and a summary of this persona's goals, expectations, desires, and so on. It's much more relatable and memorable than a market segmentation, and it allows everyone to focus on a human instead of a market. I find the process itself even more interesting than the end result because it encourages the marketing and development teams to find an alignment. Having the *user* and the *experience* defined by the teams concerned is an excellent start for having a solid UX strategy for the project. This method is usually applied during conception or preproduction phases. You might want to have several personas—for example, a primary persona for the core audience, a secondary persona for a broader reach, and an anti-persona who would be the person you are *not* targeting. One word of warning is to remember that a persona is not a real person, yet because they have a name and a personality, designers may treat them as such. This can be good, but it can also result in designing for a persona rather than for the actual people that the persona is supposed to represent. To counter this, make sure the data that informs the persona are also available, accurate, and kept up to date. Also, encourage developers to come watch UX tests so they can also see some actual people playing their game.

14.2.6 Analytics

Analytics is a very powerful tool, especially used in combination with UX tests and surveys. It uses telemetry to gather data remotely about what players do when playing a game on their own—outside of UX labs and observers' scrutiny. We will discuss analytics in greater detail in Chapter 15.

14.3 Final User Research Tips

Whatever method you will be using, the important part is to prepare by working with the people who will later read your report or survey results. You cannot test and measure everything, so you need to focus your efforts on what is important for the teams to explore. Work with them, ask them what sort of information they need to improve the game, what features they do not need feedback at the moment, and so on. The more they participate in the preparation, the more relevant the feedback will be for them, and the more trusting a relationship you will build.

Also, after a test is done and the report sent, do not stop there. Book a meeting with the main stakeholders to go through the issues and get their feedback on the findings. This is when you will be able to learn what they don't want to fix now because that feature will be redone soon, what they will fix, and what you can retest at the next UX test. Finally, follow up on the issues to fix. Propose to enter bugs or tasks in the project-tracking software used in the studio so you can see the progress made and the team can see it also. Feeling a sense of progression is important for game developers, too.

If you are not a user researcher yourself and if you cannot afford to hire UX specialists or user researchers, or to build a fancy lab, you can still make sure to regularly look at your game from an audience's perspective. Test your designs, prototypes, and early builds with people around you that don't know anything about your game (as long as they are representative of your target audience) by using a do-it-yourself version of the methods described earlier. It's never too early to test, but it can often be too late to make meaningful changes! Just make sure to remove as many biases as possible when you test your game; otherwise, you might end up drawing the wrong conclusions. Avoid using friends and family, if possible, because these people like you and they will make more effort to figure things out to please you. And they will likely not be very harsh in their feedback. You can find good resources if you wish to learn more about user research (see, e.g., Amaya *et al.* 2008; Laitinen 2008; Shaffer 2008; Bernhaupt 2010), and you can connect with the game user research community online (gamesuserresearchsig.org). Also, remember the usability and engage-ability pillars; they can guide you throughout your iteration cycles and make sense of what might not work the way you expected or intended in your game.

15

Game Analytics

15.1 The Wonders and   15.2 UX and Analytics
      Dangers of Telemetry

Data are everywhere. An impressive amount of data is collected about our behavior when we shop, interact with our friends on social media, read news online, click on an advertisement, or when we play games. Game studios are increasingly using telemetry to collect everything possible to collect about player behavior. And this represents the main limitation today with game analytics— how to make sense of all of this data. Displaying complicated graphs during an executive meeting sure looks impressive, and seeing where players drop out of your game is a wake-up call like no other, but truly finding meaning in data for what you are trying to accomplish is not that simple. So, make sure to welcome and empower data analysts as you get excited about game analytics because you will surely need them.

Analytics is an umbrella term covering collection of data and making sense of it. It can be considered as part of the business intelligence team whose job is to help business make marketing/publishing decisions based on the information extracted from data. Analytics is also a powerful ally for user researchers, helping them—along with the game team—make decisions concerning gameplay. User experience (UX) managers can have an important role in building bridges among the analytics team, the game team, and the publishing/business intelligence team, to make sure that everyone stays on track regarding what experience is intended.

15.1 The Wonders and Dangers of Telemetry

Telemetry (i.e., gathering data remotely) potentially can be both powerful and dangerous. It's powerful because it is the only tool that can inform us of what players are really doing once the game is live, as it is experienced in people's homes, on a large scale. It's your reality check, your moment of truth. How many people are playing? How long are they playing on average? Is there a specific event in the game that makes them churn (i.e., quit playing)? And so on. However, it can be perilous when it is consumed without caution, without careful analysis, and without understanding data mining limitations. Some developers have a tendency to overuse the term game analytics while forgetting that it does, in fact, require analysis (e.g., statistical analysis, predictive modeling, etc.). As Drachen *et al.* (2013) put it, "Analytics is the process of discovering and communicating patterns in data, towards solving problems in business or conversely predictions for supporting enterprise decision management, driving action and/or improving performance." "Big data" has become a buzzword because we often hear about some successful companies that are amassing terabytes of data about their customers' behaviors. However, merely collecting data doesn't necessarily lead to success. You need to extract the value out of data because *data are not information*. As pointed out by Lambrecht and Tucker (2016), "Only when big data is combined with managerial, engineering, and analytic skill will it be valuable to business." The issue is that individuals who have a basic understanding of statistics (and little to no awareness about cognitive biases) are given data visualization tools to play around with raw data at will. My position is that, unless they are adequately trained, they should let data analysts extract meaningful information for them and interpret the information with them, or they take the risk of drawing wrong or partially wrong conclusions. Knowing the difference between mean, median, and mode is a start, but it's usually not good enough.

15.1.1 Statistical Fallacies and Other Data Limitations

In his book, *How to Lie with Statistics* (1954), Darrell Huff explains that statistics are very appealing but are unfortunately often used to sensationalize, inflate, confuse, and oversimplify. In that way, statistics have a lot in common with neuroscience … There are several basic things to keep in mind when looking at data:

- Sample representativeness. Were the data collected from a sample truly representative of your intended audience? Especially when your game is in the closed beta stage, the population engaged with the game might have a more extreme behavior than the mainstream audience who will play once the game is live. Overgeneralizing results obtained on a self-selected small sample (as it is often the case in the closed beta stage) to the wider population that will play your game can be delicate. Sample randomness is important.
- Is the result statistically significant? The mean difference in behavior collected between two groups might not actually be significant if there is

too much variation within the groups. For example, consider two teams of four people who played a player versus player (PvP) game. On Team A, two players got 13 kills each and the two others got 15 kills each. On Team B, one player got 2 kills, one got 4, one got 17, and one got 33 kills. In both cases, their average (mean) is 14 kills, but you can clearly see that the individuals from Team A do not deviate much from the mean, whereas Team B is much more heterogeneous. So, when you are looking at data comparing sets of population, knowing the variance within each group is important because the difference in the averages shown could simply be random. Confidence intervals help you understand how much uncertainty lies in your data, as we already mentioned in Chapter 14.

- Correlation is not causation. Let's say that you are looking at data coming from a PvP shooter, and that you find that the more players spend time customizing their weapons (variable A), the less they die in matches (variable B). In other terms, variable A and B correlate. However, simply observing a correlation doesn't tell you what sort of relationship these variables have. Variable A could be the one causing B, or B could be causing A, or both A and B could be caused by a third variable, or the correlation observed could just be due to chance. Correlation does not imply causation.

- Data are not information and information is not insight. Information has to be extracted from raw data, mostly by removing the redundant parts of the data. Information extracted from data then needs to be interpreted, and the irrelevant information (noise) has to be removed. If what is left is valuable for making a decision, then insights are gained. Gathering tons of data just because of the big data hype will not be a good use of your time and resources.

- Bad data are worse than no data. If the telemetry hooks were not implemented and tested properly, if there is a bug within the data collection system, then you could look at polluted data without even realizing it. To use a completely fictional example, you could wrongly believe that 65% of your players who started the tutorial mission completed it, simply because no event was fired when players quit the mission in a certain way (say, by quitting the game instead of quitting the mission first); therefore, many players who did not complete the tutorial might have slipped through the cracks, consequently inflating your tutorial completion rate.

- Data analysis is good at telling *what* is going on but not necessarily *why*. Telemetry data lack context. For example, in the data, you might see fewer players than usual engaged with your game on a certain day. Why this happened is another story. Maybe a blockbuster was released and part of your audience tried it out instead of playing your game; maybe there was a sports event that lured them away from their console; maybe there were some server issues on the back end that impacted players' connections or framerate; maybe it's just a bug in your data collection; maybe it's a mix of a few of these factors; or maybe this drop is just random.

- When you conduct an experiment, remember to always have a control group with which to compare your experimental groups. For example, if you want to find out what are the characteristics of your most engaged players (e.g., what type of games do they usually play, what game activities do they prefer, etc.), you cannot just send a survey to this population without sending it to players less engaged with your game as well because you need to compare the results of the two groups to verify if the characteristics found in your engaged players are specific to them.

These are just a few very basic statistical fallacies and limitations, enough to encourage you to have a studio strategy regarding how you will treat your data so you can extract maximum insights from it. But even then, you will need to pay close attention to human limitations, especially cognitive biases.

15.1.2 Cognitive Biases and Other Human Limitations

Remember that perception is subjective and that it is influenced by our prior knowledge and our expectations, which could make us interpret a chart incorrectly, for example (hence the need to also take data visualization seriously). Because of our tendency to seek minimum workload (math and critical thinking usually requires heavy cognitive resources!), we might draw hasty conclusions that can turn out wrong or not nuanced enough. Take the self-fulfilling prophecy for example: Let's say that you fear your game is not appealing to players who like competition because you believe the game is lacking competitive features. To verify this, you ask your favorite user researcher to send out a survey to all the players who have signed up for the closed beta (which should hopefully be representative of your core audience). In this survey, the researcher includes a nonleading question about what sort of features they mostly care about in games. The results come back and show that most of the respondents do not really care about competitive features. You conclude that you do not need to worry then because your target audience is not the competitive type. Except that, most of the time, only the players who are the most engaged in playing your game are also the most likely to answer your surveys. And maybe your most-engaged players are precisely the ones that do not care about competitive features (and this is why they are still engaged with your game). Competitive players that had signed up for the beta but who did not truly engage in your game because something was missing for them might not have actually answered your survey. And this population ends up being left untapped. It's the same sort of circular argument I often hear regarding female gamers. There is a strong assumption that a large majority of MMORPG (massively multiplayer online role-playing game) or MOBA (multiplayer online battle arena) players are teenage male gamers. Therefore (?), the reasoning is that you need to have overly sexualized female characters in the game to appeal to this core audience. (Sex is certainly a strong drive but we saw in Chapter 6 that we have many others.) Except that *maybe* you should consider the fact that exposing female flesh all over your game *might* deter some *potential* female gamers from engaging with your game, thus leaving this population untapped. Just a thought.

Speaking of strong assumptions, we also have a very annoying cognitive bias called the "confirmation bias" that influences us to seek out information confirming our preexisting beliefs while ignoring other information that could bring some nuance or even contradict our belief. Confirmation bias is a plague in the age of the Internet because if you believe that, say, human activity is not causing global warming on Earth, you will find a piece of information that goes your way while ignoring the overwhelming evidence suggesting that humans are, in fact, causing global warming (i.e., at least 97% of climate scientists agree on this)—especially if you consume information via certain social media sites, which use specific algorithms predicting what information is more likely to grab your interest and earn your click. This is useful for targeted advertisement but not so much for exposing people to a more objective view of the world (or at least different perspectives). We did not have to wait for social media to experience confirmation bias, but they certainly made it easier for us to stay comfortably in our bubble. As the late statistician Hans Rosling once said in a TED (Technology, Entertainment, Design) conference in 2006, "The problem for me was not ignorance, it was preconceived ideas." Confirmation bias alone should make you careful when trying to make sense of piles of data.

You also need to take into account cognitive biases experienced by your audience as they make decisions in your game, so you can get closer to understanding why they behaved the way they did and what you should do (or not do) about it. Let's take the example described by Dan Ariely (2008) regarding a subscription offer for a magazine as seen on its website. Three options were proposed:

A. One-year subscription to the *online* version, for $59
B. One-year subscription to the *print* edition, for $125
C. One-year subscription to both online *and* print versions, for $125

Options B and C have the same price ($125), although Option C clearly has more value than B. Intrigued by this offer, Ariely ran a test on 100 students from MIT to see which option they would pick. Most students chose Option C (84 students), 16 students chose Option A, and none of them chose Option B, which therefore seems a useless option; who would want to pay the same price for less value anyway? So Ariely removed Option B and ran the test again using new participants. This time, most students chose Option A (68 students) while 32 students chose Option C. People's behavior can be influenced by the environment, and this specific case is called the "decoy effect," whereby a distracting (decoy) option (B) makes one other option (C) seem more attractive than it would be without the presence of the decoy. This example is just a way for me to illustrate that looking at what players do won't necessarily help you make the right decisions, if you don't try to understand first where their behavior comes from. Indeed, if by simply looking at the conversion numbers in the subscription example you had decided to remove Option B that no one liked, you would have ended up losing revenue.

We live in the "Age of Information" and we consume a lot of it. In many game studios, it is considered a good practice to enable anyone to look at game or business analytics so decisions can be made swiftly and autonomously. The problem with this "data self-service" approach is that, if individuals are not trained to recognize analytics fallacies and cognitive biases, it could do more harm than good. Someone could have detected an artificial pattern in the data and consequently convinced a few developers to make a change that was not useful and even maybe detrimental to the user experience or to monetization. Moreover, even trained individuals, if they do not communicate and collaborate with the different teams (analytics, user research, game team, marketing, etc.), could miss some valuable information someone else had and that would have helped them to see the data in a new light. Companies are usually proud to say that they are *data-driven* because it's so chic these days. However, if you let data *drive* you, it means that you are controlled by data, and that you are just reacting. My colleague Ben Lewis-Evans often expresses the sentiment that a studio should be *data-informed* instead, implying that decision-makers should stay in control and make *informed* decisions based on data. I would add that you should aim to make decisions based on *insights* and careful analysis of information coming out of data, against predetermined hypotheses. This means that you cannot simply consider analytics alone; you need to consider all the information coming from different sources, which can be helped by having a good UX-analytics collaboration in the studio and an overall UX strategy.

15.2 UX and Analytics

Using game telemetry can be of tremendous help in understanding where players are experiencing too much frustration. In a Gamasutra blog post, Jonathan Dankoff explains how game telemetry was used during the development of the *Assassin's Creed* games at Ubisoft (Dankoff 2014). For example, by clearly identifying which mission players were massively failing or what unintended navigation paths they were taking, it helped the team improve the game accordingly. To garner all the insights power analytics can provide, it's usually a good practice to make the different teams communicate and collaborate closely. UX practitioners have an important role to play here because they are supposed to work with the development team to understand what experience is intended, with the marketing team to understand precisely who the user is, and—hopefully—with the publishing team to understand what the business goals are. Because both the user research and the analytics teams provide insights using the scientific method—although using different tools, they should work together to drive this initiative. User research and analytics complement each other. The analytics team provides insights from quantitative data collected from a large sample of users playing in their natural habitat (e.g., their homes). Its main strength is to inform about *what* players are doing in real-life situations. For example, it can call out that many players often die at a certain point in the game. However, as mentioned earlier, quantitative data lack context, and if it's great at telling what is happening, it cannot always easily explain why. By contrast, the user research team provides insights mainly from qualitative data collected via UX tests regularly conducted with small samples of users playing in the lab, while being observed, and without an easy way for them to stop playing should they want to. Its main strength is to inform *why* players do the things they do (see Chapter 14). For example, it can identify that a usability issue makes players go to their death at a certain point in the game (e.g., they need a special weapon to defeat a specific enemy but cannot figure out where to find the weapon). However, user research cannot easily predict how important a behavior observed in the lab will be on the scale of a larger audience, especially beyond clear usability issues. Mixed-method research, combining quantitative data with qualitative user research, can greatly help connect the dots (see Hazan 2013; Lynn 2013). It implies, for example, that at least one user researcher and one data analyst pair up to work closely with the development team, or that researchers with hybrid skill sets are embedded in the team (see Mack 2016). User research and analytics combined can guide the development, marketing, and publishing teams into defining their hypotheses as well as their metrics, which later will help everyone make sense of data, find *the right* problem to solve, and try a solution.

15.2.1 Defining Hypotheses and Exploratory Questions

Trying to find a *relevant* pattern among tons of data will likely be like finding a needle in a haystack if you don't define hypotheses and exploratory questions beforehand. You don't need to collect all the data from all the actions possible in your game; you need to collect the meaningful data according to your gameplay and business goals. You should seek data that will give you the information you need to make the right decisions according to your intent. As business intelligence analyst Marie de Léséleuc mentions in the below essay, you need to define questions and hypotheses. Beyond well-defined hypotheses, you will have to run (I mean, let your data analyst run) exploratory analyses—for example, to determine clusters, distinct groups of players that behave in a certain way and engage with certain activities and spend money differently. Running a factor analysis will also be very useful to determine what significant factors are impacting player retention the most (i.e., what players who churn early are doing in the game, or not doing, as compared to players who stay engaged, for example). You will also want to know what path players are mostly taking, what items they unlock the most, what missions they play, which heroes they pick, and so on. But even then, defining your hypotheses will help you save time while structuring your thought process. (Implementing telemetry hooks in the game and testing them does take time, so prioritizing hooks will help.) This is because, with hypotheses in mind, you can anticipate the impact of certain behaviors and the absence of behavior, which will help you prioritize what to address first and will help you make the right decisions faster. You will have to define different hypotheses, mainly gameplay hypotheses and business hypotheses. Here are examples of such hypotheses.

Gameplay hypotheses:

- Players who do not understand how [insert feature] works will more likely disengage with the game.
- Players who lose their first PvP match are less likely to retain.
- Players who friend someone within the first ten minutes are more likely to retain longer.
- And so on.

Business hypotheses (in the case of a free-to-play game):

- Players who retain longer are more likely to convert (to paying customers).
- Players who engage with [marketing event] will be more likely to buy [item] pack.
- Offering beta keys to the most engaged players will result in user acquisition because they will invite their friends to play.
- And so on.

You will, of course, end up with a large number of hypotheses and exploratory questions, which you will need to prioritize, and you will have to associate them with the relevant events in the game that need tracking. Finding the right events to track for a certain question or hypothesis will not always be easy. For example, the first gameplay hypothesis might be tricky to track accurately depending on what feature we are talking about. If it's a simple mechanic, such as using a specific ability (e.g., double jump or sprint), you just need to track if the ability is used, when the ability is used, in what context (e.g., against what enemy), and maybe also where it is used (unless your levels are procedurally generated). If it's a game rule such as the tower aggro rules for a MOBA, it will be more difficult to track. You can sure track the deaths to towers, but it's usually more complicated to determine, for example, if players targeted a tower while minions were absent from the tower range (therefore drawing tower aggro). But thankfully, your user research team can tell you what were the common usability issues observed when players encountered towers, and what specific rules they usually did not understand easily. This illustrates why a mixed-method research, combining analytics and user research, will bring you the best insights. For each hypothesis and exploratory question, you can define which tools in your UX arsenal will give you the answer (user research or analytics in our example).

UX pillars will help you define these hypotheses and exploratory questions. You can think about what usability issues could impact game retention, list all the features that are meant to engage the player, and later on verify if certain features had the influence expected. By having clearly in mind what experience you intend to offer to what subsets of your audience, and by being able to identify some of the main ingredients that will make your game usable and engage-able (i.e., UX pillars), you will have a strong framework that will guide you in the process. It will also help you define what sort of data you need when, and how it should be visualized to provide the most meaningful information to the teams depending on what the hypothesis is (e.g., heat maps, tables, pie charts, histograms, lines, etc.).

Marie de Léséleuc, Business Intelligence
Analyst at Eidos Montreal

Hypotheses and Game Analytics

Whether calibrating the various classes of characters of a competitive online game, assessing the success of the mechanics developed over months, optimizing the economy of a game, or anticipating the sudden yet unavoidable departure of a dissatisfied player, it is difficult to make a conscientious decision without the aid of numbers and without an analyst dedicated to their interpretation in context—especially if the objective is to avoid decisions guided by personal opinion or haphazard approximations, which generally lead to a lack of information and deep knowledge of the issue at hand.

Although such initiatives may be commendable, the inherent limits and obstacles to such enterprises cannot be ignored. Hence, no analysis can be conducted without questions or prior hypothesis, without the establishment of clear and precise objectives, and—of course—without a concerted effort among such diverse actors as developers, researchers, users, and managers. Equally, such studies, by definition, are grounded in a contrived format from which simple and universal answers to complex issues cannot be expected. All the results of a study must therefore go through a process of critical analysis that prevents decision-making based on blindly following patterns on a chart but that is based instead on the benefits and potential of a refined knowledge of the motivations and the actions of players to whom games are marketed.

15.2.2 Defining Metrics

After you are done listing your hypotheses and questions, you will be able to define the gameplay and business metrics you will need to measure. Gameplay metrics are highly dependent on your game. For example, you might want to measure how often people die (number of deaths), weapon accuracy (hits/shots), weapon power (kills/hits), deaths per types (number of deaths by bullet, by melee, by fall, etc.), progression (an event is fired as a mission is started and another when it's completed), and so on. On the business side (i.e., business intelligence), the metrics are usually about player retention and conversion (when they buy things in the game) for free to play games. You already should know all about these metrics, or key performance indicators (KPIs) but, just in case, here are the main ones used (see Fields 2013).

- **DAU**
  Daily active users, number of unique users per day (no minimum play time).
- **MAU**
  Monthly active users, number of users (unique or coming back) in a month.

- **Retention rate**
  For example, the DAU over MAU ratio is a high-level indicator of how engaging the game is. It informs what percentage of players on average engage with the game every day.
- **Conversion rate**
  This is the percentage of players who convert to paying customers.
- **ARPU**
  Average revenue per user. It's the total revenue for a given time divided by the total number of users who engaged with the game over that same period.
- **ARPPU**
  Average revenue per paying user. Same as ARPU, except that the revenue is divided by the total number of paying users during that period.

By setting up your hypotheses and your metrics correctly, you will be able to conduct a lot of interesting experiments, such as A/B testing whereby you test which variable (between condition A or condition B, and sometimes more) influences the desired behavior the most (e.g., do players convert more if the button is green vs. if the button is red). There are many other things to say about game analytics and how to coordinate it with UX, but let me just use one last example of what can be done. The user research team can put together surveys to send out regularly to players. If you can find a way to match survey answers to gameplay data (without compromising your customers' confidentiality), you will be able to see who is doing what and what did they say they loved or hated or found confusing about your game. For example, you might find out that most of the players who encountered a particularly difficult challenge early in their experience were also more negative in their survey answers. Don't forget to invite your friends from customer service and marketing at the table because they, too, can provide insightful information about what players complain about in forums and what they have to say when they reach out specifically to customer services. Be mindful about one caveat with such data though: It's sometimes the same players that complain passionately about the same things; therefore, such feedback is not necessarily representative of what the majority of your players are experiencing. That being said, it can be very interesting for you and exciting for your audience to encourage your community to participate in improving the game.

16

UX Strategy

16.1 UX at the Project Team   16.3 UX at the Studio Level
      Level
16.2 UX in the Production
      Pipeline

Having a user experience (UX) mindset is not only about offering compelling experiences to your audience, it is also about good business (Hartson and Pyla 2012). UX practices can help developers ship a game that contains less friction points and is more engaging and that will be more likely to reach a broader audience and make more revenue. Moreover, the earlier UX issues are identified, the less it costs to fix them. Therefore, user experience should have a strategic position within a project—across the development stages and at the studio level. Striving for a great user experience requires coordination. UX is not just about art, design, engineering, and defining and implementing the experience; it's not just about marketing defining the target audience and what makes them tick; it's not just about business intelligence defining the monetization strategy; and it's not just about executives defining business goals and company values. It's about all of this. UX should be at the intersection of all of these disciplines and should be the concern of everyone. Because, in the end, it is how your audience will experience your games, products, and services that will matter. It is your players' perception, understanding, behavior, and emotion that will count. This is why merely having a separate UX team in the organization—although constituting a good starting point—likely will not make enough of an impact. UX practitioners can help provide some invaluable insights and methods, but these tools need to be embraced by everyone in order to reach a common goal.

16.1 UX at the Project Team Level

Having a UX mindset can help the development team stay focused on what will matter for the player experience and for the studio's financial health. You cannot design a free-to-play game the same way you design a paid-upfront game, for example. Similarly, if your game is about team play at its core, building a player-versus-player mode might not be the most important feature on which to focus. Developing a game is all about making choices and making trade-offs. Keeping in mind what experience you want to offer can guide you in making the tactical choices that make the most sense for your goals. For example, the publishing team might need the development team to add some event features they believe will drive monetization. However, user researchers might also be raising flags about critical issues that they believe are going to impact player retention. Knowing that developers also want to add more features before a deadline, and that you can only implement one feature or fix one thing, which one do you choose? There is no one-fits-all solution, but this example illustrates why you need to establish a collaborative and centralized UX strategy in order for everyone to be aware of the trade-offs, sort tasks in terms of priority depending on how impactful they will be for the player experience as a whole, and to make the decisions that have the biggest bang for the buck.

Another thing to consider is that game developers utilize a lot of internally developed tools to create games. It will then be important to consider the user experience of developers using these tools so that *their* experience can be less frustrating (and even pleasurable) as well as more efficient (see Lightbown 2015). A lot of precious time can be wasted if these tools are not usable, so make sure that your tools programmer is knowledgeable about UX.

16.2 UX in the Production Pipeline

I mentioned UX misconceptions in Chapter 10, but it is also important for UX representatives to debunk preconceived opinions they might have about production. My colleague, Heather Chandler, senior producer on *Fortnite* (Epic Games), explained these misconceptions about production in the Game Developers Conference 2016 talk we presented together. For example, it's not necessarily that the development team members don't want to listen to UX feedback, but they are already extremely busy just trying to put everything together—sometimes while having a lot a pressure on their shoulders to ship on time. Because they are often swamped, the development team cannot spend hours reading excruciatingly long UX reports. They need applicable and straight-to-the-point feedback, allowing them to make quick decisions. This is sometimes tough for researchers because they cannot sacrifice too much rigor; but a compromise needs to be found. For example, you can send a big detailed report followed by an e-mail highlighting the top five issues needing immediate attention. The feedback given should also be aligned with the team's development cycle and should favor immediately applicable feedback over comments on a feature that will be redone in a month anyway.

(However, when it's time for this feature to be reworked, retrieve the old associated UX feedback to avoid redoing some of the same UX mistakes in the next iteration.) In order to be efficient and avoid putting additional pressure on the team, a good UX process needs to be integrated into the production schedule. For example, UX tests should be planned well in advance for each milestone the project will reach, which is also usually when the build is the most stable. After a UX test is conducted, UX issues are identified, and changes are suggested; those fixes that everyone agrees upon need to be tasked. If there is a strong commitment to UX in the studio, the development team will be encouraged to strive for the quality of the experience they want to offer, instead of for quantities of features crammed in that do not always meaningfully support the core game pillars. In any case, a UX process and strategy must follow the game development rhythm and understand its constraints. Different UX tools and methods can be used for different phases (see Chapters 14 and 15 describing these tools). A few examples are listed here. Note that the UX methods used in each phase are not mutually exclusive, and that there can be a lot of permeability among the phases. This is just a broad overview with a few examples.

16.2.1 Conception

During conception, UX practitioners can help develop personas, and they can help the core team communicate their plan to the stakeholders. For example, it can be tricky to explain the core pillars for a game having a deep systemic design to a publishing team that does not necessarily have the same design expertise level. UX is a process that is not only useful for enhancing your audience's experience, it can also be applied to improve internal communications. In some cases, UX practitioners can help the core team define what they are after—what core experience they want players to feel. For example, if they want players to feel compassion, moral dilemma, or warfare domination, UX practitioners can use their knowledge of psychology to help outline the impactful variables that could make players experience these feelings.

16.2.2 Preproduction

At this stage, a lot of rapid internal tests can be conducted to evaluate early prototypes (paper or interactive ones). As features start to be implemented, task analyses (i.e., a type of UX test, see Chapter 14) and short usability tests can be conducted at gray box levels and gym levels in order to tweak the game feel—especially control, camera, and character (the 3Cs; see Chapter 12). In parallel, the iconography (form follows function) and heads-up display configuration can also begin to be tested using surveys, for example.

Toward the end of preproduction, it could be useful to map the entire game in such a way as to offer a zoomed-out visualization of what the experience will be like as a whole. My former Ubisoft colleague, Jean Guesdon, creative director on the *Assassin's Creed* franchise, developed an interesting method. It consists of printing a large poster showing an overview of the gameplay loops and systems, the important features, how the player will be progressing (toward what goals), and so on. It will help the development team regain perspective instead of being constantly zoomed-in on a specific task, which can sometimes make developers lose sight of the big picture and how the feature they are working on contribute to it. It might help the different smaller teams (i.e., strike team agile methodology) to coordinate more easily and hopefully break the silos that can sometimes get erected. Beyond the development team, it will help everyone who is contributing to the project, including support teams such as marketing and business intelligence, to stay focused on the user experience on the horizon. Of course, this zoom-out overview of the game can change as discoveries are made during prototyping or when it turns out that the game needs to shift direction for whatever reason. Therefore, it will be important to update the poster as the game is being refined.

Jean Guesdon, Creative Director at Ubisoft

Zoom-In/Zoom-Out Philosophy

As I was trying to formalize my way of working when designing things, and especially since I joined the *Assassin's Creed* family 10 years ago, I came to realize that my "philosophy" or "method" (probably shared by many) could be defined as a never-ending "zoom-in/zoom-out" back and forth.

To visualize what it is, first imagine a vertical axis. This axis is a *continuum* that unites the conception process from the original dream to realistic constraints. At the TOP, you have the level of VISION, where everything is possible, and where you define the goals of an endeavor. This extremity of the axis is about high-level view, global thinking, concepts, purpose; it's about defining the "why."

In the MIDDLE, you have the level of ORGANIZATION, where you need to define the means that will be used to reach your high-level goals. It's all about systems and subsystems, links among components, organizational chart, flow chart, rationalization; this is the "how."

At the BOTTOM, you're in the real world. This is the level of EXECUTION where your dreams have to accept being limited in order to be produced and finally exist.

This is about breakdowns, lists of assets, bullet points, Excel files, and all the constraints that you have to deal with (technical, legal, human resources, etc.). This is the "what."

The important thing is: *You need to be able to navigate as fast and fluidly as possible along this axis.* The more you can explain the high level when talking about constraints without forgetting the concrete stuff when dreaming, the more you're able, I find, to unify things and to dream big while making sure you'll deliver on the promise. Everybody is able, to some extent, to do this, but I think that the bigger your amplitude and your speed along this axis, the better you'll be at designing things, whatever they are.

16.2.3 Production

The production phase is when UX tests go full-blown. The focus is more on usability and game feel at first but, as the systems start to take shape and cogwheels are meshing properly, "engage-ability" will get more attention. Toward the end of production is also when all the analytical hypotheses and questions need to be defined, so that telemetry hooks can be scheduled for implementation and testing—both for gameplay and business intelligence.

16.2.4 Alpha

Once the game is feature complete (and even before), playthrough tests will be very useful to see how players progress and where the game stops being engaging. The results from these tests can help refine the telemetry hooks that might be missing. Marketing and publishing chime in more heavily from that moment on. The analytics pipeline should be ready and reliable.

16.2.5 Beta/Live

As soon as the game starts being experienced by players from the outside world without you watching over their shoulders, you need to begin making sense of analytics data, helped by UX insights from tests. Difficulty balancing, progression balancing, monetization, and so on, will then be the main focus, assuming that most critical UX issues discovered by user research during the previous stages are already solved. (Although that's often not the case.) Watching the health of your beta or live game can be nerve-wracking. Without solid hypotheses, panic can take over and reactive decisions that could damage the user experience and revenue might be made instead of carefully analyzing where predictions went wrong. Although being responsive is important, drawing hasty conclusions and rushing to act on them could very much cost you more time in the end (and potentially more money) than carefully considering all the factors at play. Remember that identifying the *right problems* that need solving is what counts.

16.3 UX at the Studio Level

In order to have a true user experience mindset at the studio level—one that is player-centered, executives need to recognize the importance of this new discipline in game development. They need to understand its strengths and limitations. Convincing upper management that adopting such a mindset will likely help the studio ship engaging games more efficiently can be tough. Within the game team, it's always possible to find some developers interested in UX who will agree to try a few things. After small wins demonstrating the benefit of UX practices, which can happen fast given the multiple iterative cycles, trust can be built more easily. With upper management, though, a clear win can often be demonstrated only when the game is live, when business intelligence metrics are gathered, and when some UX issues likely can be linked to a drop in retention or revenue. And even then, given the number of factors influencing these metrics, it can be complicated to make your point. You could try to calculate the return on investment of UX, but it's not particularly easy to do that either. Gaining reliance on a UX approach is usually a long road, one that requires staying true to the scientific approach and offering neutral and less-biased insights informed by data and cognitive science.

Corporate UX maturity takes time. According to Jakob Nielsen (2006), there are eight stages that organizations need to go through, from hostility toward usability (Stage 1) to ultimately becoming a user-driven corporation (Stage 8). Nielsen suggests that it could take a company about 20 years to reach Stage 7, where user-centered design is integrated and the quality of the experience is tracked, and another 20 years to go from Stage 7 to Stage 8. The UX maturity model that I've been using is the "Keikendo Maturity Model," described by UX expert Juan Manuel Carraro (2014) as the product of over a decade of shared experience in organizations (see Figure 16.1). This model offers a very usable visualization of the different maturity stages, which helps when discussing UX strategy with the upper management because it clearly explains the benefits and barriers at each level and how to overcome the latter. This model has five stages, from "Unintentional UX" to "Distributed UX."

- **Unintentional**
  User experience is not considered proactively but emerges out of necessity. The common barrier is unawareness or rejection of UX (probably because of misconceptions, see Chapter 10). The tools for advancement are to train employees, communicate extensively, and to explain what it is about (and what it is not about).
- **Self-referential**
  User experience is considered, but developers use their own perspective—as if the end users will act and think the way they do, instead of recognizing

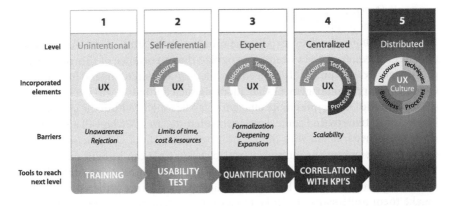

Figure 16.1

An illustration of the Keikendo Maturity Model.

that users do not have the same mental model they have. The common barriers are time, budget, and resource constraints. The main tool for advancement is to conduct user research—and I would add to preferentially conduct research on small projects or subtasks to demonstrate quick wins.

- **Expert**
  User experience has a dedicated small team, or team of one. At that stage, the UX process is not deep enough or a consistent part of the production cycle. The main tool for advancement would be to quantify user research and to regularly compare projects that are using UX testing with those that aren't in order to demonstrate value.

- **Centralized**
  User experience is represented across different roles that aren't confined within a separate team, such as interaction designer, information architecture designer, and user researcher. User research is consistent and part of the design process at that stage, but the barrier remaining is scalability. Not enough resources and skills are then dedicated to the UX mindset, and UX is seen as an internal service instead of a strategic area with its own budget, just like production or marketing. The main tool for advancement is to link UX metrics to business intelligence key performance indicators (KPIs) to expose the impact of UX (e.g., show links between UX issues and a drop in retention).

- **Distributed**
  User experience is at the same level as finance, production, or marketing. Consolidating UX as a strategic area within the organization will be important to obtain the senior executives' buy-in.

The first stages can actually go quickly in the context of the game industry; building trust and allowing for quick wins that developers can own should make things go a long way. However, the last two stages—and particularly the last one—are much harder to reach. Donald Norman, in his talk at the Game UX Summit (Norman 2016), argued that UX deserves a place at the management table and that it should be represented by a dedicated executive position. Senior executives should be ready to change their mindset for this to happen, not to mention that UX managers should also be ready to endorse that responsibility. Although we are not there yet in most cases, UX has greatly developed in the game industry and is now seriously considered.

If you are a "UX team of one" trying to mature the UX process in a studio, here is my subjective advice (based on a sample size of one): Start by listening to what developers need, the challenges they encounter, and the problems they have to solve before starting to implement any process. Explain what UX is about, debunk misconceptions, make them experience their own brain limitations (e.g., show them the basketball passes video with the gorilla discussed in Chapter 5), and make them understand that you are not here to design the game for them, but that you are at their service to help them achieve their goals by using science. Try to make UX concepts fun and don't be viewed as the "usability police," reporting UX misconduct to upper management. Instead, you are in the trenches with the developers; you should not use your science against them. Demonstrate quick wins (e.g., test icons, highlight usability issues so the UI designer can iterate, and retest the new versions, hoping issues are now solved) and celebrate all small UX victories with them. Once the teams become interested in conducting user research, you can more easily get permission to arrange a dedicated space in order to control the test environment better. Then, maybe you will get the budget to build a UX lab, with one-way mirrors and a dedicated space for developers to watch the tests live and to discuss. And you might also be able to convince upper management that hiring UX designers would make the design process more efficient. At some point, when more requests for user research are pouring in, you can more easily propose the development of a dedicated team. Then, you can implement a more integrated UX process, with a specific plan for what needs testing when. All through this process, coordinate with other teams focused on user experience, such as the analytics team, and enable cooperation and communication across the studio. Your last step will be to have a voice at the upper management table and to use that voice to be one of the players.

The science behind user experience is serious business, but the discipline does not have to be dull. I've found that making UX fun has many advantages. First, it will be more fun for you and, second, people are more likely to listen to what you have to say when they are relaxed and feel that you are not always there to criticize their work (so to speak). For example, after the UX lab was built at Epic Games, the UX team organized parties in the "secret/viewing room" (which we called the "speakeasy room" because that seemed appropriate). During these after-hours parties, we would simply invite developers to join us to listen to some music and have a few beers. Because the UX lab can sometimes be a painful place as we watch players struggling with some interface, this also allowed the lab to be considered a place to have fun. This allows colleagues to share something other than problems needing to be solved, and that's important. But I'm also a fan of parties, so I might be biased.

One last thing that has helped me communicate more clearly about UX is to regularly question *why* the target audience would care about a new feature, a multiplayer event, a marketing campaign, or items on sale (see Sinek 2009). For example, if the game team wants to add a feature (which will likely take resources away from fixing UX issues), ask them for what purpose the players would use that feature. If upper management believes that the game needs a new mode, ask them why players would care and if it would fit the overall experience—and so on. Game development is about making a series of choices and trade-offs under some level of uncertainty. It can be easy to lose focus regarding what the goals ultimately are. Of course, goals need to be refined too, and the overall strategy for a game can (and probably will) shift as development progresses. However, chasing too many rabbits can result in a mediocre product that ends up not offering any compelling experience on any level. Therefore, it can be critical to stay focused on the core experience, on *why* players you are targeting will care before making any key decision about the game—especially because time, budget, and technical constraints can be quite significant in video game development. Aiming for the "why" will allow for a thought process and an iterative process focused on the meaning for players, which is very important for motivating and engaging your audience (see Chapter 12). It could also be useful for marketing to have this mindset when selling the game because focusing on *what* players can do in the game (e.g., shoot, explore, craft, etc.) might not be as compelling as focusing on the ultimate purpose, the meaningful fantasy (e.g., conquering territories, becoming a mastermind, becoming the hero who saves the world, etc.). It is no coincidence that I started this book by explaining *why* I believe you should care about UX, instead of by explaining *what* it is right away.

The most important thing for developing UX maturity in a company is to build trust with the development team first and then across all the other teams. In his book, *Creativity, Inc.*, Ed Catmull explains that they have a specific group at Pixar called the "Braintrust" that meets every few months to assess each movie they are making (Catmull and Wallace 2014). I find this concept compelling, especially because it puts two important UX notions next to each other: *brain* and *trust*. Even though the creative process is different at Pixar than in the video game industry, I would find it interesting to explore it at a UX strategy level. For example, a group of people, all concerned about the user experience, could meet at certain times to assess games in development and live games. Another thing to consider for UX strategy is to determine a clear creative vision for the studio and think about how it would impact user experience. For example, in the essay at the end of this chapter, Ubisoft's chief creative officer, Serge Hascoët, explains why he cares about simplicity in design.

In any case, the main objective for UX managers is to support production efforts and to help everyone accomplish business goals. If they can provide the right tools at the right time to the right group of people, as well as prove the value of the UX process and mindset, people will listen—eventually.

Serge Hascoët, Chief Creative Officer at Ubisoft

"Simplicity Is the Ultimate Sophistication," Leonardo da Vinci

There was a time when a game controller didn't have any buttons; then there was one, then two, then three ... Today, a modern console controller has 21 buttons. We humans are very good at creating efficient tools, allowing us to build wonders. Unfortunately, we are also very good at making them more complex—at overspecializing them iteration after iteration.

Why did it become so complicated? We are often getting lost on creative paths; maybe we are confounding innovation and complexity. Instead of reflecting on how to apply variation on already existing tools in a game, we add more tools. Thinking that we are innovating, we very easily add, without considering consequences enough, an action and thus a button. We are already running out of buttons on game controllers! This added complexity forces designers to use a button for two or more actions; tapping or holding a button would result in different actions, for example. Consequently, this requires tutorials to explain these invisible and unnatural rules. This puts more load and complexity on the learning curve and can potentially discourage some from continuing to play.

Many people believe that games are too complex, and they are right. Each time that we went back to simpler inputs and interface, naturally usable, we conquered new players massively—for example, with the Wii Remote, the touch screen, the *Minecraft* interface.

I believe that this pledge for simplicity is sane—not only for hardware interface but also for software interface. This requires a strong vision centered toward the user. This vision must be placed at the center of the creative process. If there is one aspect where there shouldn't be any compromises, it would be regarding simplicity of use and simplicity of comprehension. We are entering an era of a virtual reality revolution whereby natural movements of our body, our hands, our head, and soon our fingers will allow unbelievable experiences.

17

Concluding Remarks

17.1 Key Takeaways
17.2 Playful Learning
(or Game-Based
Learning)
17.3 "Serious Games" and
"Gamification"

17.4 Tips for Students
Interested in Game UX
17.5 Parting Words

Throughout this book, I have proposed *a* user experience (UX) framework to help you design magical experiences by providing some basic knowledge about the brain and UX guidelines. This framework has been useful to me, and I'm hoping it will also be useful for you. But it certainly needs refinement, and you will likely need to adjust it to your own challenges. I'm certainly open to your feedback and suggestions, and I would be curious to know what worked or didn't work for you, what feels irrelevant, and what might be missing. Keep in mind, though, that this framework is not an empirically validated one. I am using some academic knowledge about the brain and renowned UX heuristics (especially the usability ones) complemented by other fuzzier concepts that are less proven empirically (such as game flow). It's a framework put together from my practice of UX in the game industry during the past decade or so, and it's focused on communication and collaboration among teams, while keeping in mind the capabilities and limitations of the brain. So, do not hesitate to challenge it. It is, after all, the whole point of the scientific method to challenge theories, even those originating from practice. And as Don Norman (2013) said, "In theory, there is no difference between theory and practice. In practice, there is."

The focus of this book is to identify the most impactful ingredients contributing to the success of a video game. But there is no *one* recipe. The recipe for providing the compelling game experience you want to offer to a specific audience will be for *you* to find out, using the ingredients and methods provided in this book. Designing an engaging experience will be particularly challenging (more so than offering good usability), but having a UX mindset and process will certainly help you along the way.

To me, UX is a philosophy more than a specific discipline. It is about shifting from our ego-centered perspective toward a player-centered one by using a scientific approach. It is about having empathy for our audience and being generous. Anyone on any team can have a UX mindset; UX practitioners are only here to support the initiative by providing the right tools and enabling the right process and strategy.

17.1 Key Takeaways

UX guidelines are based on human capabilities and limitations, which is the reason why understanding how the brain works overall is paramount, if only to avoid designing interfaces that won't be efficient for human interaction.

- **The brain, key takeaways**
  Key takeaways about the brain are described in greater detail in Chapter 9. To sum up, playing a video game is a learning experience whereby the gamer's brain is "processing" a lot of information. Information "processing" and learning starts with the perception of a stimulus and will ultimately end with a synaptic modification—a change in memory. The level of attentional resources dedicated to the stimulus will likely determine the strength of the memory for it. Two other main factors will also have an impact on the quality of learning: motivation and emotion. Lastly, by applying learning principles (impacting the different factors), the whole "process" can be improved. Remember that:
  - Perception is subjective, memory fades, and attention resources are scarce. Account for brain capabilities, performance, and limitations in your game.
  - Motivation directs our behavior in a complex way that we currently have difficulty predicting exactly. Meaning is key to motivation.
  - Emotion influences (and is influenced by) cognition, and it guides our behavior.
  - Learning by doing, in context and with meaning, provides the best learning principle to apply to games.
- **A UX framework, key takeaways**
  UX is a mindset more than anything else and should be the concern of everyone in the studio. UX practitioners can provide tools and a process to empower developers. UX guidelines rely on human–computer interaction principles and the scientific method. To offer a compelling game user experience, two main components of UX need to be considered: usability (ease of use) and "engage-ability" (ability for the game to be engaging), as shown in Figure 17.1.

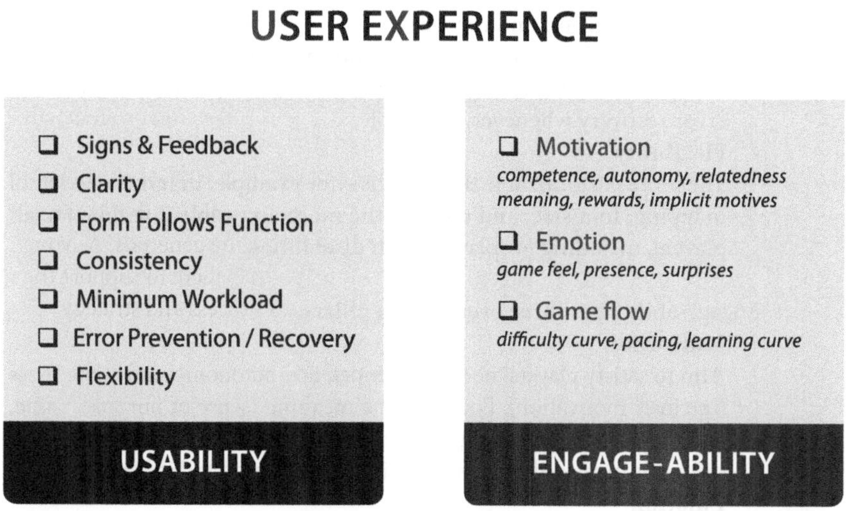

USER EXPERIENCE

USABILITY

- ❑ Signs & Feedback
- ❑ Clarity
- ❑ Form Follows Function
- ❑ Consistency
- ❑ Minimum Workload
- ❑ Error Prevention / Recovery
- ❑ Flexibility

ENGAGE-ABILITY

- ❑ Motivation
  *competence, autonomy, relatedness
  meaning, rewards, implicit motives*
- ❑ Emotion
  game feel, presence, surprises
- ❑ Game flow
  difficulty curve, pacing, learning curve

Figure 17.1

A UX framework.

Game usability has seven main pillars:

- **Signs and feedback**
  All the visual, audio, and haptic cues that inform about what is going on in the game (i.e., informative signs) or that encourage players to execute a specific action (i.e., inviting signs) and give a clear reaction of the system to players' actions (i.e., feedback). All features and possible interaction in a game should have signs and feedback associated with them because they guide players throughout their experiences.
- **Clarity**
  All signs and feedback should be perceptible and clear to avoid player confusion.
- **Form follows function**
  The form of an item, character, icon, and so on, should accurately convey its function. Design for affordance.
- **Consistency**
  The signs, feedback, controls, interface, menu navigation, world rules, and overall conventions in a video game must be consistent.
- **Minimum workload**
  Player's cognitive load (i.e., attention and memory) and physical load (e.g., number of button clicks needed to execute an action) must be taken into account and minimized for tasks that are not part of the core experience, especially during the onboarding part of the game.

- **Error prevention and recovery**
  Anticipate what errors players could make and prevent them from happening for tasks that are not core to the experience. Allow for error recovery whenever applicable.
- **Flexibility**
  The more customizable the game is—for example, in terms of control mapping, font size, and colors—the more accessible it will be for all players, including for players with disabilities.

Engage-ability has three overarching pillars:
- **Motivation**
  Aim to satisfy players' need for competence, autonomy, and relatedness (intrinsic motivation). Focus on the meaning (sense of purpose, value, and impact) for anything players need to do or have to learn. Offer meaningful rewards. Account for individual needs and implicit motives.
- **Emotion**
  Polish the game feel (control, camera, and character—the 3Cs, presence, physical reality) and enable discovery and surprises.
- **Game flow**
  Implies accounting for the level of challenge (difficulty curve) and the amount of pressure (pacing), and it requires distributed learning by doing (learning curve), preferentially through level design.

You can use this framework to collaborate across teams. It can guide iterative design, user research, and analytics. It should also help you elaborate a UX strategy across the studio so that user experience becomes the concern of everyone.

This framework, important for commercial games, should also be considered when designing games having an educational or social change purpose.

17.2 Playful Learning (or Game-Based Learning)

With video games having such a central place in children and young adults' entertainment lives, many people—from teachers to politicians—want to harness their engaging powers to educate, especially because extremely successful games can offer some great educational value and are sometimes already used at school (such as *Minecraft*, *SimCity*, or *Civilization*). Many books, academic papers, conferences (e.g., Games for Change Festival), and companies are now dedicated to the use and creation of video games to educate or, more broadly, change the world (e.g., Shaffer 2006; McGonigal 2011; Blumberg 2014; Mayer 2014; Guernsey and Levine 2015; Burak and Parker 2017). There is no doubt that video games have an important role to play in education, and the main reason is because to play is inherently to learn. Play allows the brain to experiment with new and usually more complex situations than the ones encountered in real life. According to researcher and psychiatrist Stuart Brown, "When we stop playing, we start dying" (Brown and Vaughan 2009). And during infancy and childhood, play is even more critical because the brain is developing and is much more malleable than later in life (see Pellegrini *et al.* 2007, for a review). This is why I will focus on children more specifically in this section, although the concepts tackled can be applied to adult learning. Play allows the child to assimilate reality (Piaget and Inhelder 1969) and remains the leading source of development for preschoolers (Vygotsky 1967). Play is critical for learning and is also one of the necessary elements in building a culture (Huizinga 1938/1955). With video game play currently being one of the most popular types of play, it is naturally considered as a great medium for education. The other reason why video games can be powerful for educating is because they give immediate feedback on a user's actions, which is a critical element to efficient learning. There is one main problem, though; most playful learning initiatives using video games rely on their power to engage their audience. However, we know how difficult it is to actually make engaging games.

The game industry, which is in the business of manufacturing fun, often struggles to reach its goal. Commercial games are not necessarily fun, even those with substantial development and marketing budgets. They can fail to engage or fail to retain their audience. This whole book is dedicated to defining ingredients and methods that can help professional developers improve the player experience and make games more successful. These challenges are also true for educational video games—even more so because they are usually developed with a very tight budget. Introducing any type of video games (even badly designed ones) might have been considered engaging for schoolchildren in the past because using games in a classroom then had the exciting taste of novelty. However, today, video games are everywhere. Just because children are attracted and engaged by many video games that doesn't mean they will be by all of them. Therefore, merely disguising math exercises by adding a thin video game layer on top won't be enough to be engaging. The problem with many of the so-called educational games is that they either aren't truly educational, or they aren't truly fun to play. Or both.

17.2.1 Making Educational Games Engaging

To create fun educational games, I would argue that using a UX framework is as important as it is for commercial games (see Hodent 2014). Like any other interactive products, educational games need to polish their usability and engage-ability to provide an engaging learning experience. Otherwise, the game could end up being too frustrating to play or boring. Motivation, for example, is a particularly important pillar to nail to make the game engaging (see Chapters 6 and 12). Education needs the power of video games mostly because many children may be less engaged in the school curriculum as delivered in a traditional way. Therefore, they need to be motivated to play the game that educators are hoping will teach them similar curriculum in a way that the children will find meaningful. Another critical pillar for education is game flow (see Chapter 12). The concept of keeping players within the flow zone (whereby the game is not too easy but not too hard) is very similar to the concept of the zone of proximal development (ZPD), which is well-known in developmental psychology. This concept was introduced by psychologist Lev Vygotsky (1978), who described the ZPD as the zone between that which the child can already do without assistance from a more experienced individual such as a teacher (too easy) and that which she or he cannot yet accomplish without assistance (too hard). When children are structured to be within this zone, they presumably are able to develop new abilities with the help of an adult or a more advanced learner. According to Vygotsky, play becomes a means by which to extend the ZPD. We could argue that keeping players in the flow zone, where the appropriate level of challenge occurs, is the best way to have them engaged in overcoming difficulties as they are learning new skills. Therefore, measuring engage-ability, such as using questionnaires relative to game flow, should provide some indication whether an educational game is engaging and provides an enjoyable learning experience (see, e.g., Fu *et al.* 2009). Additionally, the game flow pillar considers the learning curve so that which is taught in the game has both context and meaning and is distributed over time. In that regard, game UX is using the learning principles already well-known by educators (such as behavioral psychology, cognitive psychology, and constructivist psychology principles; see Chapter 8).

17.2.2 Making Game-Based Learning Truly Educational

A lot of so-called educational games merely put some cute animations on a quiz and are *instructing* children more than truly educating them. Even when the game does have some educational value, what the player will learn will not necessarily *transfer* to new situations (see Blumberg and Fisch 2013; Hodent 2016). However, transfer of learning—the extension of what was learned in one context to a new one—is the ultimate goal for educators because they want children to apply the content learned to many different (and real-life) situations. Consider a game with a true educational value like *ST Math* (Peterson 2013). This game, developed by MIND Research, is meaningful because performance in the game is claimed to facilitate performance on state math tests (if we accept that standardized academic tests measure what is important for children to learn).

Another approach would be to design games in which players have to actively use classroom curriculum in order to accomplish meaningful goals. Seymour Papert, mathematician and educator, used such an approach as early as the 1960s. Inspired by Jean Piaget's constructivist theory, Papert held a constructionist approach to learning, by which learning is more efficient through discovery when the curriculum is manipulated in contextual and meaningful situations, as we saw in Chapter 8. Instead of having the computer control the child, Papert (1980) wanted the child to program the computer. With the Logo computer language he developed at MIT, Papert did not try, for example, to make geometry rules fun by adding an interactive layer to traditional teaching. Instead, he enabled children to discover these rules on their own through an iterative trial-and-error process as they tried to accomplish goals *they* had determined and that were *meaningful* to them. Unsurprisingly, schoolchildren and students who developed strategies in the context of Papert's playful experience were able to transfer these strategies to other contexts (Klahr and Carver 1988).

A growing number of researchers and educators recognize that video games have the potential to offer a meaningful experience in which children can progress at their own pace, adjusting their actions depending on the immediate feedback games offer. Games can also allow children (and adults) to manipulate elements and concepts that they cannot in real life. For example, Jonathan Blow's *Braid* requires manipulating time to solve complex puzzles, and Valve's *Portal* requires solving spatial puzzles in a three-dimensional environment. However, there are many hurdles that need to be overcome before unleashing the true educational potential of video games, and we are barely scratching the surface. Overcoming these challenges might be more easily achieved by a better understanding of UX, applying a UX framework to educational games, and by considering transfer of learning.

17.3 "Serious Games" and "Gamification"

I perceive most serious games as sloppy or failed playful learning experiences because, as their name suggests, they are letting the fun and engagement out (although I would admit that my perspective might be a bit extreme). It's "serious" business; you need to learn something as you play! This is why I do not like to use this term at all. Serious games are games that are supposed to provoke a change in the player, whether it is about teaching math, encouraging working out, or enabling empathy. In all cases, though, when a change in perception, cognition, and behavior is desired, we are talking about learning. Therefore, serious games should always be considered for the playful learning experience they provide. Calling them "serious games" is not only contradictory, it also does not encourage developers of such games to challenge a game's engagement and educational values.

Gamification is another term that I do not particularly like. To me, this term mostly refers to applying extrinsic rewards and basic game progression metaphors to boring activities in order to increase people's motivation to complete them. It's mostly about giving points, badges, or achievements as people progress doing their tasks. My issue with gamification is that it often does not make any effort to consider how an activity could become more meaningful (or else it would be a playful learning experience), but instead focuses on short-term behavioral changes. Carrots and sticks surely work to change behavior within a certain context, as we saw in Chapter 6; however, the transfer of skills onto a different context using this approach can be particularly weak. Maybe you will exercise more often as long as you are using the new app applying gamification to make you run around, but it is also likely that, as soon as you stop using this app, you won't transfer any learning or change in behavior to other situations (i.e., life without this app). This is the problem with some extrinsic rewards: As soon as the rewards are taken away, motivation to keep doing the behavior could vanish with them (although it depends on the context). The main advantage of gamification is to provide immediate feedback on performance and progression—for example, because we know how important it is to motivation—in games and in real life (see Chapters 6 and 13). You just need to be aware of its limitations.

Being playfully and meaningfully engaging is the important element to favor, in my opinion, if the goal is to truly be educational or to provoke long-lasting changes in people—that is, having the spirit of play instead of trying to "gamify" everything. One example that I like to mention is the "Blackawton Bees project," during which children conducted a collaborative scientific study on bumblebees' visuospatial abilities. Through play and real experimentation (using the scientific method), children learned about science while doing a truly meaningful activity greater than themselves; they even published their findings in a scientific journal (Blackawton *et al.* 2011). Games are amazing tools to immerse players in new environments and to allow them to experiment. They can be shaped into meaningful situations that sustain players' curiosity and the pleasure of learning, but only if we can harness their true power and magic by considering the user experience, not by merely scratching their surface.

17.4 Tips for Students Interested in Game UX

Students frequently ask me what they should do to become a game UX specialist. Here are a few suggestions. If you are interested in game user research, you need to have excellent knowledge of human factors, human–computer interaction, and cognitive psychology. Therefore, students coming from these fields are more likely to find an internship or an entry-level user research job (which usually mainly consists of observing UX tests and compiling observations to assist the UX researcher in charge). You also need to have some good academic research background in order to understand and be able to apply the scientific method. Lastly, having at least a basic understanding of statistics will also be important. If you have a data science background, you can surely enter the game industry as well—either through the user research door or the analytics one. In any case, students must have a *good gaming culture*, which means they need to play different types of games on different platforms regularly. (Tip: Mention the types of games you play the most on your resume.) Students also need to be ready to learn about game design and to avoid pretending that they know about it just because they have played so many games. This mindset is usually frowned upon because it's like saying you can cook because you like eating food. Of course, do express your passion about games but show that you are eager to learn about how to make them. Remember that UX researchers are not supposed to give subjective opinions or try to design the game in place of the game team; they are there to help the team.

If you are more interested in UX design, then you need a design background and a good understanding of human–computer interaction principles. To find a job in the game industry, you will need to develop a portfolio showing off your skills, preferably with different types of projects on different platforms and, even more preferably, projects related to games. What is usually appreciated in a portfolio is being able to see your design thinking and process. Show the sketches, paper prototypes, and interactive prototypes; explain why you made the choices you made and so on, instead of simply showing the end result. Usually, you will be given a test to complete (i.e., provide a rough interactive prototype and design process for a feature) when you apply for a UX design job. If your test is good and you get an interview, be ready to clearly communicate your design choices (i.e., you must have good reasons for them) while staying open to other perspectives and being aware of the strengths *and* limitations of your design. Design is about making trade-offs, so you should be able to communicate clearly about the trade-offs you chose to make and why (regarding the player's experience).

In all cases, remember to customize your resume. A resume targeted to a game studio should not look the same as one targeted to a social media company, for example. In the game industry, as far as UX is concerned, we mostly care about the following (more or less—depending on the UX specialty):

- Your understanding of human factors, human–computer interaction, cognitive psychology.
- Your expertise in academic research (scientific method).
- Your understanding of data science.
- Your design expertise and design process (for UX designers).
- Your level of knowledge and passion for video games. This one is valid for *all* UX jobs and is often the information missing on resumes. (I'm guessing it's because these resumes are designed to be sent to any type of industries, including the gaming industry, but that is not a good strategy.)

Avoid throwing UX key words everywhere on your resume to make you look professional. Mention only the UX knowledge, techniques, tools, and so on, that you have truly mastered. If you have some professional experience, mention what you did and try to be concise because people usually do not like to read walls of text. Less is more. And if you are seeking a UX position, your resume should absolutely provide a good experience. If it's messy and unclear, it will indicate that you cannot walk the talk. UX is a philosophy, and it should be expressed on your resume, too.

Lastly, meet with UX practitioners at conferences and conventions, connect with them on social media, start a blog, take part in the conversation. The game UX community is still small; go reach out to people.

17.5 Parting Words

I would like to warmly thank you for your interest in this book and for reading it all the way until the end. I hope that I have met your expectations and that I offered you a pleasant experience, one with enough challenging content to keep you engaged. It was truly an honor to be able to express my love for science, video games, and user experiences to you here. Together, let's keep fighting for the user!

Acknowledgments

What led me to the writing of this book is quite a journey, and I have so many people to thank. Because I'm not sure if I'll have such another great opportunity to thank them properly, this section may be a bit long. Let me start with the people who welcomed me in the game industry: Caroline Jeanteur and Pauline Jacquey from Ubisoft HQ were the first persons to give me a voice. I started my career at the Strategic Innovation Lab led by Caroline and filled with other passionate, curiosity-driven, and amazing women (Isabelle, Lidwine, and Laura, at the time). It was a great cocoon, allowing me to get my bearings in this industry (and to express my creativity with fun videos about the brain and psychology—thanks, François!). So, thank you girls for the brain stimulation and the fun. I will always fondly remember the Mentos-in-Diet-Coke stunt. I would also like to thank Yves Guillemot, Ubisoft's CEO, because I believe the Lab originated from his desire to have a think tank. His interest in psychology certainly helped me feel comfortable. The first games I worked on at Ubisoft were from the *Games for Everyone* department, led by Pauline. Her passion and determination were surely contagious. I loved collaborating with her team; it sparked so many interesting conversations. Sébastien Doré and Emile Liang, in particular, were passionate and fun partners in crime as we were trying to enhance the educational value of the games we were working on (by the way Seb, I believe it's your turn to buy lunch). Ubisoft's editorial team brought fun craziness in my life, and working with these guys (and gals) was a really exciting learning experience. In particular, I would like to thank all the people involved in the "Design Academy," from those who put the content together, to those who taught it, those who had to coordinate and prioritize initiatives (hi, Mattheo!), and all the developers who attended the training session. Thank you for letting me talk about the brain and for laughing at my stupid jokes in certain slides ... As I moved to Ubisoft Montreal, I met other crazy and smart people, some of whom changed my horizon—among them, Christophe Derennes and Yannis Mallat, who are incredibly sharp and also know how to throw a party. Of course, I'd like to thank all the people from the user research lab and from the *Rainbow Six* prod—and most especially, Marie-Pierre Dyotte, director of the lab at the time I joined, who trusted me and gave me autonomy. All the people I met at Ubisoft, and especially those who engaged with me after some of my ramblings about the brain, contributed to my thought process, and I owe them a lot. There are way too many people to mention here, so I hope they will recognize themselves.

There is one person at Ubisoft in particular whom I owe much more to than anyone else. I'm talking about the irreplaceable Serge Hascoët, Ubisoft's chief creative officer—the heart and soul of design at Ubi, so to speak. Serge has been an amazing mentor for me while allowing me to challenge his own thinking, which I truly find humbling and inspiring. His deep love for design—for worlds—combined with his passion for science has always represented a mesmerizing beacon for me. Thank you, Serge, for your empathy, your generosity, your curiosity, your playfulness, your profound care for games but also for those who make them, and, of course, for your love of wine. You have been a model for me to follow, and I feel profoundly lucky to have been able to witness some of your genius. I can still mimic the cry of the dolphin much better than you, so that should count for something.

Moving on to my short yet endearing experience at LucasArts (abruptly interrupted because the studio *had* to close), I met some other passionate people (and intense *Star Wars* geeks!) who also indulged me by listening to my stuff while feeding my UX thoughts. I met people there who love to "salsa dance," say "dude!" all the time, and book "binary meetings"; and they made a difference for me. This was also the first time I truly interacted with the publishing branch and started to elaborate the beginning of a UX strategy encouraged by Mary Bihr (whom I suspect only did so in exchange for having me play the *Assassin's Creed* parts she had some difficulty in overcoming; I now understand what you did there, Mary!). One of the key elements of my UX strategy then was to organize Pecha Kucha sessions with beer. I still believe it was a good move, and I would like to thank all the people who participated in these sessions (and those who constantly bailed—you know who you are). I would also like to deeply thank Fred Markus, who has been an active supporter of my endeavors for years. We first met at Ubisoft, where he was the head of prototyping. Then he was the one who hired me at LucasArts and later at Epic Games; and he let me have carte blanche. I reckon that Fred likes interacting with me mostly because I've been listening with interest to his Nintendo rabbit stories and because I've been laughing at his jokes. Well, okay, not at *all* of his jokes. (Seriously, Fred, sometimes you have lousy jokes.) Fred has a passion for understanding *how* things are made and, through his constant questioning about cognitive psychology and UX, he helped me refine and push the boundaries of my thinking. So I guess I owe you a bottle of wine, Fred. Probably two. Although I did introduce you to *Spinal Tap*; so, maybe we can call it even?

During my time at Epic Games, I met with the most hardcore and passionate developers. Many of the people at Epic mostly live for their craft. It's truly humbling—although sometimes a bit intimidating, I have to admit. Epic's upper management let me build up a really neat UX lab and start a team (thank you, Farnz, in particular, for your constant support). I want to thank all the amazing individuals who helped me build this team: Rex, Laura, Tom (aka "Mr. Tyler"), and Stephanie. They were the first SUX people ("Super UX"), and they helped me in this grand adventure. Then, the team grew up (thanks to those who passed by: Brian, Matt, Maurita, Jessica, Ed, Will, Julie, and the others) and is now composed of some of the most badass UX practitioners in the industry (and I'm absolutely not biased)—in order of appearance (I think): Alex Trowbridge, Paul Heath, Ben Lewis-Evans, Jim Brown, and our current lab and data analysts Brandon Newberry, Bill Hardin, and Jonathan Valdivieso. I am so fortunate to have been able to bring such a kick-ass team together. They not only rock at their job, but they are amazing human beings too, and they inspire me daily with their wit—not to mention, of course, their smartness and their nerf gun aiming skills. So thank you for trusting me and joining the team. I would also like to thank the *Fortnite* team, who were the first to buy into the UX fun and are still today as I write this our greatest partners. They worked with us, accepted our poking, and challenged us back, and it's been a true pleasure to work with them—in particular, Heather Chandler, who greatly helped me implement a UX process, and Darren Sugg, Pete Ellis, and Zak Phelps, who are always stopping by the UX lab whenever a test is happening. I would like to thank the Epic UX designers for spreading some UX love within the teams—in particular, Laura Teeples, Robbie Klapka, Derek Diaz, Matt "Twin-Blast" Shetler, and Phillip Harris, who are the UX designers I interacted with the most. There are too many people to thank at Epic, but I would like to call out our regular Speakeasy customers. (Don't forget that password!) Lastly, I would like to thank Donald Mustard for coping with my impatience so elegantly, and Tim Sweeney, Epic's CEO, for his support and for the inspiration he gave me. (Gotta protect open platforms and mind that Metaverse!) I will also keep fond memories of Karolina Grochowska and Joel Crabbe, who were amazing people, both at work and in life, and who left us all too soon while we were developing *Fortnite*. (Hugs to you, Gina.)

A warm thank you to all the people who gave me feedback on this book—especially to Ben Lewis-Evans, who put in way more effort than anyone else, but also to Fred Markus, Chad Lane, Jim Brown, Andrew Przybylski, Anne McLaughlin, Darren Clary, Darren Sugg, and Fran Blumberg. (Thanks, Fran, for your constant support and spot-on feedback!) I would also like to thank those who agreed to write a short essay for this book: Serge Hascoët, Darren Sugg, Anouk Ben-Tchavtchavadze, Jean Guesdon, Ben Lewis-Evans, John Ballantyne, Tom Bible, Ian Hamilton, Fred Markus, Marie de Léséleuc, Andrew Przybylski, and the intrepid genius Kim Libreri (Academy Award winner!!). A huge thanks to Delphine Seletti (Create and Enjoy) for the coolest illustrations that she did for this book. Of course, thank you Sean Connelly for giving me this opportunity (and for the drinks!).

Loving thanks to my friends and family, many of whom aren't quite sure what it is I'm doing exactly, yet they have always supported me. (Special thanks to my playful and geek parents who first introduced me to video games through the Magnavox Odyssey^2/Philips Videopac!) Thanks also to my game dev friends who *do* know what I'm doing and encouraged me along the way.

Lastly, I would like to thank all the people I met during all these years—whether at work, after work, at conferences, or online, those who invited me to give a talk or gave me a voice somehow, those who helped me organize and run the Game UX Summit (Ellen, Rachel, Dana, and Daniel in particular), those who agreed to speak at this event (Don Norman and Dan Ariely, in particular), and those who simply took the time to chat with me. Thank you to the UBM/GDC crew for letting UX becoming a summit at GDC (especially Meggan Scavio and Victoria Petersen), to Anouk for advising with me, and to the UX summit speakers and audience. You all have contributed to this book in some manner—so I hope you will like it.

Thank you.

References

Abeele, V. V., Nacke, L. E., Mekler, E. D., & Johnson, D. (2016). Design and Preliminary Validation of the Player Experience Inventory. In *ACM CHI Play '16 Proceedings of the 2016 Annual Symposium on Computer-Human Interaction in Play* (pp. 335–341), Austin, TX.

Alessi, S. M., & Trollip, S. R. (2001). *Multimedia for Learning: Methods and Development*. Boston, MA: Allyn and Bacon.

Amabile, T. M. (1996). *Creativity in Context: Update to the Social Psychology of Creativity*. Boulder, CO: Westview Press.

Amaya, G., Davis, J. P., Gunn, D. V., Harrison, C., Pagulayan, R. J., Phillips, B., & Wixon, D. (2008). Games User Research (GUR): Our experience with and evolution of four methods. *In* K. Ibister & N. Schaffer (Eds.), *Game Usability*. Burlington, MA: Morgan Kaufmann Publishers, pp. 35–64.

Anselme, P. (2010). The uncertainty processing theory of motivation. *Behavioural Brain Research, 208*, 291–310.

Anstis, S. M. (1974). Letter: A chart demonstrating variations in acuity with retinal position. *Vision Research, 14*, 589–592.

Ariely, D. (2008). *Predictably Irrational: The Hidden Forces that Shape Our Decisions*. New York: Harper Collins.

Ariely, D. (2016a). *Payoff: The Hidden Logic that Shapes Our Motivations*. New York: Simon & Schuster/TED.

Ariely, D. (2016b). *Free Beer: And Other Triggers that Tempt us to Misbehave*. Game UX Summit (Durham, NC, May 12th). Retrieved from http://www.gamasutra.com/blogs/CeliaHodent/20160722/277651/Game_UX_Summit_2016__All_Sessions_Summary.php-11-Dan Ariely (Accessed May 28, 2017).

Atkinson, R. C., & Shiffrin, R. M. (1968). Human memory: A proposed system and its control processes. In K. W. Spence & J. T. Spence (Eds.), *The Psychology of Learning and Motivation*, Vol. 2. New York: Academic Press, pp. 89–195.

Baddeley, A. D., & Hitch, G. (1974). Working memory. In G. H. Bower (Ed.), *The Psychology of Learning and Motivation: Advances in Research and Theory*, Vol. 8. New York: Academic Press, pp. 47–89.

Baillargeon, R. (2004). Infants' physical world. *Current Directions in Psychological Science, 13*, 89–94.

Baillargeon, R., Spelke, E., & Wasserman, S. (1985). Object permanence in five-month-old infants. *Cognition, 20*, 191–208.

Bartle, R. (1996). *Hearts, Clubs, Diamonds, Spades: Players Who Suit MUDs.* Retrieved from http://mud.co.uk/richard/hcds.htm (Accessed May 28, 2017).

Bartle, R. (2009). Understand the limits of theory. In C. Bateman (Ed.), *Beyond Game Design: Nine Steps to Creating Better Videogames.* Boston: Charles River Media, pp. 117–133.

Baumeister, R. F. (2016). Toward a general theory of motivation: Problems, challenges, opportunities, and the big picture. *Motivation and Emotion, 40*, 1–10.

Benson, B. (2016). *Cognitive Bias Cheat Sheet. Better Humans.* Retrieved from https://betterhumans.coach.me/cognitive-bias-cheat-sheet-55a472476b18#.52t8xb9ut (Accessed May 28, 2017).

Bernhaupt, R. (Ed.). (2010). *Evaluating User Experience in Games.* London: Springer-Verlag.

Blackawton, P. S., Airzee, S., Allen, A., Baker, S., Berrow, A., Blair, C., Churchill, M., et al. (2011). Blackawton bees. *Biology Letters, 7*, 168–172.

Blumberg, F. C. (Ed.). (2014). *Learning by Playing: Video Gaming in Education.* Oxford, UK: Oxford University Press.

Blumberg, F. C., & Fisch, S. M. (2013). Introduction: Digital games as a context for cognitive development, learning, and developmental research. In F. C. Blumberg & S. M. Fisch (Eds.), *New Directions for Child and Adolescent Development, 139*, pp. 1–9.

Bowman, L. L., Levine, L. E., Waite, B. M., & Gendron, M. (2010). Can students really multitask? An experimental study of instant messaging while reading. *Computers & Education, 54*, 927–931.

Brown, S., & Vaughan, C. (2009). *Play: How It Shapes the Brain, Opens the Imagination, and Invigorates the Soul.* New York: Avery.

Burak, A., & Parker, L. (2017). *Power Play: How Video Games Can Save the World.* New York, NY: St. Martin's Press/MacMillan.

Cabanac, M. (1992). Pleasure: The common currency. *Journal of Theoretical Biology, 155*, 173–200.

Carraro, J. M. (2014). *How Mature Is Your Organization when It Comes to UX? UX Magazine.* Retrieved from http://uxmag.com/articles/how-mature-is-your-organization-when-it-comes-to-ux (Accessed May 28, 2017).

Castel, A. D., Nazarian, M., & Blake, A. B. (2015). Attention and incidental memory in everyday settings. In J. Fawcett, E. F. Risko & A. Kingstone (Eds.), *The Handbook of Attention.* Cambridge, MA: MIT Press, pp. 463–483.

Catmull, E., & Wallace, A. (2014). *Creativity, Inc.: Overcoming the Unseen Forces that Stand in the Way of True Inspiration.* New York: Random House.

Cerasoli, C. P., Nicklin, J. M., & Ford, M. T. (2014). Intrinsic motivation and extrinsic incentives jointly predict performance: A 40-year meta-analysis. *Psychological Bulletin, 140,* 980–1008.

Chen, J. (2007). Flow in games (and everything else). *Communication of the ACM, 50,* 31–34.

Cherry, E. C. (1953). Some experiments on the recognition of speech, with one and two ears. *Journal of the Acoustical Society of America, 25,* 975–979.

Craik, F. I. M., & Lockhart, R. S. (1972). Levels of processing: A framework for memory research. *Journal of Verbal Learning and Verbal Behavior, 11,* 671–684.

Craik, F. I. M., & Tulving, E. (1975). Depth of processing and the retention of words in episodic memory. *Journal of Experimental Psychology: General, 104,* 268–294.

Csikszentmihalyi, M. (1990). *Flow: The Psychology of Optimal Experience.* New York: Harper Perennial.

Damasio, A. R. (1994). *Descartes' Error: Emotion, Reason, and the Human Brain.* New York: Avon.

Daneman, M., & Carpenter, P. A. (1980). Individual differences in working memory and reading. *Journal of Verbal Learning and Verbal Behavior, 19,* 450–466.

Dankoff, J. (2014). Game telemetry with DNA tracking on Assassin's Creed. *Gamasutra.* Retrieved from http://www.gamasutra.com/blogs/JonathanDankoff/20140320/213624/Game_Telemetry_with_DNA_Tracking_on_Assassins_Creed.php (Accessed May 28, 2017).

Darrell, H. (1954). *How to Lie with Statistics.* New York: W.W. Norton & Co.

Deci, E. L. (1975). *Intrinsic Motivation.* New York: Plenum.

Deci, E. L., & Ryan, R. M. (1985). *Intrinsic Motivation and Self-Determination in Human Behavior.* New York: Plenum.

Denisova, A., Nordin, I. A., & Cairns, P. (2016). The Convergence of Player Experience Questionnaires. In *ACM CHI Play '16 Proceedings of the 2016 Annual Symposium on Computer-Human Interaction in Play* (pp. 33–37), Austin, TX.

Desurvire, H., Caplan, M., & Toth, J. A. (2004). Using Heuristics to Evaluate the Playability of Games. *Extended Abstracts CHI 2004, 1509–1512.*

Dillon, R. (2010). *On the Way to Fun: An Emotion-Based Approach to Successful Game Design.* Natick, MA: A K Peters, Ltd.

Drachen, A., Seif El-Nasr, M., & Canossa, A. (2013). Game analytics—The basics. In M. Seif El-Nasr, A. Drachen & A. Canossa (Eds.), *Game Analytics— Maximizing the Value of Player Data.* London: Springer, pp. 13–40.

Dutton, D. G., & Aaron, A. P. (1974). Some evidence for heightened sexual attraction under conditions of high anxiety. *Journal of Personality and Social Psychology, 30,* 510–517.

Dweck, C. S., & Leggett, E. L. (1988). A social-cognitive approach to motivation and personality. *Psychological Review, 95*(2), 256–273.

Easterbrook, J. A. (1959). The effect of emotion on cue utilization and the organization of behaviour. *Psychological Review, 66,* 183–201.

Ebbinghaus, H. (1885). *Über das Gedächtnis.* Leipzig: Dunker. *Translated* Ebbinghaus, H. (1913/1885) *Memory: A Contribution to Experimental Psychology.* Ruger HA, Bussenius CE, translator. New York: Teachers College, Columbia University.

Ekman, P. (1972). Universals and Cultural Differences in Facial Expressions of Emotions. In Cole, J. (Ed.), *Nebraska Symposium on Motivation.* Lincoln, NB: University of Nebraska Press, pp. 207–282.

Ekman, P. (1999). Facial expressions. In T. Dalgleish & M. J. Power (Eds.), *The Handbook of Cognition and Emotion.* New York: Wiley, pp. 301–320.

Eysenck, M. W., Derakshan, N., Santos, R., & Calvo, M. G. (2007). Anxiety and cognitive performance: Attentional control theory. *Emotion, 7,* 336–353

Fechner, G. T. (1966). *Elements of psychophysics* (Vol. 1). (H. E. Adler, Trans.). New York: Holt, Rinehart & Winston. (Original work published 1860).

Federoff, M. A. (2002). Heuristics and usability guidelines for the creation and evaluation of fun in videogames. Master's thesis, Department of Telecommunications, Indiana University.

Festinger, L. (1957). *A Theory of Cognitive Dissonance.* Stanford, CA: Stanford University Press.

Fields, T. V. (2013). Game industry metrics terminology and analytics case. In M. Seif El-Nasr, A. Drachen & A. Canossa (Eds.), *Game Analytics— Maximizing the Value of Player Data.* London: Springer, pp. 53–71.

Fitts, P. M. (1954). The information capacity of the human motor system in controlling the amplitude of movement. *Journal of Experimental Psychology, 47,* 381–391.

Fitts, P. M., & Jones, R. E. (1947). Analysis of factors contributing to 460 "pilot error" experiences in operating aircraft controls (Report No. TSEAA-694-12). Dayton, OH: Aero Medical Laboratory, Air Materiel Command, U.S. Air Force.

Fu, F. L., Su, R. C., & Yu, S. C. (2009). EGameFlow: A scale to measure learners' enjoyment of e-learning games. *Computers and Education, 52,* 101–112.

Fullerton, T. (2014). *Game Design Workshop: A Playcentric Approach to Creating Innovative Games.* 3rd edn. Boca Raton, FL: CRC press.

Galea, J. M., Mallia, E., Rothwell, J., & Diedrichsen, J. (2015). The dissociable effects of punishment and reward on motor learning. *Nature Neuroscience, 18,* 597–602.

Gerhart, B., & Fang, M. (2015). Pay, intrinsic motivation, extrinsic motivation, performance, and creativity in the workplace: Revisiting long-held beliefs. *Annual Review of Organizational Psychology and Organizational Behavior, 2,* 489–521.

Gibson, J. J. (1979). *The Ecological Approach to Visual Perception.* Boston, MA: Houghton Mifflin.

Goodale, M. A., & Milner, A. D. (1992). Separate visual pathways for perception and action. *Trends in Neuroscience, 15,* 20–5.

Greene, R. L. (2008). Repetition and spacing effects. In J. Byrne (Ed.) *Learning and Memory: A Comprehensive Reference.* Vol. 2, pp. 65–78. Oxford: Elsevier.

Green, C. S., & Bavelier, D. (2003). Action video game modifies visual selective attention. *Nature, 423*, 534–537.

Gross, J. J. (Ed.). (2007). *Handbook of Emotion Regulation*. New York: Guilford Press.

Guernsey, L., & Levine, M. (2015). *Tap, Click, Read: Growing Readers in a World of Screens*. San Francisco, CA: Jossey-Bass.

Hartson, R. (2003). Cognitive, physical, sensory, and functional affordances in interaction design. *Interaction Design, 22*, 315–338.

Hartson, R., & Pyla, P. (2012). *The UX Book: Process and Guidelines for Ensuring a Quality User Experience*. Waltham, MA: Morgan Kaufmann/Elsevier.

Hazan, E. (2013). Contextualizing data. In M. Seif El-Nasr, A. Drachen & A. Canossa (Eds.), *Game Analytics—Maximizing the Value of Player Data*. London: Springer, pp. 477–496.

Hennessey, B. A., & Amabile, T. M. (2010). Creativity. *Annual Review of Psychology, 61*, 569–598.

Heyman, J., & Ariely, D. (2004). Effort for payment. A tale of two markets. *Psychological Science, 15*, 787–793.

Hodent, C. (2014). Toward a playful and usable education. In F. C. Blumberg (Ed.), *Learning by Playing: Video Gaming in Education*. pp. 69–86. Oxford, UK: Oxford University Press.

Hodent, C. (2015). 5 Misconceptions about UX (User Experience) in video games. *Gamasutra*. Retrieved from http://www.gamasutra.com/blogs/CeliaHodent/20150406/240476/5_Misconceptions_about_UX_User_Experience_in_Video_Games.php

Hodent, C. (2016). The elusive power of video games for education. *Gamasutra*. Retrieved from http://www.gamasutra.com/blogs/CeliaHodent/20160801/278244/The_Elusive_Power_of_Video_Games_for_Education.php#comments

Hodent, C., Bryant, P., & Houdé, O. (2005). Language-specific effects on number computation in toddlers. *Developmental Science, 8*, 373–392.

Horvath, K., & Lombard, M. (2009). *Social and Spatial Presence: An Application to Optimize Human-Computer Interaction*. Paper presented at the 12th Annual International Workshop on Presence, 11–13 November, Los Angeles, CA

Houdé, O., & Borst, G. (2015). Evidence for an inhibitory-control theory of the reasoning brain. *Frontiers in Human Neuroscience, 9*, 148.

Huizinga, J. (1938/1955). *Homo Ludens: A Study of the Play Element in Culture*. Boston, MA: Beacon Press.

Hull, C. L. (1943). *Principles of Behavior*. New York: Appleton.

Isbister, K. (2016). *How Games Move Us: Emotion by Design*. Cambridge, MA: The MIT Press.

Isbister, K., & Schaffer, N. (2008). What is usability and why should I care?; Introduction. In K. Ibister & N. Schaffer (Eds.), *Game Usability*. pp. 3–5. Burlington: Elsevier.

Izard, C. E., & Ackerman, B. P. (2000). Motivational, organizational, and regulatory functions of discrete emotions. In M. Lewis & J. M. Haviland Jones (Eds.), *Handbook of Emotions*. pp.253–264. New York: The Guilford Press.

Jarrett, C. (2015). *Great Myths of the Brain*. New York: Wiley.

Jenkins, G. D., Jr., Mitra, A., Gupta, N., & Shaw, J. D. (1998). Are financial incentives related to performance? A meta-analytic review of empirical research. *Journal of Applied Psychology, 83*, 777–787.

Jennett, C., Cox, A. L., Cairns, P., Dhoparee, S., Epps, A., Tijs, T., & Walton, A. (2008). Measuring and defining the experience of immersion in games. *International Journal of Human-Computer Studies, 66*, 641–661.

Johnson, J. (2010). *Designing with the Mind in Mind: Simple Guide to Understanding User Interface Design Guidelines*. Burlington, NJ: Elsevier.

Just, M. A., Carpenter, P. A., Keller, T. A., Emery, L., Zajac, H., & Thulborn, K. R. (2001). Interdependence of non-overlapping cortical systems in dual cognitive tasks. *NeuroImage, 14*, 417–426.

Kahneman, D. (2011). *Thinking, Fast and Slow*. New York: Farrar, Straus and Giroux.

Kahneman, D., & Tversky, A. (1984). Choices, values, and frames. *American Psychologist, 39*, 341–350.

Kandel, E. (2006). In *Search of Memory: The Emergence of a New Science of Mind*. New York: W. W. Norton.

Kelley, D. (2001). *Design as an Iterative Process*. Retrieved from http://ecorner. stanford.edu/authorMaterialInfo.html?mid=686 (Accessed May 28, 2017).

Kirsch, P., Schienle, A., Stark, R., Sammer, G., Blecker, C., Walter, B., Ott, U., Burkhart, J., & Vaitl, D., 2003. Anticipation of reward in a nonaversive differential conditioning paradigm and the brain reward system: An event-related fMRI study. *Neuroimage, 20*, 1086–1095.

Klahr, D., & Carver, S. M. (1988). Cognitive objectives in a LOGO debugging curriculum: Instruction, learning, and transfer. *Cognitive Psychology, 20*, 362–404.

Koelsch, S. (2014). Bain correlates of music-evoked emotions. *Nature Reviews Neuroscience, 15*, 170–180.

Koster, R. (2004). *Theory of Fun for Game Design*. New York: Paraglyph Press.

Krug, S. (2014). *Don't Make Me Think, Revisited: A Common Sense Approach to Web Usability*. 3rd edn. San Francisco, CA: New Riders, Peachpit, Pearson Education.

Kuhn, G., & Martinez, L. M. (2012). Misdirection: Past, present, and the future. *Frontiers in Human Neuroscience, 5*, 172. http://dx.doi.org/10.3389/fnhum. 2011.00172

Laitinen, S. (2008). Usability and playability expert evaluation. In K. Ibister & N. Schaffer (Eds.), *Game Usability*. pp. 91–111. Burlington: Elsevier.

Lambrecht, A., & Tucker, C. E. (2016). *The Limits of Big Data's Competitive Edge*. MIT IDE Research Brief. Retrieved from http://ide.mit.edu/sites/ default/files/publications/IDE-researchbrief-v03.pdf (Accessed May 28, 2017).

Lavie, N. (2005). Distracted and confused? Selective attention under load. *Trends in Cognitive Sciences, 9*, 75–82.

Lazarus, R. S. (1991). *Emotion and Adaptation*. Oxford, UK: Oxford University Press.

Lazzaro, N. (2008). The four fun keys. In K. Ibister & N. Schaffer (Eds.), *Game Usability*. Burlington: Elsevier, pp. 315–344.

LeDoux, J. (1996). *The Emotional Brain: The Mysterious Underpinnings of Emotional Life*. New York: Simon & Schuster.

Lepper, M., Greene, D., & Nisbett, R. (1973). Undermining children's intrinsic interest with extrinsic rewards: A test of the "overjustification" hypothesis. *Journal of Personality and Social Psychology, 28*, 129–137.

Lepper, M. R., & Henderlong, J. (2000). Turning "play" into "work" and "work" into "play": 25 years of research on intrinsic versus extrinsic motivation. In C. Sansone & J. M. Harackiewicz (Eds.), *Intrinsic and Extrinsic Motivation: The Search for Optimal Motivation and Performance*. San Diego, CA: Academic Press, pp. 257–307.

Levine, S. C., Jordan, N. C., & Huttenlocher, J. (1992). Development of calculation abilities in young children. *Journal of Experimental Child Psychology, 53*, 72–103.

Lewis-Evans, B. (2012). Finding out what they think: A rough primer to user research, Part 1. *Gamasutra*. Retrieved from http://www.gamasutra.com/view/feature/169069/finding_out_what_they_think_a_.php (Accessed May 28, 2017).

Lewis-Evans, B. (2013). Dopamine and games—Liking, learning, or wanting to play? *Gamasutra*. Retrieved from http://www.gamasutra.com/blogs/BenLewisEvans/20130827/198975/Dopamine_and_games__Liking_learning_or_wanting_to_play.php (Accessed May 28, 2017).

Lidwell, W., Holden, K., Butler, J., & Elam, K. (2010). *Universal Principles of Design: 125 Ways to Enhance Usability, Influence Perception, Increase Appeal, Make Better Design Decisions, and Teach through Design*. Beverly, MA: Rockport Publishers.

Lieury, A. (2015). *Psychologie Cognitive*. 4e edn. Paris: Dunod.

Lightbown, D. (2015). *Designing the User Experience of Game Development Tools*. Boca Raton, FL: CRC Press.

Lilienfeld, S. O., Lynn, S. J., Ruscio, J., & Beyerstein, B. L. (2010). *50 Great Myths of Popular Psychology: Shattering Widespread Misconceptions about Human Behavior*. New York: Wiley-Blackwell.

Lindholm, T., & Christianson, S. A. (1998). Gender effects in eyewitness accounts of a violent crime. *Psychology, Crime and Law, 4*, 323–339.

Livingston, I. (2016). Working within Research Constraints in Video Game Development. *Game UX Summit* (Durham, NC, May 12th). Retrieved from http://www.gamasutra.com/blogs/CeliaHodent/20160722/277651/Game_UX_Summit_2016__All_Sessions_Summary.php-4-Ian Livingston (Accessed May 28, 2017).

Loftus, E. F., & Palmer, J. C. (1974). Reconstruction of automobile destruction: An example of the interaction between language and memory. *Journal of Verbal Learning and Verbal Behavior, 13*, 585–589.

Lombard, M., Ditton, T. B., & Weinstein, L. (2009). Measuring Presence: The Temple Presence Inventory (TPI). In *Proceedings of the 12th Annual International Workshop on Presence*. Retrieved from https://pdfs.semanticscholar.org/308b/1 6bec9f17784fed039ddf4f86a856b36a768.pdf (Accessed May 28, 2017).

Lynn, J. (2013). Combining back-end telemetry data with established user testing protocols: A love story. In M. Seif El-Nasr, A. Drachen & A. Canossa (Eds.), *Game Analytics—Maximizing the Value of Player Data*. London: Springer, pp. 497–514.

Mack, S. (2016). Insights Hybrids at Riot: Blending Research at Analytics to Empower Player-Focused Design. *Game UX Summit* (Durham, NC, May 12th). Retrieved from http://www.gamasutra.com/blogs/CeliaHodent/20160722/277651/Game_ UX_Summit_2016__All_Sessions_Summary.php-8-Steve Mack (Accessed May 28, 2017).

MacKenzie, I. S. (2013). *Human-Computer Interaction: An Empirical Research Perspective*. Waltham, MA: Morgan Kaufmann.

Malone, T. W. (1980). What Makes Things Fun to Learn? Heuristics for Designing Instructional Computer Games. *Proceedings of the 3rd ACM SIGSMALL Symposium* (pp. 162–169), Palo Alto, CA.

Marozeau, J., Innes-Brown, H., Grayden, D. B., Burkitt, A. N., & Blamey, P. J. (2010). The effect of visual cues on auditory stream segregation in musicians and non-musicians. *PLoS One, 5*(6), e11297.

Maslow, A. H. (1943). A theory of human motivation. *Psychological Review, 50*, 370–396.

Mayer, R. E. (2014). *Computer Games for Learning: An Evidence-Based Approach*. Cambridge, MA: MIT Press.

McClure, S. M., Li, J., Tomlin, D., Cypert, K. S., Montague, L. M., & Montague, P. R. (2004). Neural correlates of behavioral preference for culturally familiar drinks. *Neuron, 44*, 379–387.

McDermott, J. H. (2009). The cocktail party problem. *Current Biology, 19*, R1024–R1027.

McGonigal, J. (2011). *Reality Is Broken: Why Games Make Us Better and How They Can Change the World*. New York: Penguin Press.

McLaughlin, A. (2016). Beyond Surveys & Observation: Human Factors Psychology Tools for Game Studies. *Game UX Summit* (Durham, NC, May 12th). Retrieved from http://www.gamasutra.com/blogs/CeliaHodent/20160722/277651/ Game_UX_Summit_2016__All_Sessions_Summary.php-1-Anne McLaughlin (Accessed May 28, 2017).

Medlock, M. C., Wixon, D., Terrano, M., Romero, R., & Fulton, B. (2002). *Using the RITE method to improve products: A definition and a case study*. Presented at the *Usability Professionals Association* 2002, Orlando, FL.

Miller, G. A. (1956). The magical number seven, plus or minus two: Some limits on our capacity for processing information. *Psychological Review, 63*, 81–97.

Nielsen, J. (1994). Heuristic evaluation. *In* J. Nielsen & R. L. Mack (Eds.), *Usability Inspection Methods*. pp. 25–62. New York: Wiley.

Nielsen, J. (2006). *Corporate UX Maturity: Stages 5–8*. Nielsen Norman Group. Retrieved from https://www.nngroup.com/articles/usability-maturity-stages-5-8/ (Accessed May 28, 2017).

Nielsen, J., & Molich, R. (1990). Heuristic Evaluation of User Interfaces. *Proceedings of the ACM CHI'90 Conference* (pp. 249–256), Seattle, WA, 1–5 April.

Norman, D. A. (2005). *Emotional Design: Why We Love (or Hate) Everyday Things*. New York: Basic Books.

Norman, D. A. (2013). *The Design of Everyday Things, Revised and Expanded Edition*. New York: Basic Books.

Norman, D. A. (2016). UX, HCD, and VR: Games of Yesterday, Today, and the Future. *Game UX Summit* (Durham, NC, May 12th). Retrieved from http://www.gamasutra.com/blogs/CeliaHodent/20160722/277651/Game_UX_Summit_2016__All_Sessions_Summary.php-12-Don Norman (Accessed May 28, 2017).

Norman, D. A., Miller, J., & Henderson, A. (1995). What You See, Some of What's in the Future, And How We Go About Doing It: HI at Apple Computer. *Proceedings of CHI* 1995, Denver, CO.

Norton, M. I., Mochon, D., & Ariely, D. (2012). The IKEA effect: When labor leads to love. *Journal of Consumer Psychology, 22*, 453–460.

Ochsner, K. N., Ray, R. R., Hughes, B., McRae, K, Cooper, J. C., Weber, J, Gabrieli, J. D. E., & Gross, J. J. (2009). Bottom-up and top-down processes in emotion generation. *The Association for Psychological Science, 20*, 1322–1331.

Oosterbeek, H., Sloof, R., & Kuilen, G. V. D. (2004). Cultural differences in ultimatum game experiments: Evidence from a meta-analysis. *Experimental Economics, 7*, 171–188.

Paivio, A. (1974). Spacing of repetitions in the incidental and intentional free recall of pictures and words. *Journal of Verbal Learning and Verbal Behavior, 13*, 497–511.

Palmiter, R. D. (2008). Dopamine signaling in the dorsal striatum is essential for motivated behaviors: Lessons from dopamine-deficient mice. *Annals of the New York Academy of Science, 1129*, 35–46.

Papert, S. (1980). *Mindstorms. Children, Computers, and Powerful Ideas*. New York: Basic Books.

Pashler, H., McDaniel, M., Rohrer, D., & Bjork, R. (2008). Learning styles: Concepts and evidence. *Psychological Science in the Public Interest, 9*, 105–119.

Pavlov, I. P. (1927). *Conditioned Reflexes*. London: Clarendo Press.

Pellegrini, A. D., Dupuis, D., & Smith, P. K. (2007). Play in evolution and development. *Developmental Review, 27*, 261–276.

Peterson, M. (2013). Preschool Math: Education's Secret Weapon. *Huffington Post*. Retrieved from http://www.huffingtonpost.com/matthew-peterson/post_5235_b_3652895.html

Piaget, J. (1937). *La construction du reel chez l'enfant*. Neuchâtel: Delachaux & Niestlé.

Piaget, J., & Inhelder, B. (1969). *The Psychology of the Child*. New York: Basic Books.

Pickel, K. L. (2015). Eyewitness memory. In J. Fawcett, E. F. Risko & A. Kingstone (Eds.), *The Handbook of Attention*. Cambridge, MA: MIT Press, (pp. 485–502).

Pinker, S. (1997). *How the Mind Works*. New York, NY: W. W. Norton & Company.

Prensky, M. (2001). Digital Natives, Digital Immigrants: Do they really think different? *On the Horizon, 9*, 1–6. Retrieved from http://www.marcprensky.com/writing/Prensky%20-%20Digital%20Natives,%20Digital%20Immigrants%20-%20Part1.pdf (Accessed May 28, 2017).

Przybylski, A. K. (2016). How We'll Know When Science Is Ready to Inform Game Development and Policy. *Game UX Summit* (Durham, NC, May 12th). Retrieved from http://www.gamasutra.com/blogs/CeliaHodent/20160722/277651/Game_%20UX_Summit_2016__All_Sessions_Summary.php-3-Andrew%20Przybylski#3- Andrew Przybylski (Accessed May 28, 2017).

Przybylski, A. K., Deci, E. L., Rigby, C. S., & Ryan, R. M. (2014). Competence-impeding electronic games and players' aggressive feelings, thoughts, and behaviors. *Journal of Personality and Social Psychology, 106*, 441–457.

Przybylski, A. K., Rigby, C. S., & Ryan, R. M. (2010). A motivational model of video game engagement. *Review of General Psychology, 14*, 154–166.

Reber, A. S. (1989). Implicit learning and tacit knowledge. *Journal of Experimental Psychology: General, 118*, 219–235.

Rensink, R. A, O'Regan, J. K., & Clark, J. J. (1997). To see or not to see? The need for attention to perceive changes in scenes. *Psychological Science, 8*, 368–373.

Rogers, S. (2014). *Level Up! The Guide to Great Video Game Design*. 2nd edn. Chichester, UK: Wiley.

Rosenthal, R., & Jacobson, L. (1992). *Pygmalion in the Classroom. Expanded edn.* New York: Irvington.

Ryan, R. M., & Deci, E. L. (2000). Self-determination theory and the facilitation of intrinsic motivation, social development, and well-being. *American Psychologist, 55*, 68–78.

Sacks, O. (2007). *Musicophilia: Tales of Music and the Brain*. London: Picador.

Salen, K., & Zimmerman, E. (2004). *Rules of Play: Game Design Fundamentals*, Vol. 1. London: MIT.

Saloojee, Y., & Dagli, E. (2000). Tobacco industry tactics for resisting public policy on health. *Bulletin of World Health Organization, 78*, 902–910.

Schachter, S., & Singer, J. E. (1962). Cognitive, social, and physiological determinants of emotional state. *Psychological Review, 69*, 379–399.

Schaffer, N. (2007). *Heuristics for Usability in Games*. Rensselaer Polytechnic Institute, White Paper. https://pdfs.semanticscholar.org/a837/d36a0dda35e10f7dfce77818924f4514fa51.pdf (Accessed May 28, 2017).

Schell, J. (2008). *The Art of Game Design*. Amsterdam: Elsevier/Morgan Kaufmann.

Schüll, N. D. (2012). *Addiction by Design: Machine Gambling in Las Vegas*. Princeton, NJ: Princeton University Press.

Schultheiss, O. C. (2008). Implicit motives. In O. P. John, R. W. Robins & L. A. Pervin (Eds.), *Handbook of Personality: Theory and Research*. 3rd edn. New York: Guilford, pp. 603–633.

Schultz, W. (2009). Dopamine Neurons: Reward and Uncertainty. *In:* L. Squire (Ed.), *Encyclopedia of Neuroscience*. Oxford: Academic press, pp. 571–577.

Schvaneveldt, R. W., & Meyer, D. E. (1973). Retrieval and comparison processes in semantic memory. In S. Kornblum (Ed.). *Attention and Performance IV* (pp. 395–409). New York: Academic Press.

Selten, R., & Stoecker, R. (1986). End behavior in sequences of finite prisoner's dilemma supergames a learning theory approach. *Journal of Economic Behavior & Organization*, 7, 47–70.

Shafer, D. M., Carbonara, C. P., & Popova, L. (2011). Spatial presence and perceived reality as predictors of motion-based video game enjoyment. *Presence*, 20, 591–619.

Shaffer, D. W. (2006). *How Computer Games Help Children Learn*. New York: Palgrave Macmillan.

Shaffer, N. (2008). Heuristic evaluation of games. In K. Ibister & N. Schaffer (Eds.), *Game Usability*. pp. 79–89. Burlington, NJ: Elsevier.

Shepard, R. N., & Metzler, J. (1971). Mental rotation of three-dimensional objects. *Science*, 171, 701–703.

Simons, D. J., & Chabris, C. F. (1999). Gorillas in our midst: Sustained inattentional blindness for dynamic events. *Perception*, 28, 1059–1074.

Simons, D. J., & Levin, D. T. (1998). Failure to detect changes to people in a real-world interaction. *Psychonomic Bulletin and Review*, 5, 644–649.

Sinek, S. (2009). *Start with Why: How Great Leaders Inspire Everyone to Take Action*. New York, NY: Penguin Publishers.

Skinner, B. F. (1974). *About Behaviorism*. New York: Knoph.

Stafford, T., & Webb, M. (2005). *Mind Hacks: Tips & Tools for Using your Brain*. Sebastapol, CA: O'Reilly.

Sweetser, P., & Wyeth, P. (2005). GameFlow: A model for evaluating player enjoyment in games. *ACM Computers in Entertainment*, 3, 1–24.

Sweller, J. (1994). Cognitive load theory, learning difficulty and instructional design. *Learning and Instruction*, 4, 295–312.

Swink, S. (2009). *Game Feel: A Game Designer's Guide to Virtual Sensation*. Burlington, MA: Morgan Kaufmann.

Takahashi, D. (2016). With just 3 games, Supercell made $924M in profits on $2.3B in revenue in 2015. VentureBeat. Retrieved from https://venturebeat.com/2016/03/09/with-just-3-games-supercell-made-924m-in-profits-on-2-3b-in-revenue-in-2015/ (Accessed May 28, 2017).

Takatalo, J., Häkkinen, J., Kaistinen, J., & Nyman, G. (2010). Presence, involvement, and flow in digital games. In R. Bernhaupt (Ed.), *Evaluating User Experience in Games* (pp. 23–46). London: Springer-Verlag.

Thorndike, E. L. (1913). *Educational Psychology: The Psychology of Learning*, (Vol. 2). New York: Teachers College Press.

Toppino, T. C., Kasserman, J. E., & Mracek, W. A. (1991). The effect of spacing repetitions on the recognition memory of young children and adults. *Journal of Experimental Child Psychology, 51,* 123–138.

Tversky, A., & Kahneman, D. (1974). Judgment under uncertainty: Heuristics and biases. *Science, 185,* 1124–1130.

Valins, S. (1966). Cognitive effects of false heart-rate feedback. *Journal of Personality and Social Psychology, 4,* 400–408.

van Honk, J., Will, G. -J., Terburg, D., Raub, W., Eisenegger, C., & Buskens, V. (2016). Effects of testosterone administration on strategic gambling in poker play. *Scientific Reports,* 6, 18096.

Vogel, S., & Schwabe, L. (2016). Learning and memory under stress: Implications for the classroom. *Science of Learning, 1,* Article number 16011.

Vroom, V. H. (1964). *Work and Motivation.* San Francisco, CA: Jossey-Bass.

Vygotsky, L. S. (1967). Play and its role in the mental development of the child. *Soviet Psychology, 5,* 6–18.

Vygotsky, L. S. (1978). Interaction between learning and development. In M. Cole, V. John-Steiner, S. Scribner & E. Souberman (Eds.), *Mind in Society: The Development of Higher Psychological Processes.* Cambridge, MA: Harvard University Press, pp. 79–91.

Wahba, M. A., & Bridwell, L. G. (1983). Maslow reconsidered: A review of research on the need hierarchy theory. In R. Steers & L. Porter (Eds.), *Motivation and Work Behavior.* New York: McGraw-Hill, pp. 34–41.

Wertheimer, M. (1923). Untersuchungen zur Lehre der Gestalt II, Psychol Forsch. 4, 301–350. Translation published as Laws of Organization in Perceptual Forms, In Ellis WA *Source Book of Gestalt Psychology* (pp. 71–88). London: Routledge (1938)

Whorf, B. L. (1956). *Language, Thought and Reality.* Cambridge: MIT.

Wynn, K. (1992). Addition and subtraction by human infants. *Nature, 358,* 749–750.

Yee, N. (2016). *Gaming Motivations Align with Personality Traits.* Retrieved from http://quanticfoundry.com/2016/01/05/personality-correlates/ (Accessed May 28, 2017).

Index

A

Affordances, 31–32, 178–180
Analytics, 198; *see also* Game analytics
Assassin's Creed 2, 84
Attention, 51–57, 93
    application to games, 55–57
    cocktail party effect, 51
    excessive cognitive load, 53
    functioning, 51–52
    inattentional blindness, 54
    limitations of human attention, 52–55
    multitasking, 52
    selective attention, 51
    Stroop effect, 53
    underadditivity, 53
Autonomy, 142–143

B

Behavioral psychology principles, 83–85
    classical conditioning, 84
    operant conditioning, 84–85
Bias
    cognitive, 12–15
    confirmation, 203
    hindsight, 104, 174
    ingroup, 144
    Weber–Fechner, 32–33
Big Five model of personality, 69, 70
Biological drives, 60–61
Blizzard, 63, 82, 89, 118

Blood Dragon, 88
Brain, overview about, 9–18
    brain operation, 16
    cognitive biases, 12–15
    mental models and the player-centered
        approach, 15–18
    mind myths, 9–12
Brain, takeaways, 91–94, 220
    attention, 93
    computer metaphor, 91
    emotion, 94
    learning principles, 94
    memory, 93
    motivation, 93–94
    perception, 92
"Breadcrumb trail," 113

C

Capcom, 100
Civilization, 143
Clash of Clans, 63, 81
Clash Royale, 174
Classical conditioning, 84
Closure principle, 27–28
Cocktail party effect, 51
Cognitive biases, 12–15
Cognitive dissonance, 70
Cognitive needs, 65–68
Cognitive psychology principles, 86
Competence, 138–142

Conditioned response, 84
Conditioning, 83
Confirmation bias, 203
Constructivist principles, 86–87
Control, camera, and character (3Cs),
    157, 211, 222

D

Dark Souls, 100
Dead Space, 110
Declarative memory, 40
Decoy effect, 203
Design thinking, 173–183
    affordances, 178–180
    human-centered design, 173
    iterative cycle, 175–177
    onboarding plan, 180–183
Diablo III, 118
"Diegetic" interface, 110
Difficulty curve, 163–165
"Digital natives," 12
"Dishabituation," 160
"Dopamine shots," 80

E

Educational games, 223–224
Egocentric system, 31
80/20 rule, 132
Emotion, 73–82, 94, 153–161
    application to games, 80–82
    cognition guided by emotion, 75–77
    control, camera, and character, 157
    discovery, novelty, and surprises,
        160–161
    emotional trigger, 79
    game feel, 153–160
    hormones, 76
    limbic system, influence of, 75–76
    loss aversion, 79
    oxytocin, 80
    somatic markers theory, 76–77
    when emotion "tricks" us, 77–80
Engage-ability, 135–171
    autonomy, 142–143
    competence, 138–142
    control, camera, and character, 157
    difficulty curve, 163–165
    discovery, novelty, and surprises,
        160–161

"dishabituation," 160
emotion, 153–161
"extension of identity," 157
extrinsic motivation, learned needs,
    and rewards, 149–151
game feel, 153–160
game flow, 161–171
"habituation," 160
"IKEA effect," 142
individual needs and implicit motives,
    151–152
ingroup bias, 144
intrinsic motivation, 138–149
learning curve and onboarding,
    167–170
meaning, 148–149
motivation, 137–152
pillars for game UX, 135–137
relatedness, 144–147
Environmental-shaped motivation, 61
Epic Games, 4, 102, 141, 159, 216
Experience points (XP), 33
Explicit memory, 40
Extrinsic incentives, undermining
    effect of, 65–66
Extrinsic motivation, 61–65, 149–151

F

Factor analysis, 69
Far Cry 4, 118, 119
Feedback, 116–117
Figure/ground principle, 26–27
Five-factor model, 69
Flicker, 36
Flow, theory of, 67–68, 161
Fortnite, 56, 159
FromSoftware, 100
Functional magnetic resonance
    imaging (fMRI), 23, 53

G

Game analytics, 199–208
    cognitive biases, 202–204
    confirmation bias, 203
    decoy effect, 203
    defining hypotheses and exploratory
        questions, 205–206
    defining metrics, 207–208
    statistical fallacies, 200–202

telemetry, 200–204
UX and analytics, 204–208
Game-based learning, 222–223
Game usability pillars, 221–222
Game user experience, *see* User
    experience, overview of
Game user research, 185–198
  analytics, 198
  distrust of science, 187
  heuristic evaluations, 196–197
  methodologies and tools, 187–198
  personas, 197–198
  rapid internal tests, 197
  recommendations, 198
  scientific method, 185–187
  surveys, 195–196
  UX tests, 190–195
Gamification, 225–226
Gestalt principles (perception), 26–31
  closure, 27–28
  figure/ground principle, 26–27
  multistability, 27
  proximity, 29–31
  similarity, 28
  symmetry, 28
Google Maps, 32

H

"Habituation," 160
Heads-up displays (HUDs), 23, 26, 37
Heuristics, 110, 112
Hindsight bias, 104, 174
Hormones, 62, 76
Hull's law, 61
Human-centered design (HCD), 173;
    see also Design thinking
Human-computer interaction (HCI), 99

I

Iconography, testing of, 26
IDEO Product Development, 87
"IKEA effect," 142
Implicit memory, 41
Implicit motivation, 60–61
Importance of gamer's brain, 1–5
  competition, 1
  decision making, 2
  "neuro-hype" trap, 2–4
Inattentional blindness, 54

Infamous, 143
Informative signs, 115–116
Ingroup bias, 144
Instrumental learning, 84
International Game Developers
    Association, 104–105
Intrinsic motivation, 65–68, 138–149
Inviting signs, 116

K

Key performance indicators (KPIs)
Konami, 42, 84, 143

L

League of Legends, 131
Learned drives, 61, 62
Learning curve, 167–170
Learning principles, 83–90, 94
  application to games, 87–90
  behavioral psychology principles,
    83–85
  brain-training games, 86
  cognitive psychology principles, 86
  conditioning, 83
  constructivist principles, 86–87
  negative reinforcement, 85
  Pavlov's dogs, 84
  Skinner box, 84
*The Legend of Zelda: Phantom
    Hourglass*, 140
Lexical decision task, 41
Limbic system, 75–76
Link to the Past, 116
Long-term memory, 40–42
Loss aversion, 79
"Love hormone," 80
LucasArts, 4

M

Mario Galaxy, 89
Maslow's hierarchy of needs, 60
Massively multiplayer online games
    (MMORPGs), 63
Meaning, 71–72, 148–149
Memory, 35–50, 93
  amnesic patients, 41
  application to games, 45–50
  explicit memory, 40
  flicker, 36

functioning, 35–42
implicit memory, 41
lexical decision task, 41
limitations of human memory, 42–44
long-term memory, 40–42
multistore model, 35
primacy effect, 37
recency effect, 37
reconstruction, 45
reminders, 48–50
sensory memory, 36–37
short-term memory, 37–38
spacing effect and level design,
    46–48
subliminal priming, 41
working memory, 38–40
Mental models, 15–18
Mental rotation, 32
Metal Gear Solid, 42, 84
*Metal Gear Solid V: The Phantom
    Pain*, 143
Microsoft Games Studios, 197
Middle-earth: Shadow of Mordor, 160
Mind myths, 9–12
    differences between men and
        women, 11
    learning styles and teaching
        styles, 11–12
    "left-brain right-brain" distinction, 10
    rewiring your brain, 12
    untapped brain powers, 10
MIND Research, 224
Minecraft, 56, 65
MMORPGs, *see* Massively multiplayer
    online games
MOBA game, *see* Multiplayer online
    battle arena game
Monolith, 160
Motivation, 59–72, 93–94, 137–152
    application to games, 70–71
    autonomy, need for, 66
    "Big Five" personality traits, 69
    cognitive dissonance, 70
    competence, need for, 66
    environmental-shaped motivation and
        learned drives, 61–65
    extrinsic, 61–65, 149–151
    factor analysis, 69
    flow, theory of, 67–68

implicit motivation, 60–61, 151–152
importance of meaning, 71–72
intrinsic, 65–68, 138–149
learned drive, 62
overjustification effect, 66
personality and individual needs,
    68–69
relatedness, need for, 66
rewards, 64
self-determination theory, 66–67
undermining effect of extrinsic
    incentives, 65–66
Multiplayer online battle arena (MOBA)
    game, 141
Multistability principle, 27
Multistore model (memory), 35
Multitasking, 52
"Muscle memory," 126
Myers-Briggs Personality Test, 11

N

Naughty Dog, 89, 132
Negative reinforcement, 85
Neurotransmitters, 62
Nintendo, 46, 89, 116, 138
Nintendo DS, 140
Nohboard, 194
Non-player character (NPC), 116

O

Oculus Story Studio, 174
Onboarding, 167–170, 180–183
Operant conditioning, 84–85
Overjustification effect, 66
Overwatch, 82
Oxytocin, 80

P

Paragon, 141
Pareto principle, 132
Pavlov's dogs, 84
Perception, 19–33, 92
    affordances, 31–32
    application to games, 24–33
    context, 22
    egocentric system, 31
    functioning, 19–20
    Gestalt principles, 26–31
    knowing your audience, 24–26

limitations of human perception, 20–24
"physical skeuomorphism," 31
playtesting and testing your iconography, 26
"testing rooms," 33
visual imagery and mental rotation, 32
Weber–Fechner bias, 32–33
Personality, 68–69
Personas, 197–198
"Physical skeuomorphism," 31
Pixar, 217
Player-centered approach, 15–18
Player versus player (PvP) game, 201
Playful learning, 222–223
Primacy effect, 37
Procedural memory, 41
Proximity principle, 29–31
PvP game, *see* Player versus player game

Q

Quality assurance (QA), 5, 105

R

Rapid iterative testing and evaluation (RITE), 197
Recency effect, 37
Relatedness, 144–147
Research, *see* Game user research
Resident Evil, 100
Revenues, 1

S

Scientific method, 185–187
Selective attention, 51
Self-determination theory (SDT), 66–67, 138
Sensory memory, 36–37
Serious games, 225–226
Short-term memory, 37–38
SimCity, 143
Similarity principle, 28
Skinner box, 84
Skyrim, 143
Somatic markers theory, 76–77
Sony PlayStation 4 (PS4), 25, 113
"Speakeasy room," 216

ST Math, 224
Strategy, *see* UX strategy
Stroop effect, 53
Students, recommendations for, 226–227
Subliminal priming, 41
Sucker Punch, 143
Supercell, 63, 81, 174
Super Mario Brothers, 46, 138
Surveys, 195–196
Symmetry principle, 28

T

TED (Technology, Entertainment, Design) conference, 203

U

Ubisoft, 4, 29, 84, 88, 154, 212, 217
UI, *see* User interface
Uncharted 2, 89
Uncharted 4, 132
Underadditivity, 53
Understanding the brain, *see* Brain, takeaways
Usability, 109–134
    clarity, 117–123
    consistency, 125–127
    "diegetic" interface, 110
    error prevention and error recovery, 129–131
    flexibility, 131–134
    form follows function, 123–125
    heuristics in software and video games, 110–115
    list of heuristics, 112–114
    minimum workload, 127–129
    "muscle memory," 126
    Pareto principle, 132
    pillars for game UX, 115–134
    signs and feedback, 115–117
User experience (UX), 2
User experience (UX), overview of, 97–107
    definition of game UX, 105–107
    hindsight bias, 104
    misconceptions, 100–105
    short history, 98–100
User experience (UX) framework, key takeaways, 220

User experience (UX) strategy, 209–218
    model stages, 214–215
    in production pipeline, 210–213
    at project team level, 210
    "speakeasy room," 216
    at studio level, 213–218
User interface (UI), 26, 110

V

Virtual reality (VR), 174
Visceral Games, 110

W

Weber–Fechner bias, 32–33
Working memory (WM), 38–40
World of Warcraft, 63, 89

X

XP, *see* Experience points

Z

Zone of proximal development (ZPD), 223